# GAS TANK CITY

ANDREW HOLMES

First published in 2024 by Circa Press
©2024 Circa Press Limited and Andrew Holmes

Circa Press
50 Great Portland Street
London W1W 7ND
www.circa.press

ISBN 978-1-911422-47-1



Seeing the Idea
©2024 Andrew Holmes

Homeless Representation
©2024 Thomas E Crow

The Romance of Anonymity
©1991 Mark Fisher

The Harvest of a Quiet Eye
©1986 Cedric Price

Designer: April

Printed and bound in China

# GAS TANK CITY

ANDREW HOLMES

# Seeing the Idea Andrew Holmes

July 1967 found me looking at a freehand graphite drawing of some seventy horizontal, but very slightly wobbly parallel lines on paper. The label at the side said that this miracle was by Agnes Martin, and was titled *Stone*. Three minutes earlier, in a room close by, I had seen another miracle attributed to Edward Hopper, called *Gas*. It was mid-afternoon, and I was in the Museum of Modern Art, in New York. I was on the way to my night shift to wash dishes at Café Figaro, on the corner of Bleecker Street and MacDougal, in the West Village.

Some months earlier, back in London, I had walked into the lecture hall at the Architectural Association one sunny Saturday morning to find a man unlatching a slim case that contained a guitar. There were twelve people in the room. He said, 'They call me Mississippi Fred McDowell, but I'm from Rossville, Tennessee, but it don't matter much to me'. He played for an hour. It was enchanting. I knew I was in the presence of genius. About ten days later, I spent a day listening and talking to another enchanter, this time in the AA's private dining room. He was called John Cage. I didn't understand all that much of what he said, which gently questioned everything I thought, but he did say, 'It's not either/or; it's both/and'.

I walked round the MoMA galleries, but kept going back to *Stone* and *Gas* over and over again. It was the pencil lines close up; the state of mind that was conveyed; the green of the trees; decisions about colour. There was enough time for a cup of tea and a think before going to work. Would it be possible to combine Agnes Martin and Edward Hopper as an idea, like putting together John Cage and Mississippi Fred McDowell? Was Agnes Martin really drawing a parking lot? Were Agnes and Fred really manually drawing and playing an idea about the machine? There was a struggle for a personality and individuality in a society dominated by the machine. Where did that come from, the wobbly line, the amplified rhythm of the insistent picking hand, and the over-vivid green surface of the trees? How could something be as practical and ethereal as Martin, and as real and elusive as Hopper?

An idea was there. How to do it? What to draw? What to combine? A realistic image depicted in unrealistic colours?

I experimented for four years. I tried hybrids. What would the unlikely combination of Robert Frank and Maxfield Parrish look like? *Covered Car* meets *Daybreak*. A drawing that I did make. Cars though are made in hundreds. Repetition has an effect. Bo Diddley repeated his hambone riff over and over, Phelps 'Catfish' Collins of the J.B.'s even more so later on 'Super Bad'. The ultimate discipline had an effect. Making a hundred drawings would take decades. Together they would be a history combining portrait, war, religion and landscape.

May 1976 finds me sitting in the corner booth in Zingo's on Pierce Road, Bakersfield. I'm looking out of the window, past a pick-up parked up against the glass, to a Kenworth conventional under the Truck Center sign. The sound is of a semi-truck diesel rumbling. For ten years now I have been going from the Rock Store to Big Bob's, from Sugartrux to Mario's Auto Works, Slab City to El Mirage. The car journeys are long, driving alone except for the radio, the Bakersfield Sound of Buck Owens and Merle Haggard. I drive on Route 99 to Milliken Avenue on Route 10.

It is 1980, the end of the day. The sun is going down. I've taken my camera out as usual and I'm walking between two trailers. A man appears at the end of this cul-de-sac. He's carrying a long machete. I stop. He and his friends saw me, he said, and wanted to warn me. This is a dangerous part of town, and I should be careful with the camera. He invites me to eat; they're serving steaks with a side order of melon. The steaks are grilling on inverted truck hubcaps over a fire set in a 50-gallon oil drum. The machetes are good for slicing the melons into quarters. The melon truck is right next to the drum. I've stumbled on a truck stop on South Central Avenue.

Earlier in the day I had photographed two brand-new freight cars, one red, one yellow. I was wandering over the rail tracks south of Union Station. The officers in the police car that came up along the tracks said it wasn't a good idea to be there; I should depart. I did so along a narrow alley. I had reached the end, was thinking to return after a suitable lapse of time, when the figure emerged at the other end. The man looked like a tough version of Clint Eastwood channelling Lee Van Cleef. I thought this is it. He approached, as he passed by, said, 'Makes a pretty picture, don't it?'

It is 1986. I'm sitting between two truckers. Each must weigh 250 pounds. They are complaining that it's too dry in California. They haven't met before. They're from Alabama. Their plates are okay, just, but there's not enough food on them. Their attention turns to a survey of all the truck stops they've ever visited, based on the size of the meal that's served. This naturally goes on to include the size of the waitresses and the cooks. The unanimous conclusion is that the best that meets all criteria is the one up near Detroit. Is it Arlene's I wonder? A mother and her two daughters, they say. Fine women, they say. This is the TA at Milliken and Route 10. Concorde silently slides by the window, landing at Ontario airport. At another counter across the corner is a man dressed all in black, long black hair, black straw Stetson, mirror shades, fingerless leather gloves. He says, 'funny, ain't it?' I say, 'yes', and wait. His young son has dyed his hair blond and got a Mohican haircut. Times have changed. He had been a Marine. His hair had been a buzz cut. Leaving the Army he had got a job in a warehouse. There was a new young worker there with long hair. He had teased him about it on the first morning. The man politely asked him not to rassle him. He did a second time the next day. He woke up on the floor, the young man standing over him saying, 'I told you not to rassle me'. He never did again. Times change.

Leaving the booth, through the gate out into the lot, the noise of fifty trucks with their diesels running is deafening, the heat of the sun off the asphalt blasts in the face, as does the smell of hot oil. It's 95 degrees in the shade. The cabs and the refrigerated trailers have to be kept cold. I sit on the end of a low loader. A striking looking man joins me. He tells me his great, great, great grandfather married a Cherokee girl when he was fourteen. It was just after the end of the Civil War. We talk for two hours. I am told, 'So this is Holmes World'.

September 1988. I'm on Beal Road out of Niland close to the Salton Sea. I'm staring at a brightly multicoloured painted adobe hill. The whole is covered in biblical texts, as are the broken-down cars and trailers scattered around. A wiry figure in exhausted work clothes stands beneath a straw hat. He tells me of his balloon flight that had crash-landed here two years before. It had been a sign that his mission was to build a mountain. This is Salvation Mountain. It is 115 degrees in the shade. The word GOD is in bright pink capital letters ten feet high on its summit. I am told it is there so that you have to look up. If you look up your chest will fill with air. You will be inspired. If you look down the chest collapses and you will be depressed. He walks to town, where he is given food. Builders bring paint, and road menders bring feldspar for his project. He gets water from the American Canal close by. He bathes in a natural spring. He never asks for anything. He is always given things. He is a man you know you have to help. This is important.

I explain what I do making drawings. I drive every day with my camera. I am a man on a pilgrimage he says, as Butch Hancock has been singing to me in the car. As David Greene in London says, I am a monk, but a monk in a car. Beyond is Slab City, population one hundred and fifty plus four thousand in winter. It is federal land; the sixty-five slabs are all that is left of Camp Dunlap, a Second World War military training base.

John Holt lives there now. He, his wife and daughter live in a roofless shack. One night we are gathered round a barbecue cooking. His job had been polishing truck hubcaps. He looked up one time to see two cops poking his pregnant wife with their nightsticks. He tried to stop them. The police broke both his knees. He can't work now. He says, 'I have nothing except that'. He points upwards. Above us is the full Milky Way spread out across the sky.

It is 2000. A small photograph in a magazine shows a car that has been built in LA by someone called Mario. That is all. In Santa Monica I look through all five telephone directories in the house where I am staying for a Mario. I phone Directory Enquiries. I explain to a very patient operator what I'm looking for, and for some reason it becomes her mission to solve my problem. She looks through the database, district after district. After ten minutes she says there's a Mario's Auto Works, at Montclair, about fifty miles from where I sit.

I phone the number. Come on out, they say, but come at lunchtime
or the end of the day. I drive out, and fifty minutes later I'm there,
very much the wrong side of the tracks, looking at a long blue shed
covered in graffiti. It's lunchtime.

I introduce myself to a man I meet at the sliding door to the
workshop and show him what I do. He shows me what he and his
sons do. I am introduced. It's nothing particularly remarkable, not
unlike the Bromsgrove Guild in my hometown. We talk. He walks
away, turns, beckoning with his finger. He unlocks a door to an
immaculate white room concealed within the shed. He opens the
door, and I step through. Inside are three of the most astonishing
cars I have ever seen – lowriders. Over many years I have got
to know the De Alba family and the Elite Car Club quite well.
Mario was the second man to be elected to the Lowrider Hall
of Fame. He is no longer allowed to enter competitions. He wins
them all. As we say goodbye we discover we have both been on
the Whittier Boulevard lowrider cruises in East LA, back in the early
Seventies. We remember the sound as a lowrider burbles by with
added tunes from sub-bass woofers in the trunk.

January 2024 finds me looking at a room with seven drawings
on the wall. That is two years at the wheel, alone. Each seems to
convey an emotion on pulling the car over, or turning the corner,
and seeing something astonishing. There still seems to be an air
of calm. The initial effect has been maintained over the many hours
of detailed drawing, but times have changed. The heat is the same.
Driving and seeing is the same. Fifty years later, the oil tanker trucks
have gone. Propane cylinders have taken their place. Pierce has
become Buck Owens Boulevard. Buck, the king of Bakersfield,
has gone. Merle has gone, but so too have Leonard Knight,
John Holt, Edward Hopper and Agnes Martin, all lonesome.

The rich saturated, immaculate surface of a working vehicle,
whose driver has only just left the scene, has evolved into a depiction
of something more personal, ageing and broken-down. There is
a transition from *Worth* to *Independence,* from city to desert.
The sky blue sky and the light remain the same. The subjects,

the compositions and the colour still convey something
contradictory. Emotion and rational thought are ambiguous.
Rational thought is the emotion, something as ethereal as
Martin and as elusive as Hopper. I look at the random notes
written over a coffee in a truck stop thirty years ago:

*Superficiality can be profound and worth living for*
*I mean everything is ephemeral when you look*
*at it in its proper focus*
*It just happens more quickly in LA*
*I like country because there are thought patterns*
*that people put into their music*
*I guess they're artists on the same plane as I am*
*I find that musicians are making a more cohesive statement*
*to me than many artists do, even artists I admire*
*I like it dry and simple, in a way inartistic*
*I love the Highway. I love to drive*
*Music has a way of bringing back all kinds of memories*
*We were going at slightly slower RPM then, and I like that*
*The image is a kind of windshield*
*The work is a huge field through which I drive*
*It's a Drive-In, another stop on the Highway*

## Homeless Representation Thomas E Crow

Photo-Realism as a category in art gained its currency in California, starting in the 1960s, and for many counts as a Pop-adjacent artefact of that era; shiny automobiles in perpetual sunlight, standing now for a lost utopia of shared prosperity and optimism. Some of the most distinctive work in that idiom, however, came in the years of the following decade when that economic dream began to unravel, so there existed already in its heyday a current of ironic allusion to fleeting satisfactions and lost hopes. A further transposition to London, in late autumn 1992, might have seemed too great a stretch for any level of irony, yet I found myself in Finsbury Park following run-down streets lined with small Asian clothing businesses, in search of works by Andrew Holmes, then and now the most important British producer of manually transformed photographs. His gallery lay in an eclectic new trading estate surrounded by barbed wire. For the London art scene, when the phenomenon of galleries actively colonising semi-derelict commercial districts was still new, this was the edge of the Earth.

For all its obstacles to easy accessibility, the cold, raw commercial edge of the setting was appropriate to the vision on display inside, despite Holmes siting his works in the Californian geography celebrated in those canvases of long ago. His California could be said to be the one left over after the manicured suburbs and commercial glitter have been taken out of the equation. Revealed in Holmes's vision are other forms of life, pre-eminently those occupying the mobile structures on the American highway (trucks, trailers, tanks) with their permanent industrial armature (which channels, fills, fuels, unloads, washes). These complex lines of transportation that sustain the city artificially across the harsh surrounding desert are for him the great architectural achievements of America.

Holmes renders these realities in his large drawings built up over days and weeks in seamless layers of Derwent colour pencil. Their vividness is achieved through density of application and concentration of effect. Deliberately casual, snapshot arrangements are entirely missing from his work, as is the reiteration of merely at-hand suburban exteriors. His characteristic compression of meaning results in compositions like *Tanks,* a drawing that literally figures the necessary effacement of authorial presence implicit in its technique. The subject matter is two polished tank trailers positioned beneath a gantry from which they are being filled with milk. The artist/viewer is so positioned between the two tanks as to have a close-up view of the one in front, the other being reflected from behind in its immaculate curving surface. This is, of course, an impossible vision, one that no photograph could provide, in that the viewer's image would necessarily be caught in that same play of reflection. Careful, meditated extrapolation from the visual data is required to preserve a crucial cognitive distinction between the independent life of the working apparatus and the presence of the temporary observer – and one can feel the force of the exclusion.

Much theorising about mechanical reproduction in recent art has suffered from the assumption that 'the photograph' is a pre-existing, unitary object. The source of any photography-based illusionism, Holmes points out, is the negative or transparency – usually tiny, absent, and unavailable for inspection. Consequently any enlarged, opaque print is already a reproduction, one in which information is always distorted and lost. There will be kinds of information in the source better mediated and fixed by a slow, manual process of synthesising intelligence and accumulated feeling. And the result can be put to different sorts of uses, encountered and contemplated in ways that a photographic print cannot. Large-scale and intense colour saturation, for example, can be achieved by means not indelibly associated with advertising display. This removes the otherwise automatic requirement of irony and in turn expands the range of possible subjects. The technique also allows the work to issue, where appropriate, a less insistent invitation to the viewer's attention.

*Tanks* is the attempt to get down the feelings of an architect encountering a momentary vision of an anonymous architecture beyond the powers of the profession to produce. Its anonymity derives in part from mass-produced industrial components, and thus has something in common with the early work of Richard Rogers (for whom Holmes worked at one time). But Holmes's conception proceeds from a paradox inherent in those designs, in that the tolerances involved call for refinements in custom manufacture that no architect could individually visualise. Thus their construction has depended upon practical wisdom provided by contractors and skilled workmen, and such structures are subject to rapid decay if not rigorously and sensitively maintained by other hands (the deterioration of the Centre Pompidou being the proof). The building is, therefore, not a fixed thing, but exists along a trajectory in time of purposeful social activity.

Once architecture is reconceived in this way, there is no reason not to expand the term to cover the entire system of supply by road in which the urban oasis of Los Angeles is suspended. Complex industrial structures of remarkable scale and intricacy are in continual motion through this system, manoeuvred and maintained by highly skilled individuals. As architecture, it cannot be encompassed by plan or rendering; merely to conceive its extent is to grasp one's inability to do more than glimpse temporary fragments, and it will be only through these that it can be represented. The self-denying discipline involved yields a palpable tension in the works, from the fluidly distorting mirrors of polished chrome to the achingly sustained areas of unbroken colour.

In Holmes's hands, the process of drawing is one of investing a photographic trace of the fragment with the sense of its sublime, ungraspable whole, effected via all the small decisions over emphasis, contrast, and simplification taken through the time of painstaking execution.

**Gas Tank City** Drawings 1974–2024

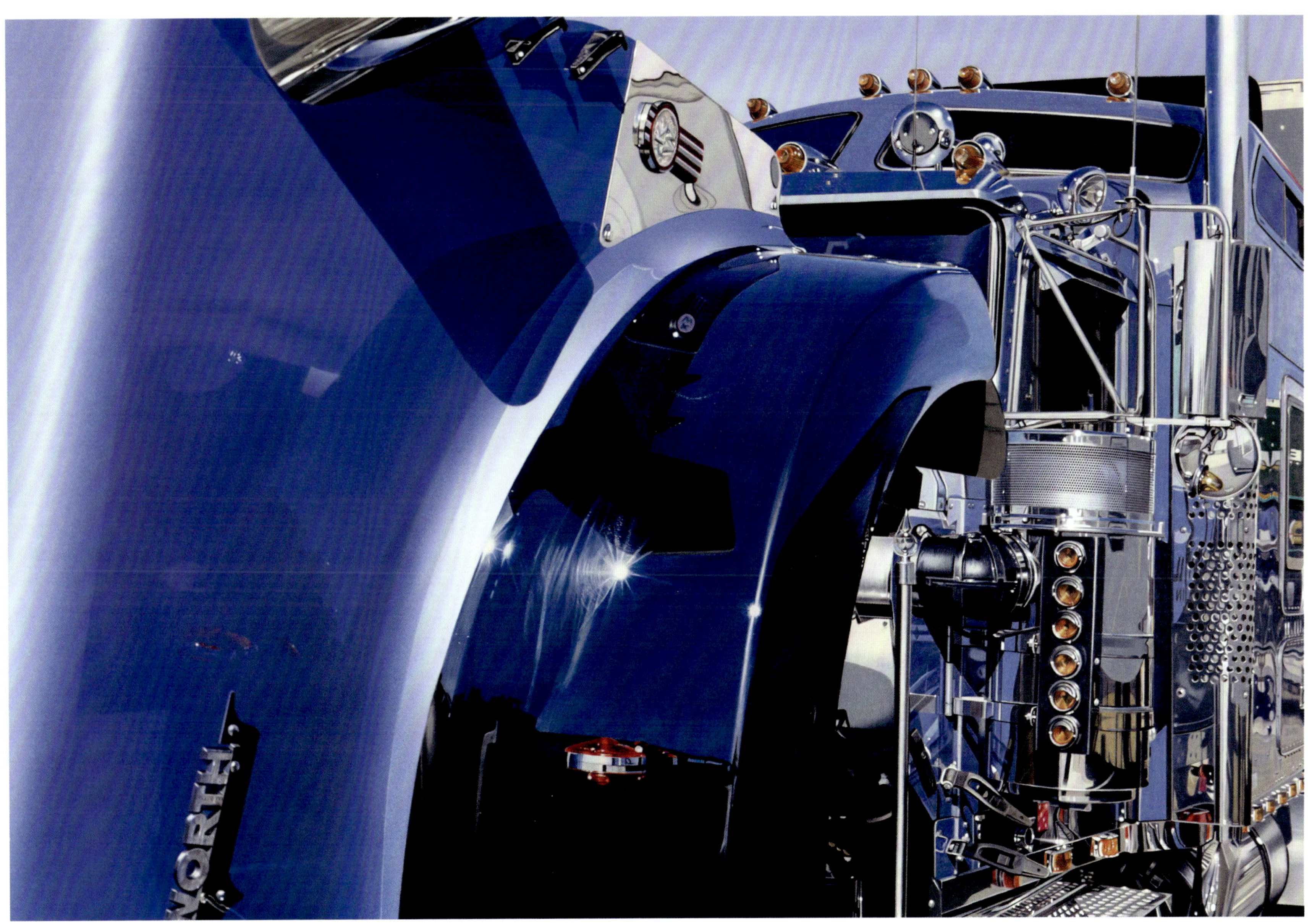

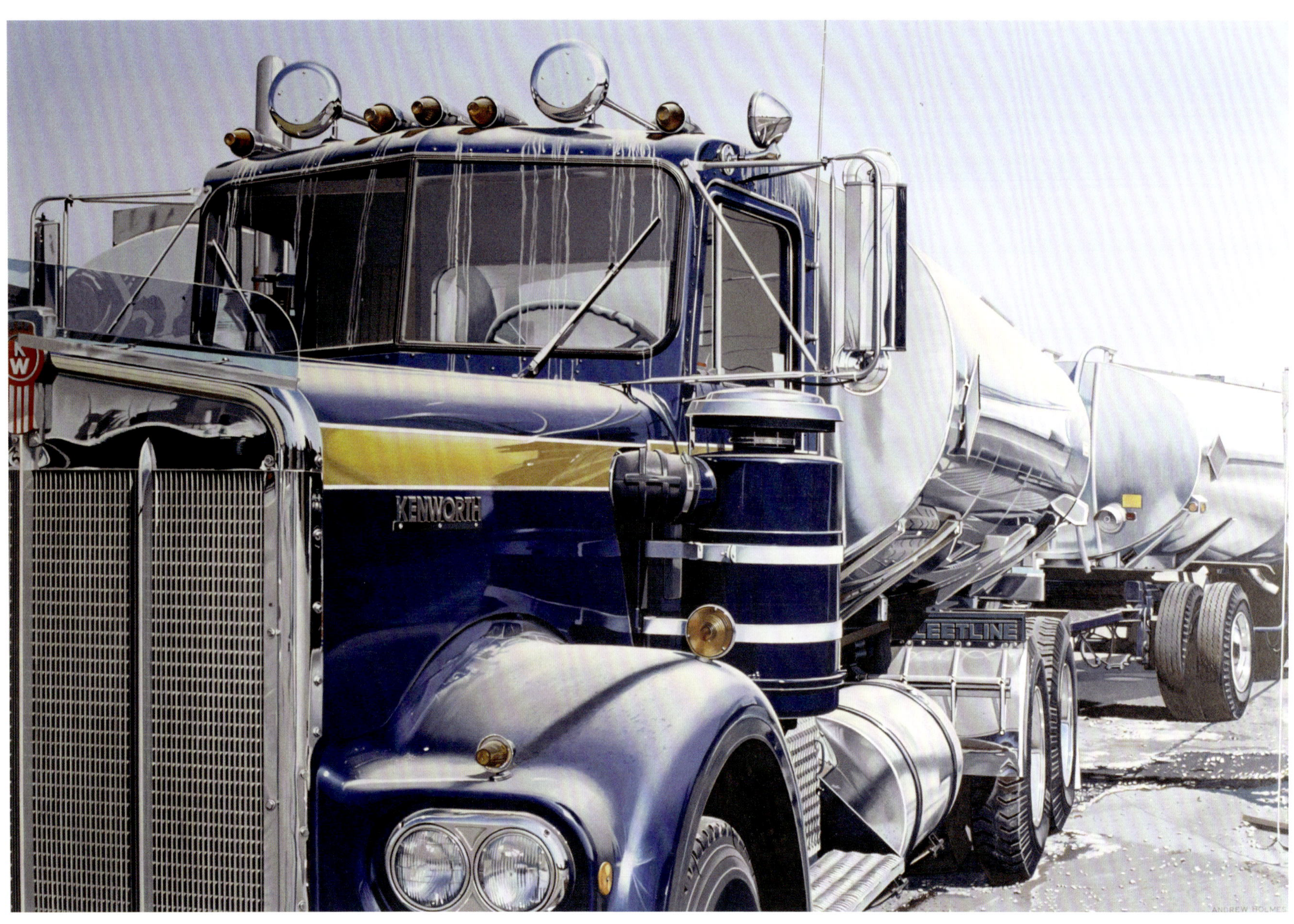
KENWORTH
FLEETLINE
ANDREW HOLMES

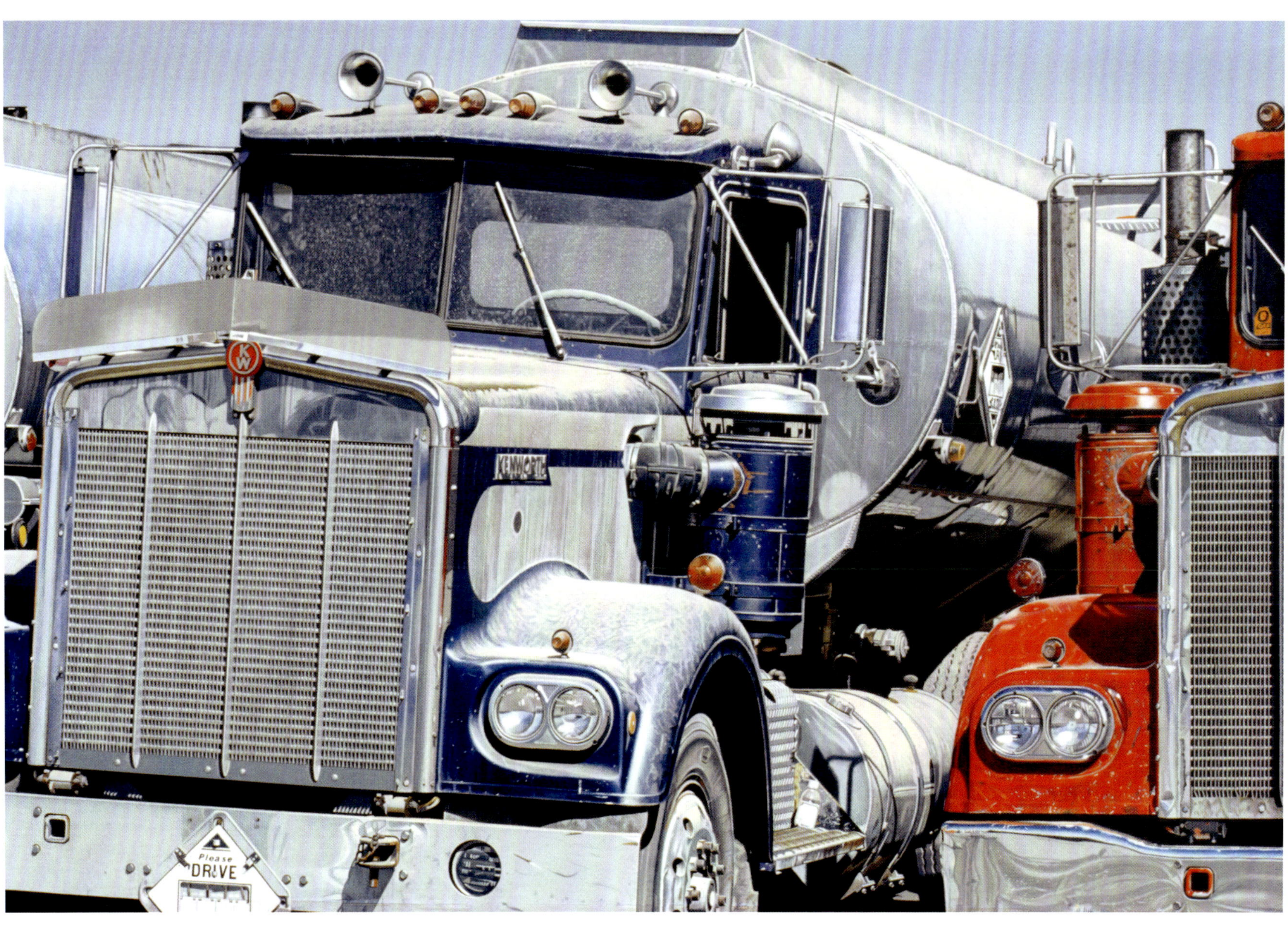

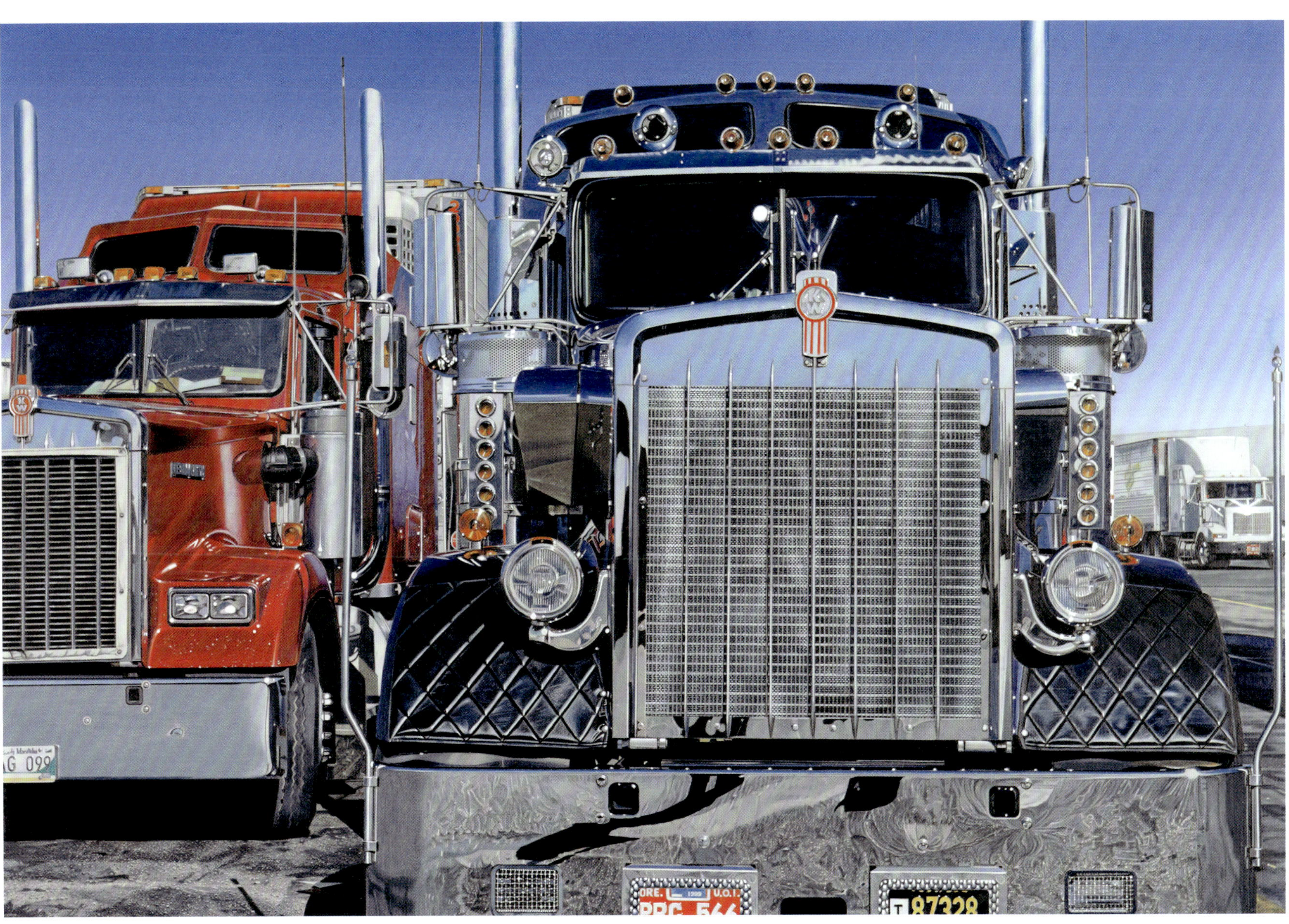

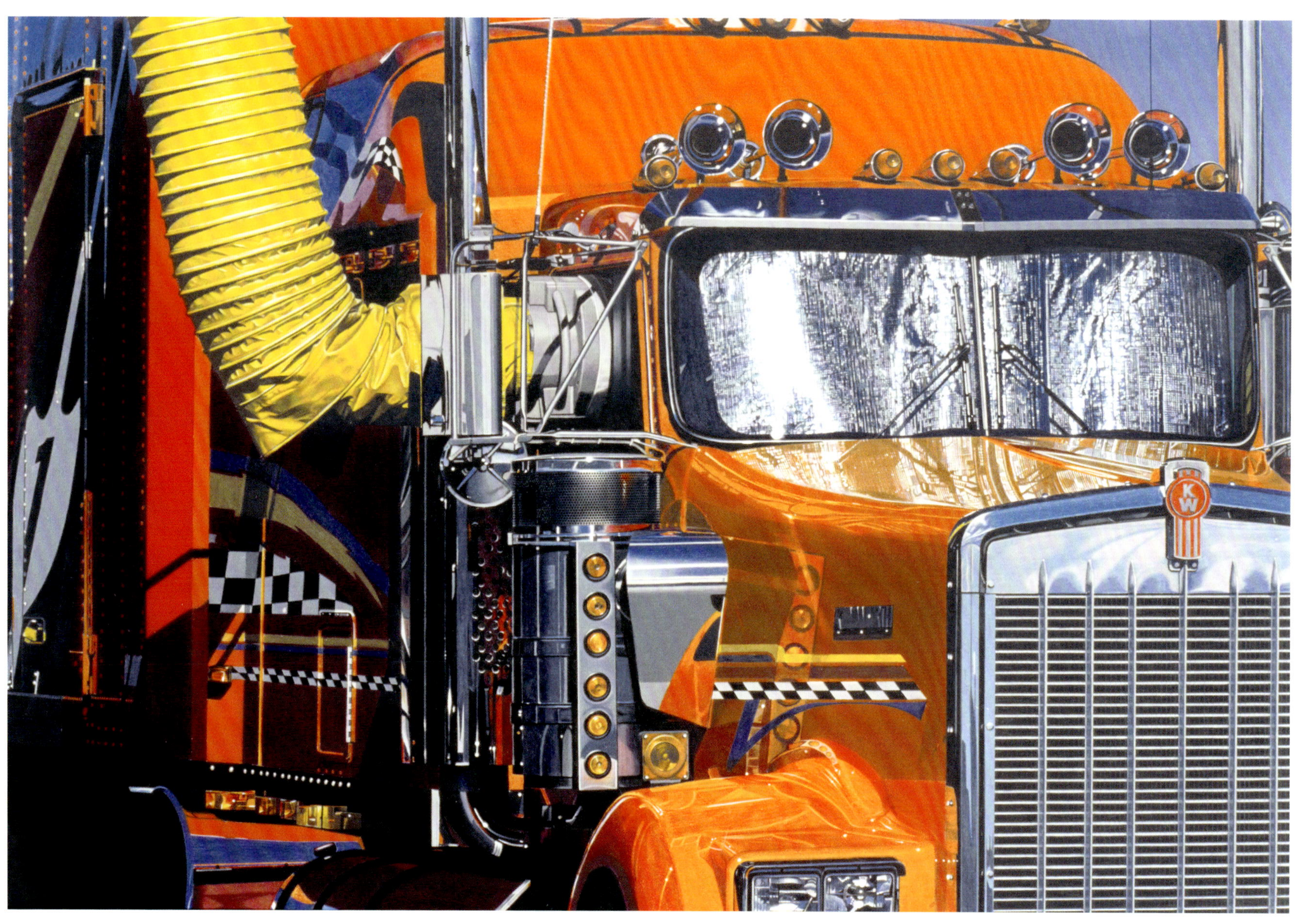

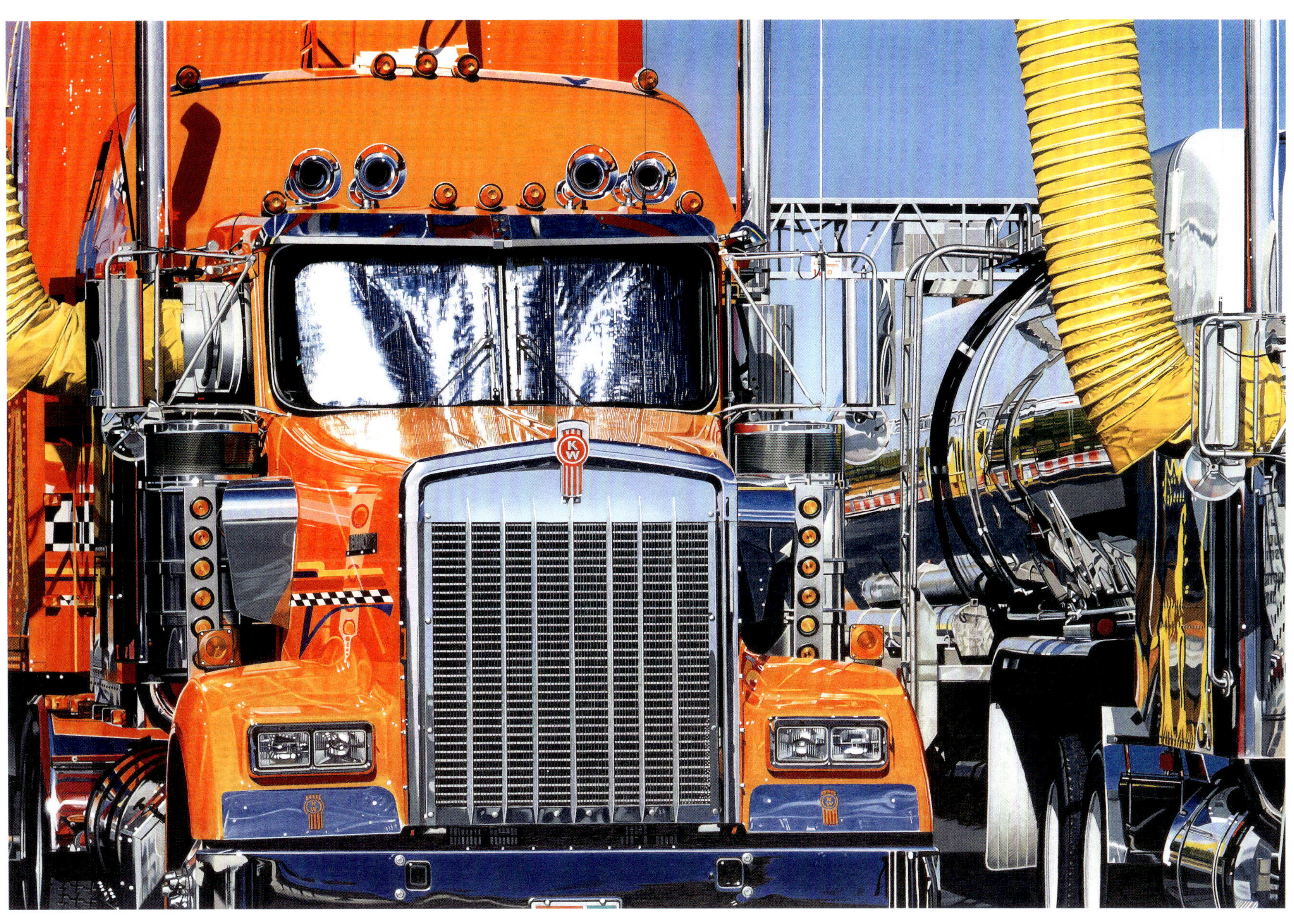

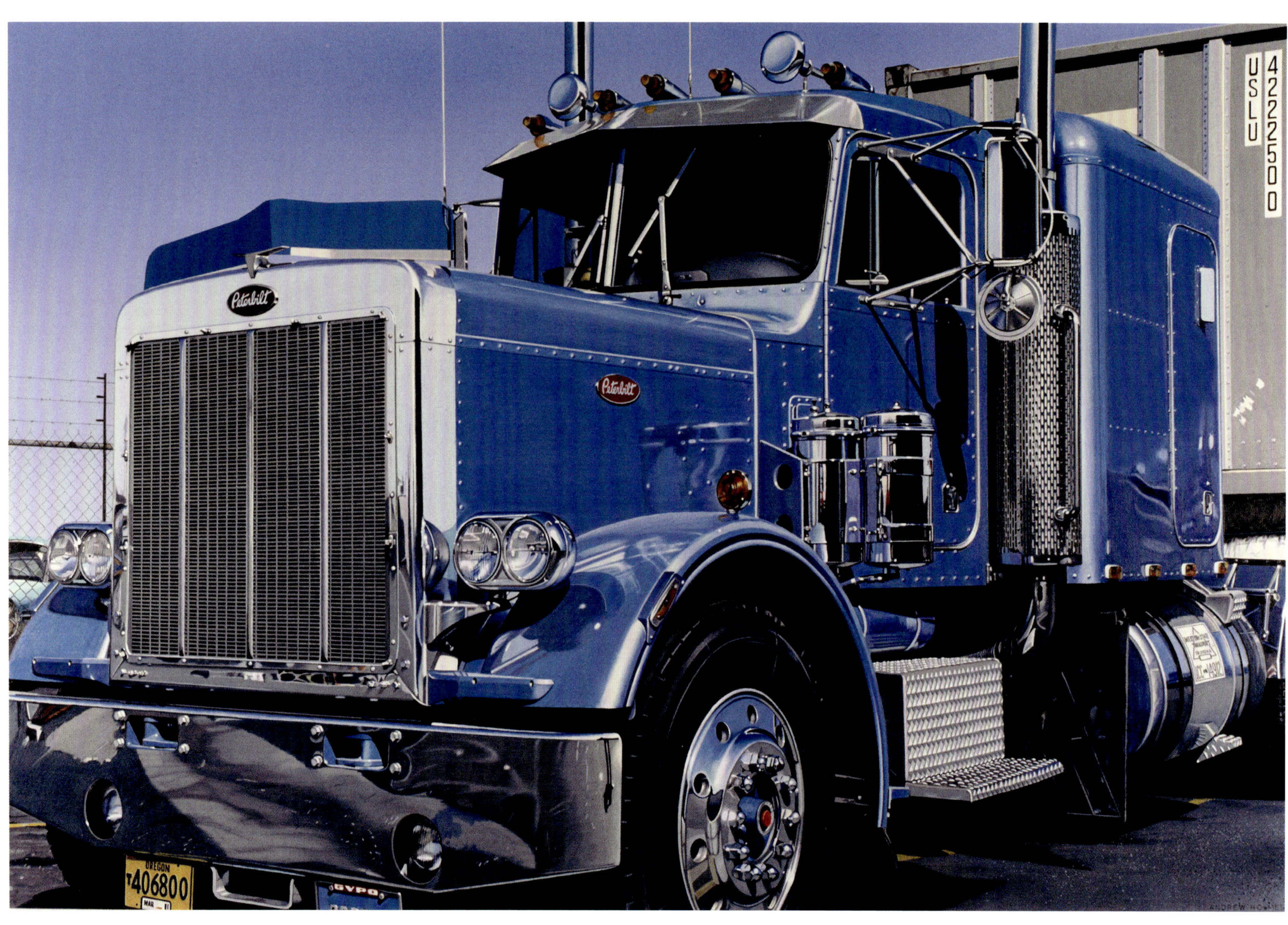

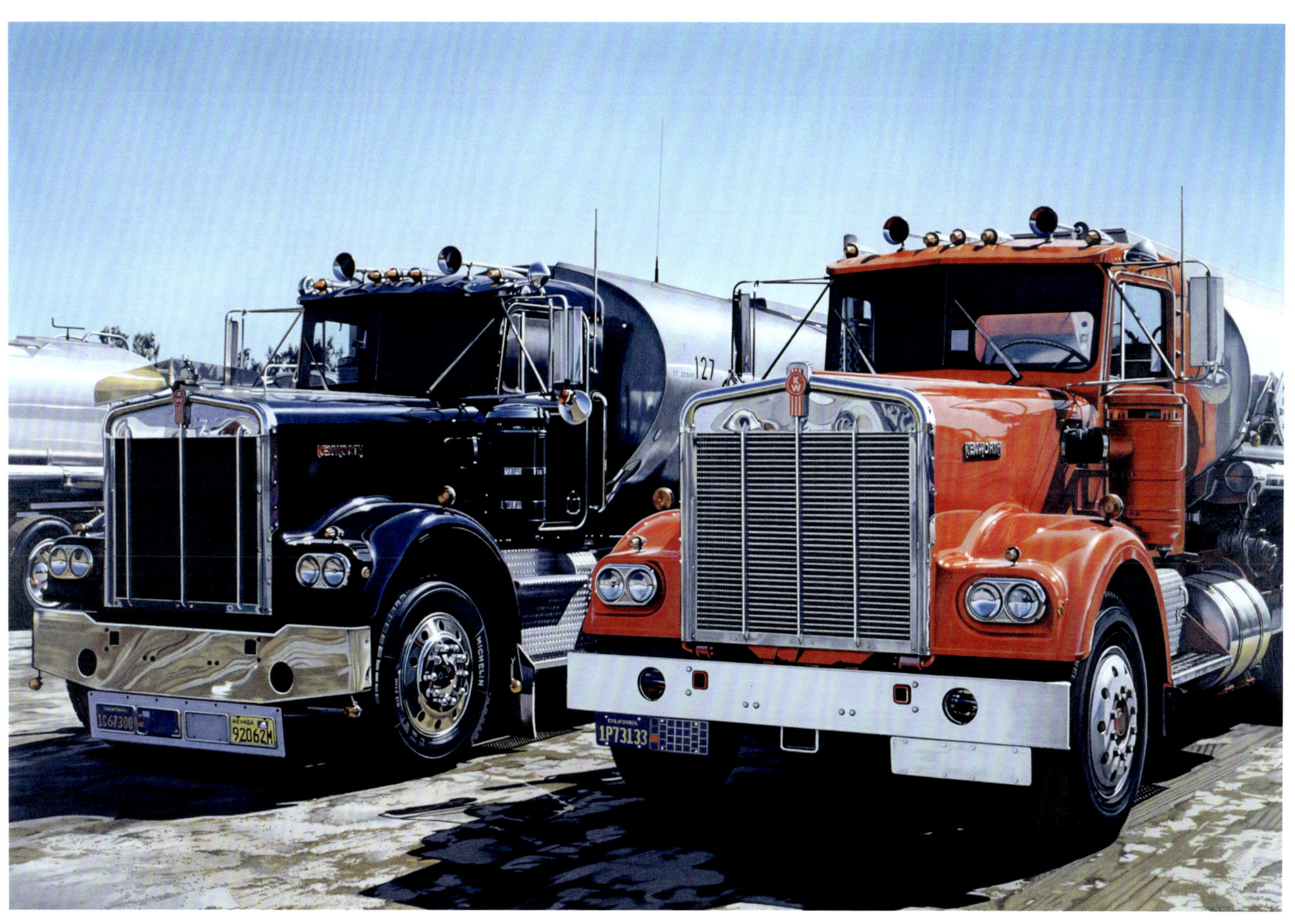

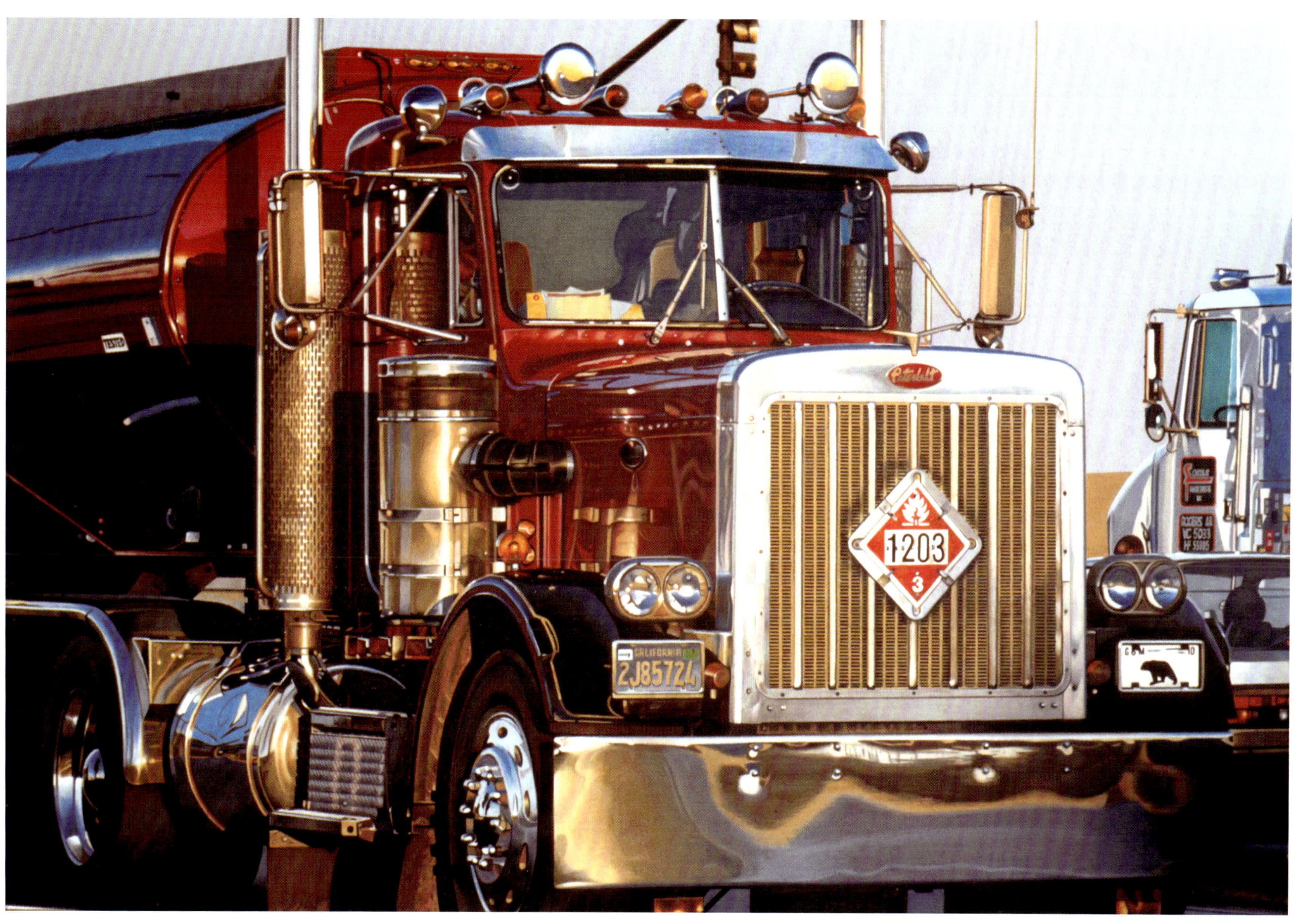

1203
CALIFORNIA 2J85724

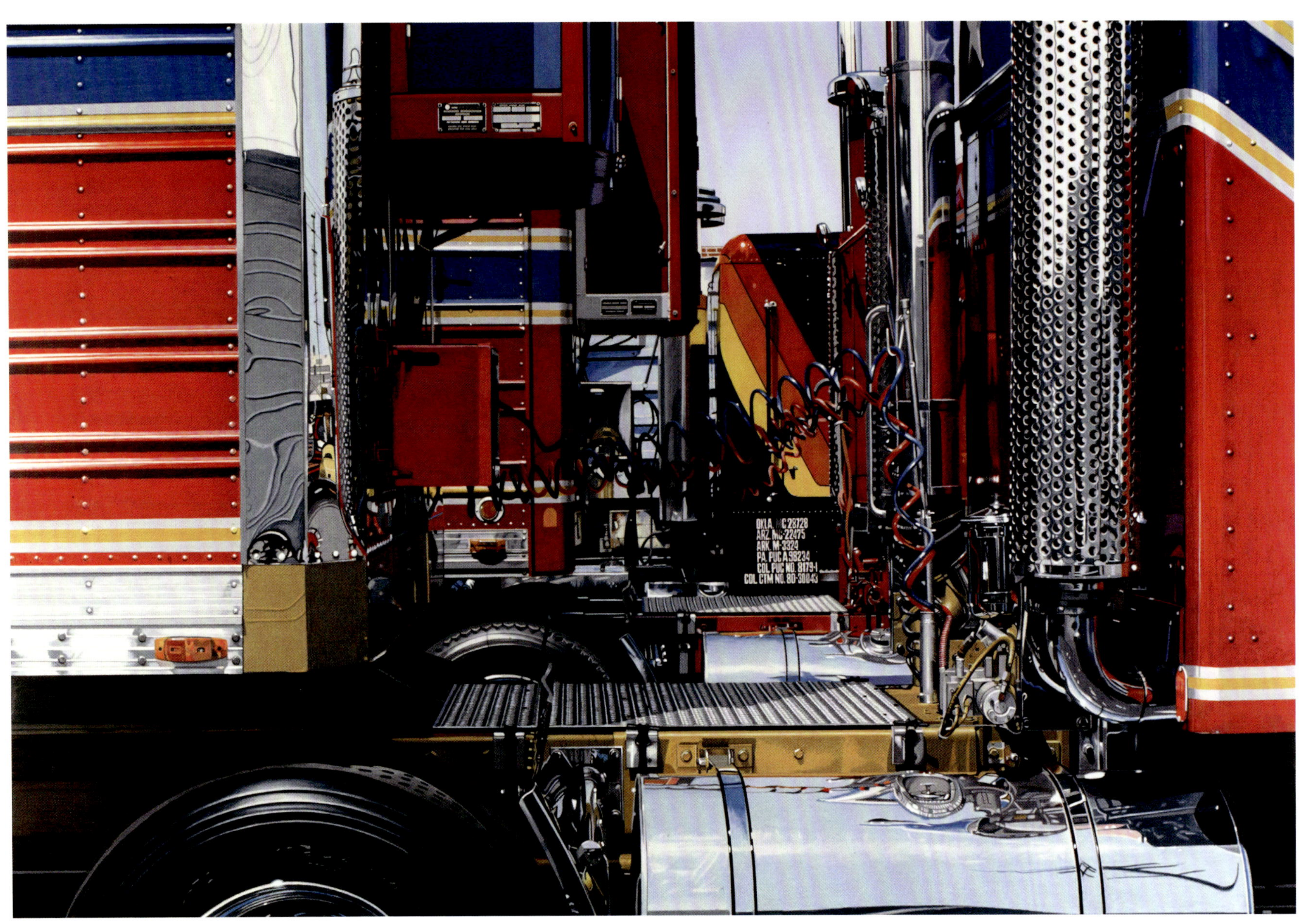

OKLA. MC 28728
ARZ. MC-22475
ARK. M-3324
PA. PUC A 98234
COL. PUC NO. 8179-1
COL. CTM NO. 80-30043

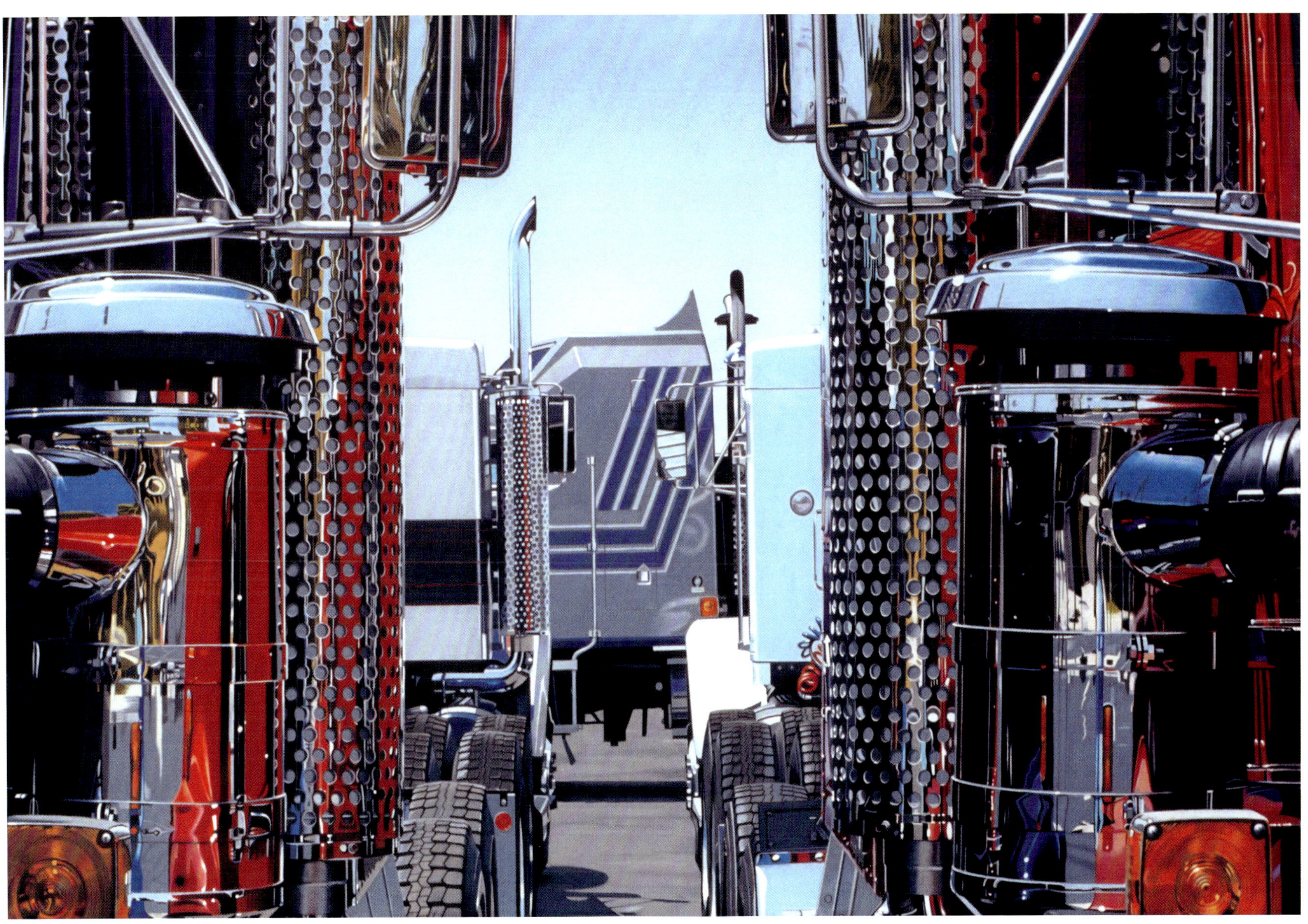

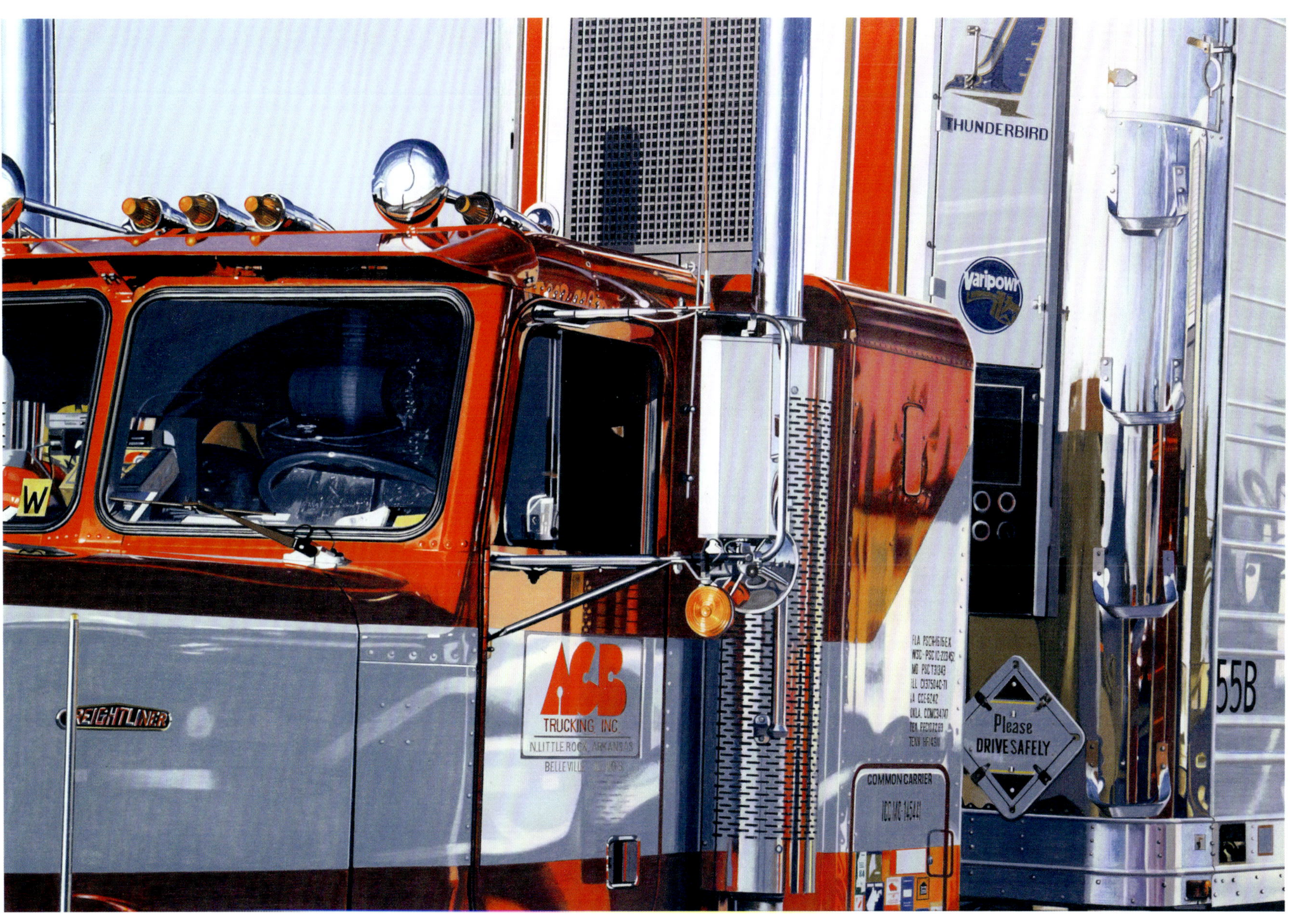

THUNDERBIRD
Varipowr
FREIGHTLINER
W
ACB
TRUCKING INC
N. LITTLE ROCK, ARKANSAS
BELLEVILLE
COMMON CARRIER
ICC MC-145441
Please
DRIVE SAFELY
55B

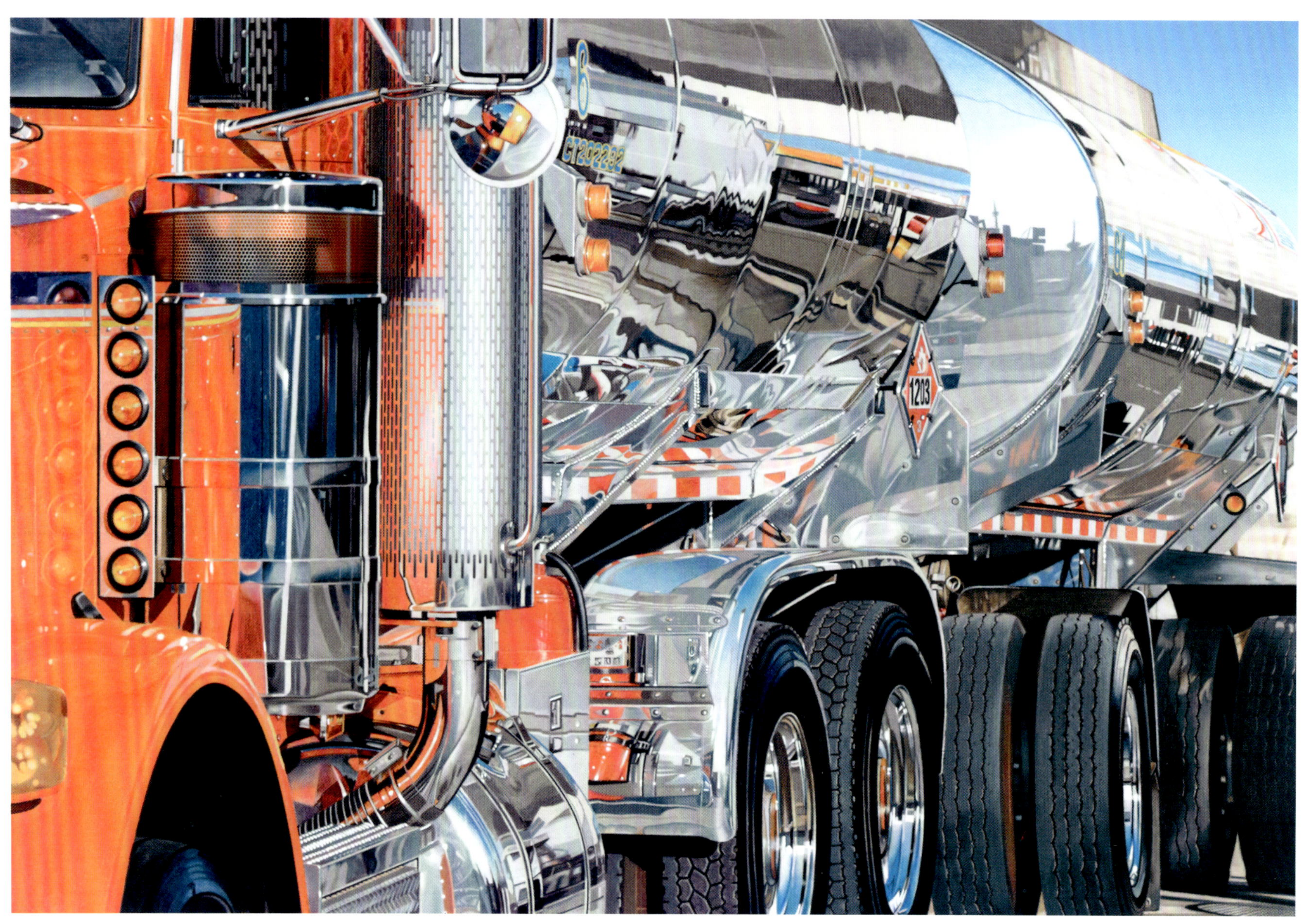

1203

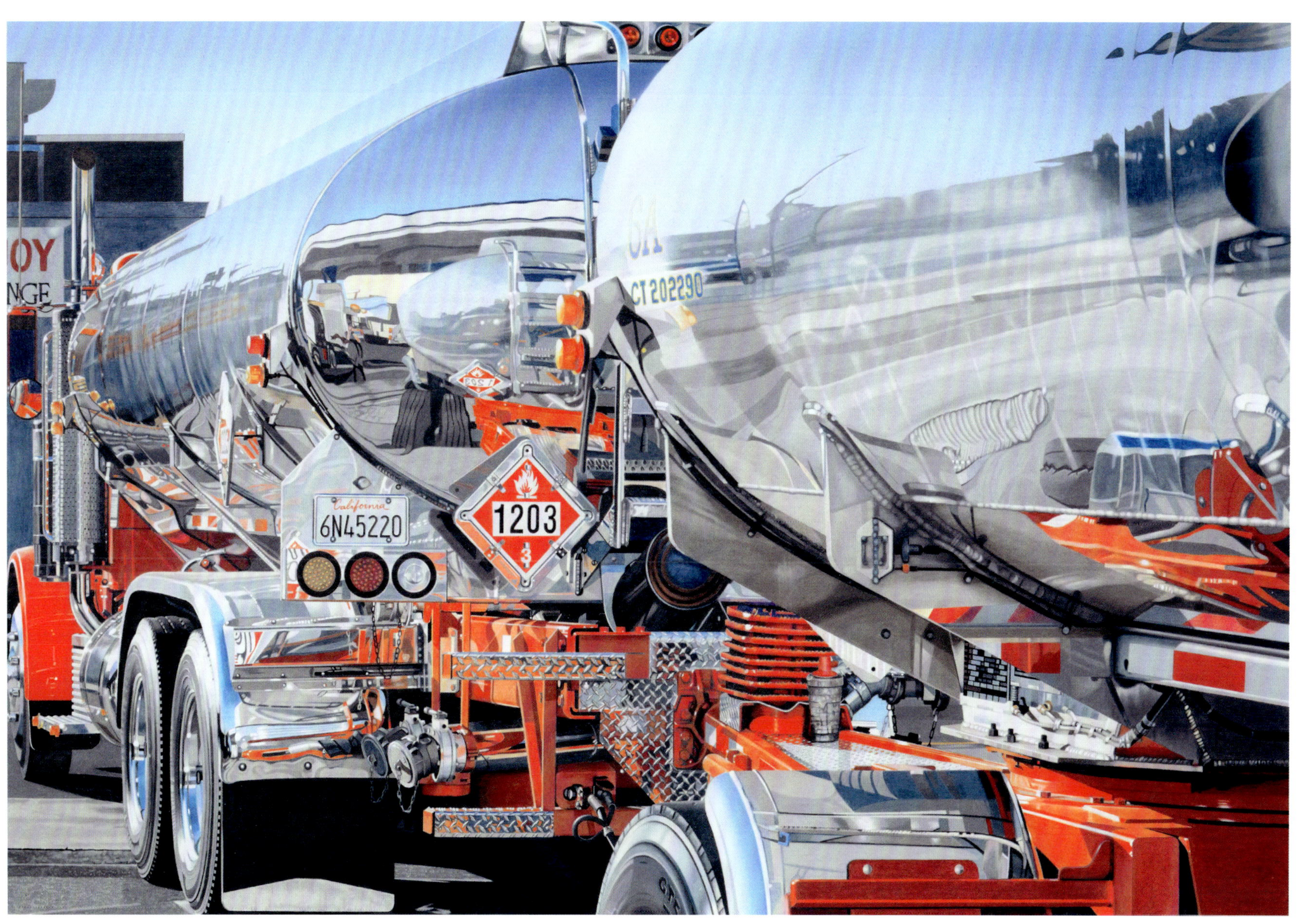

California
6N45220
1203
CT 202290

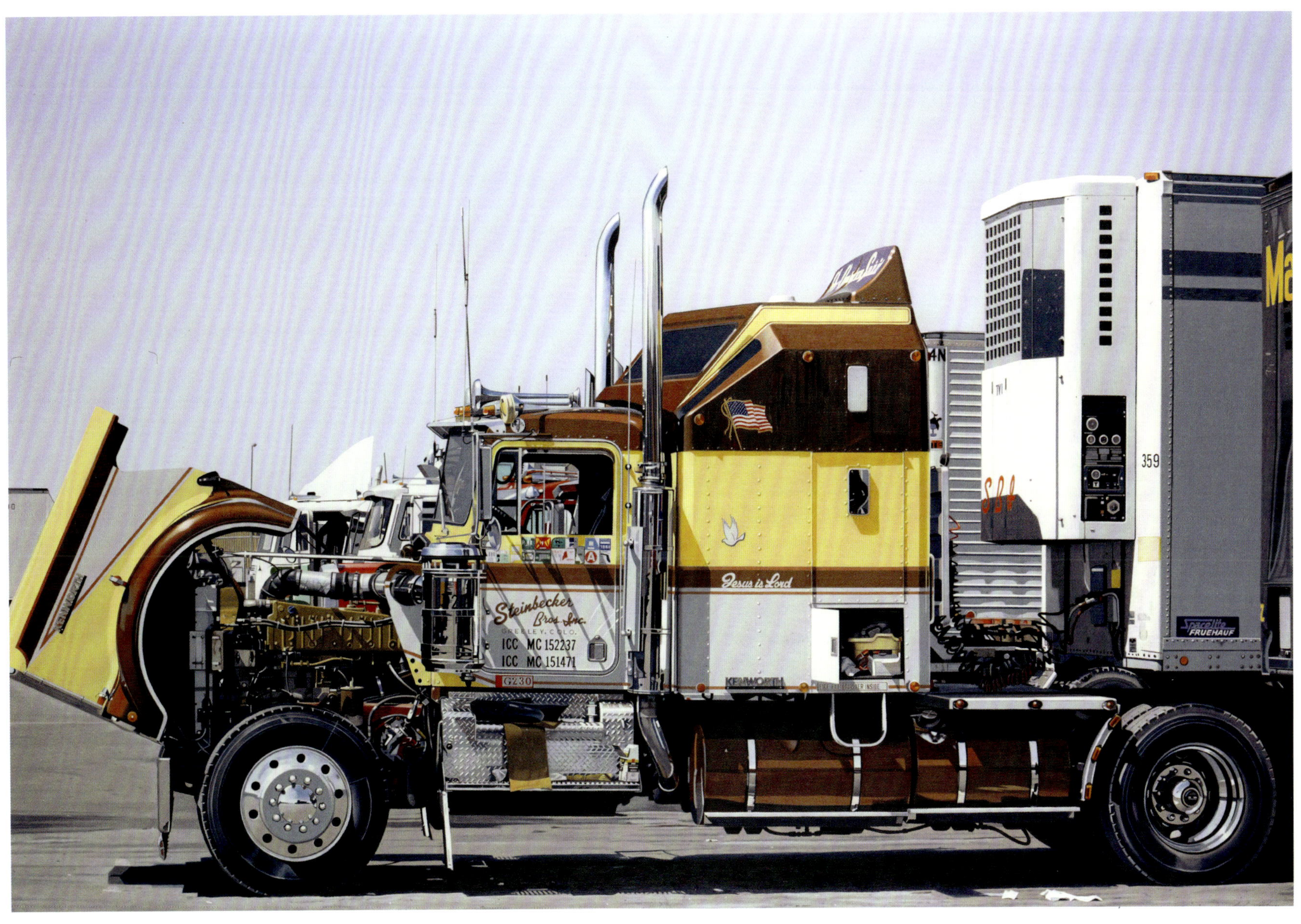

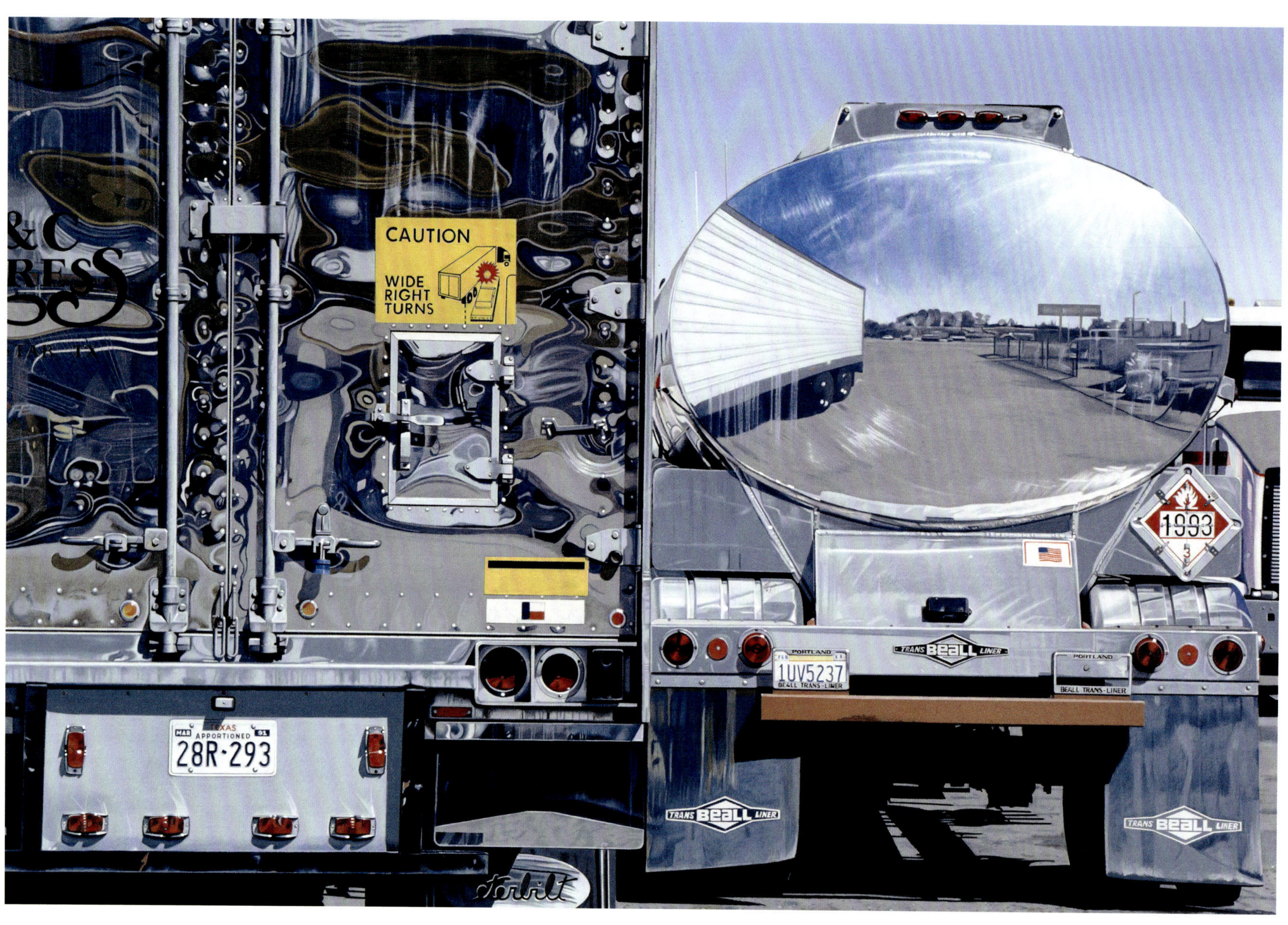
CAUTION
WIDE
RIGHT
TURNS
TEXAS
APPORTIONED
28R·293
PORTLAND
1UV5237
BEALL TRANS-LINER
TRANS BEALL LINER
1993

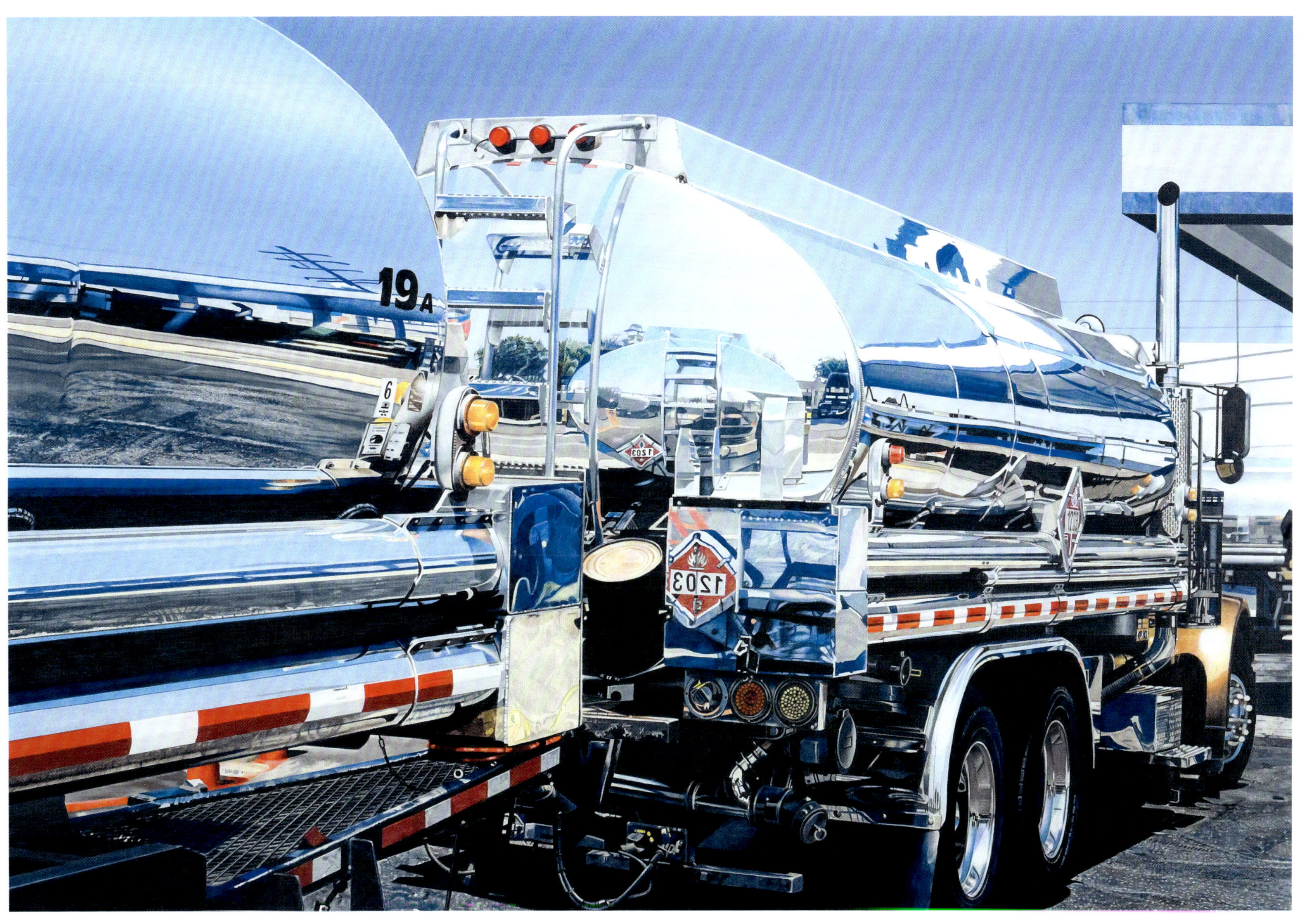
19 A
1203
1203

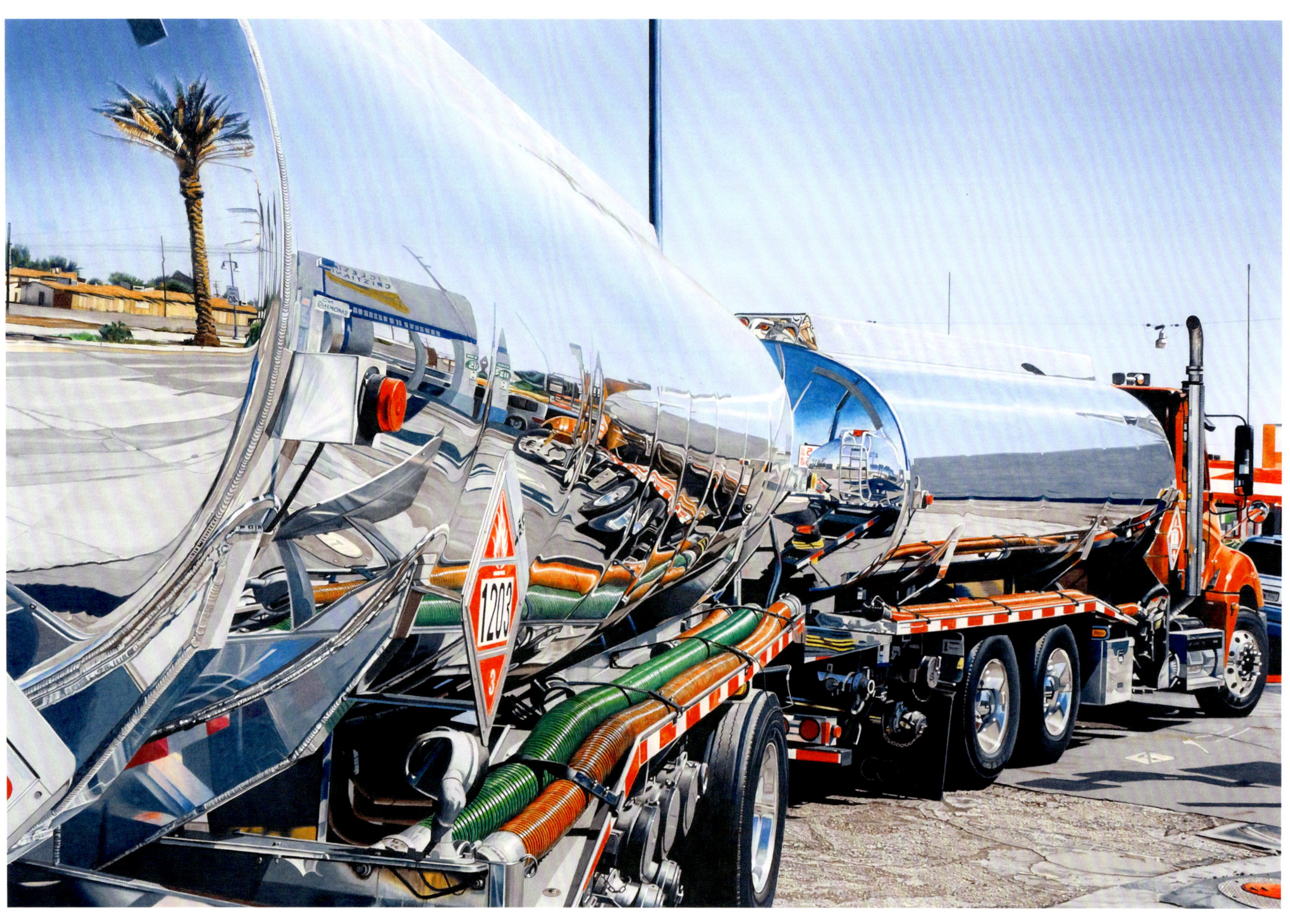

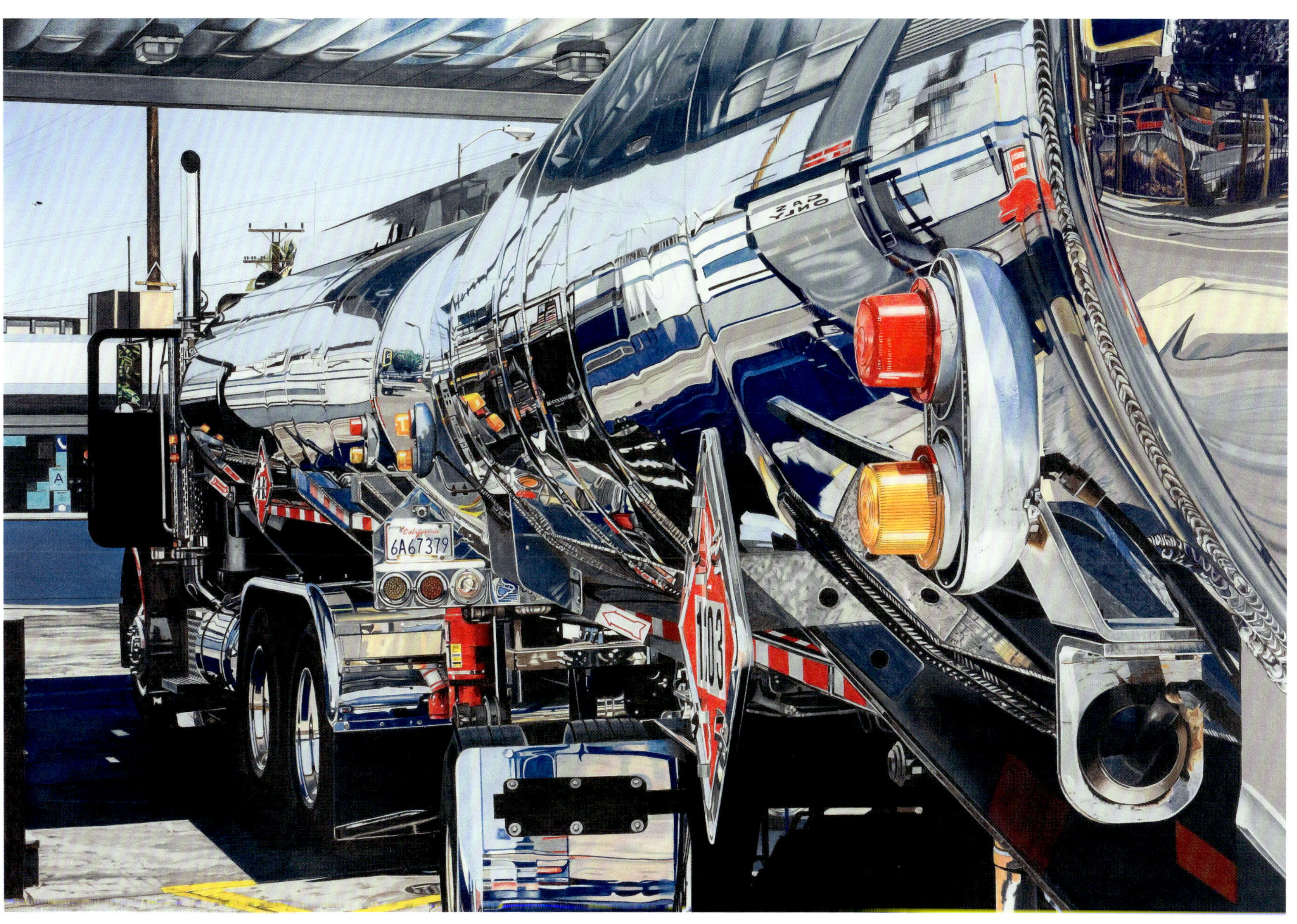

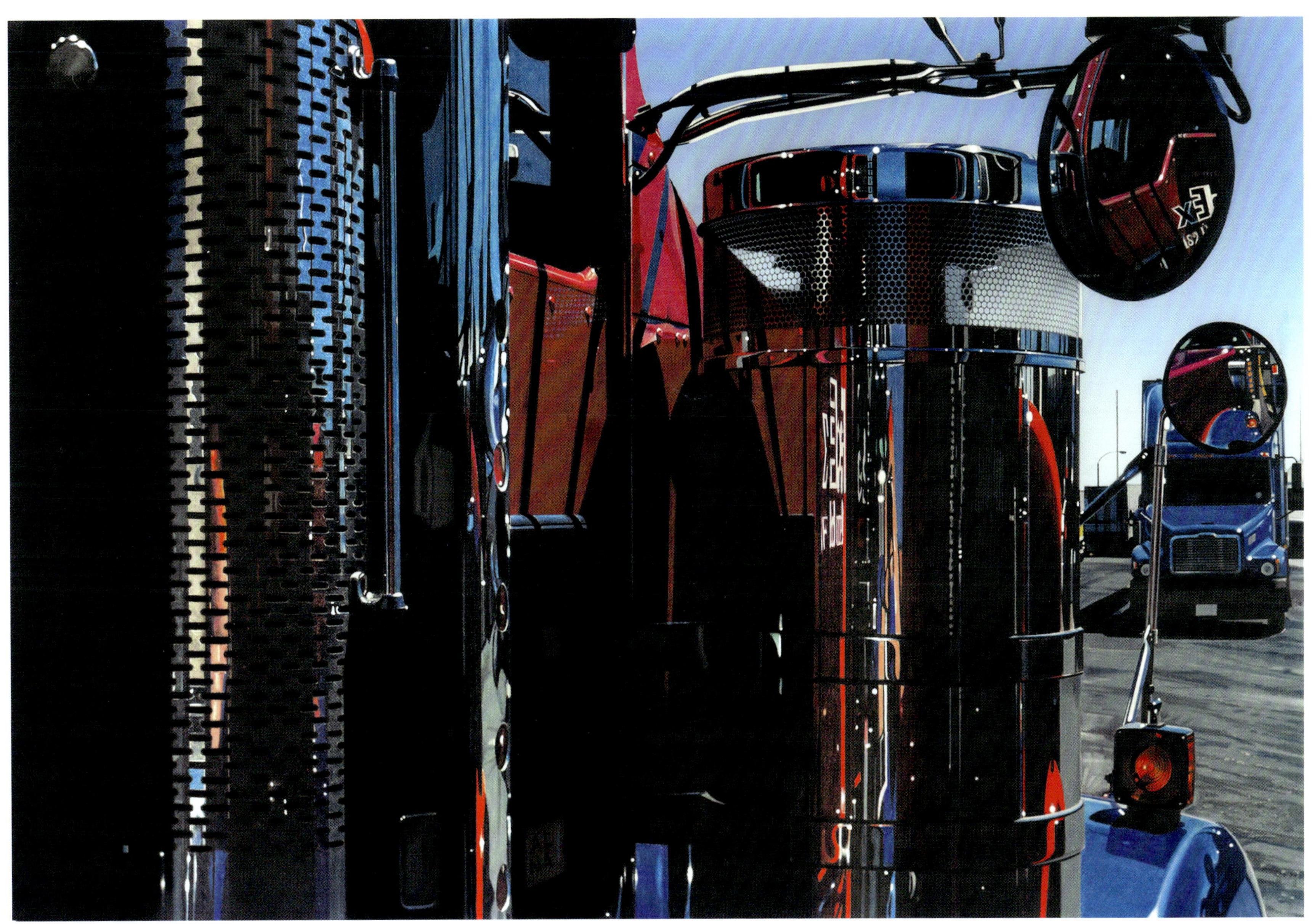

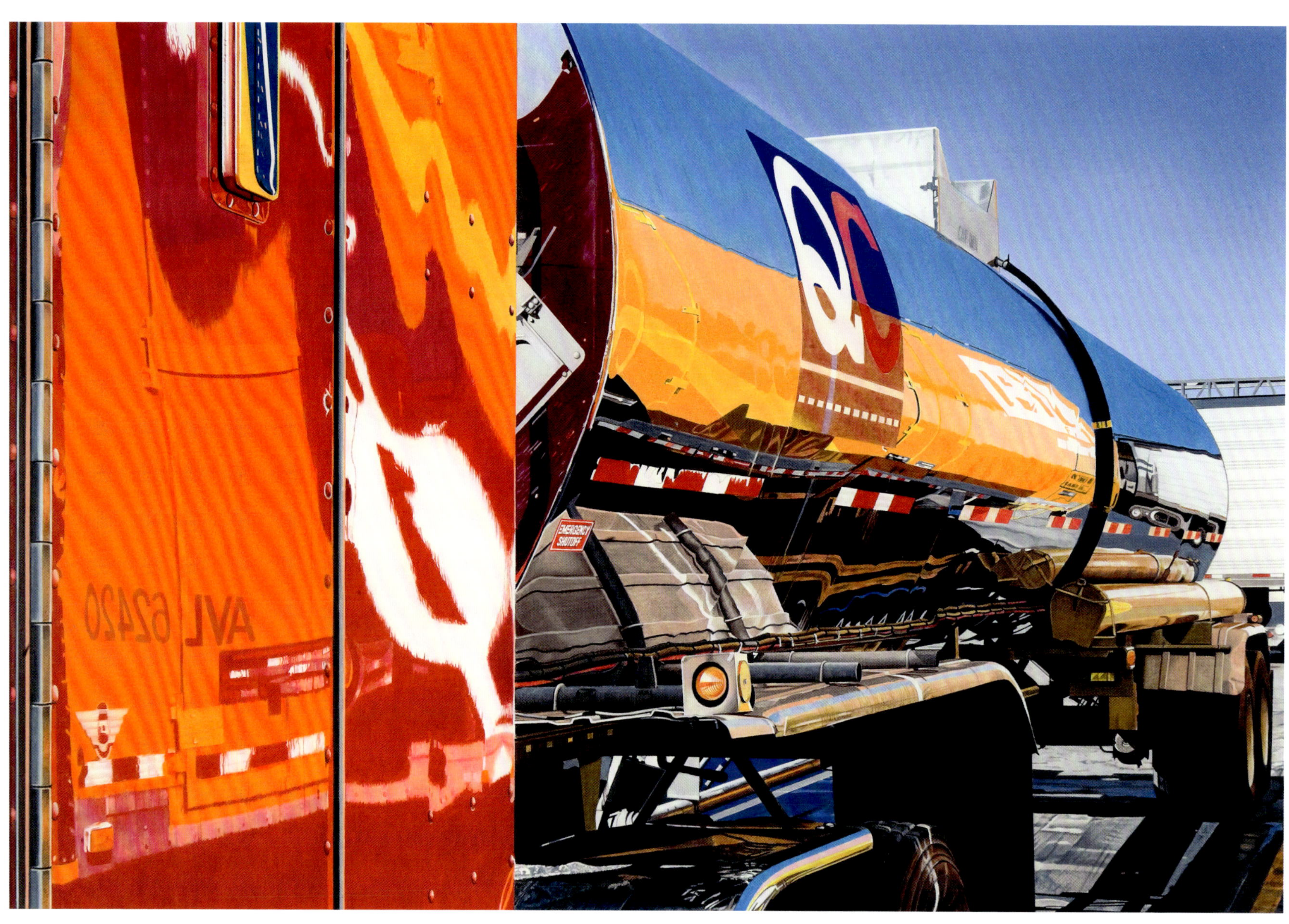

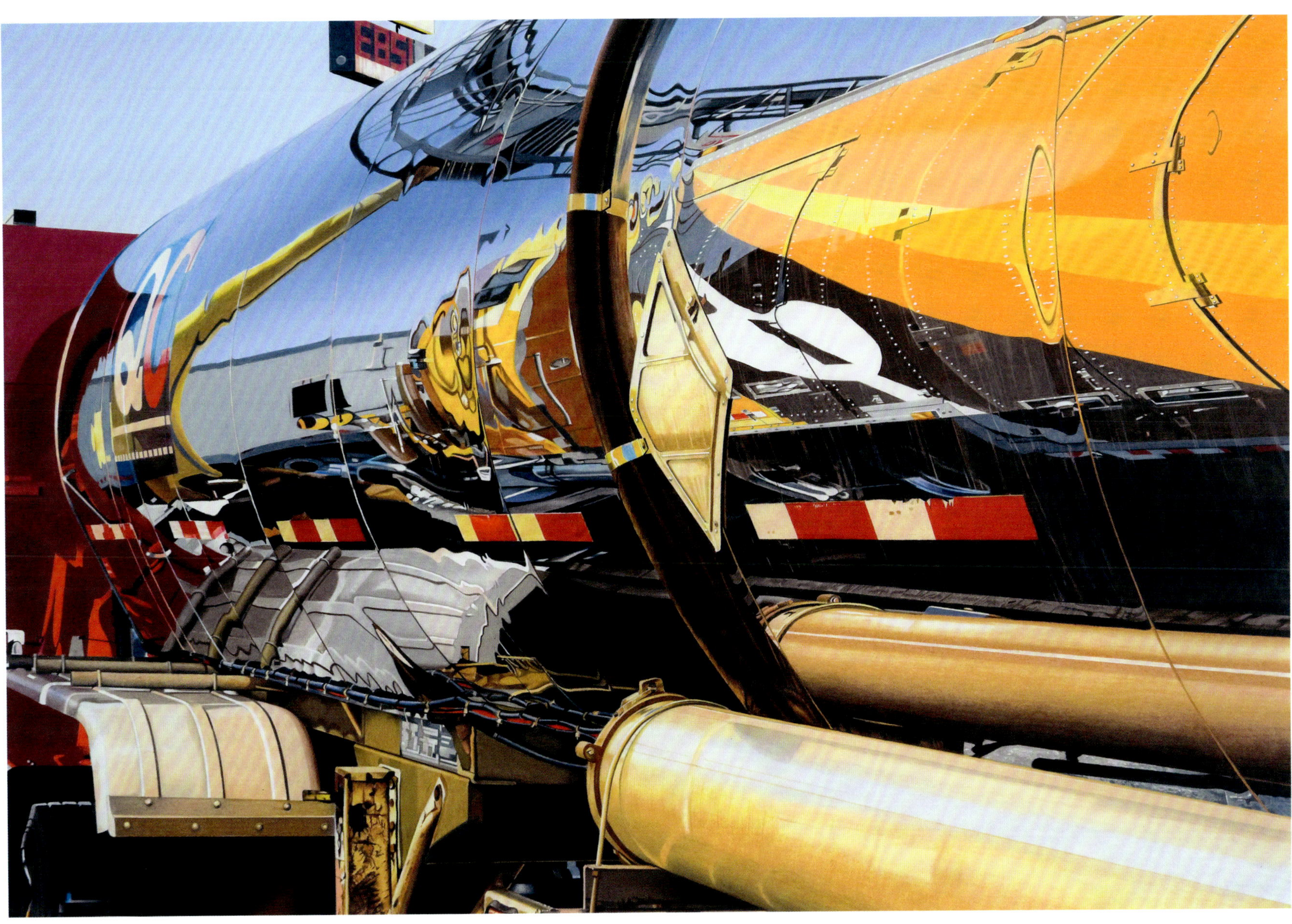

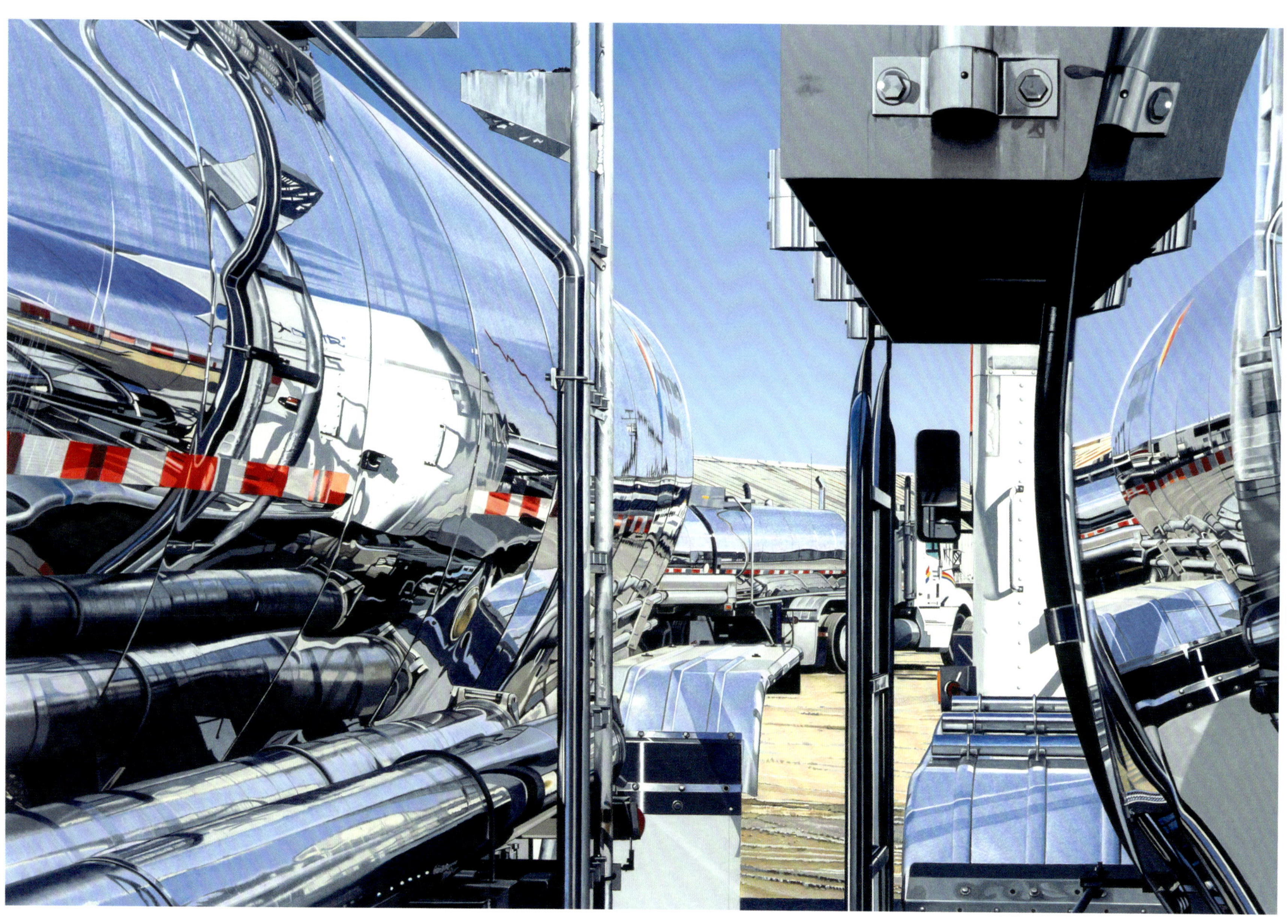

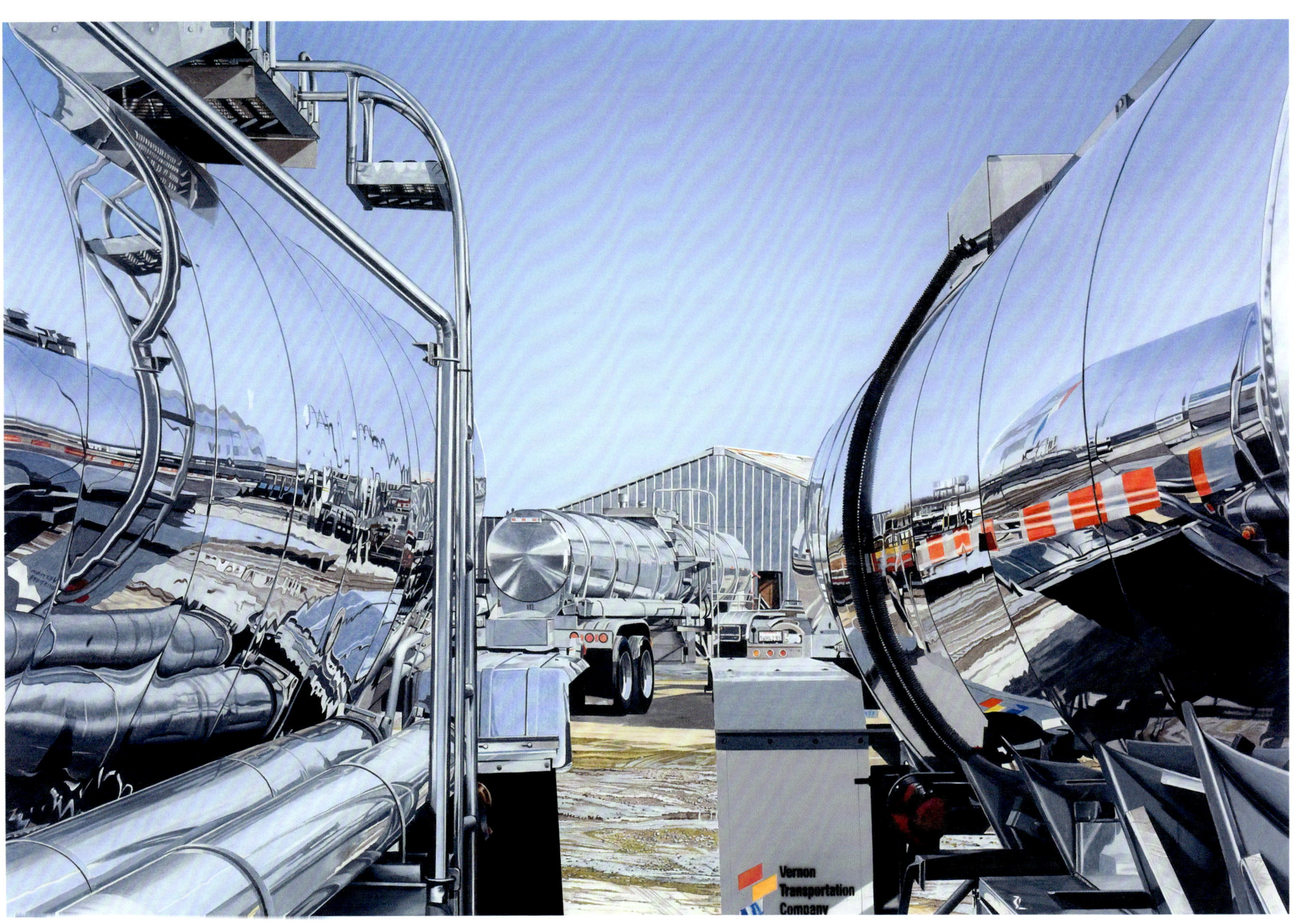

Vernon
Transportation
Company

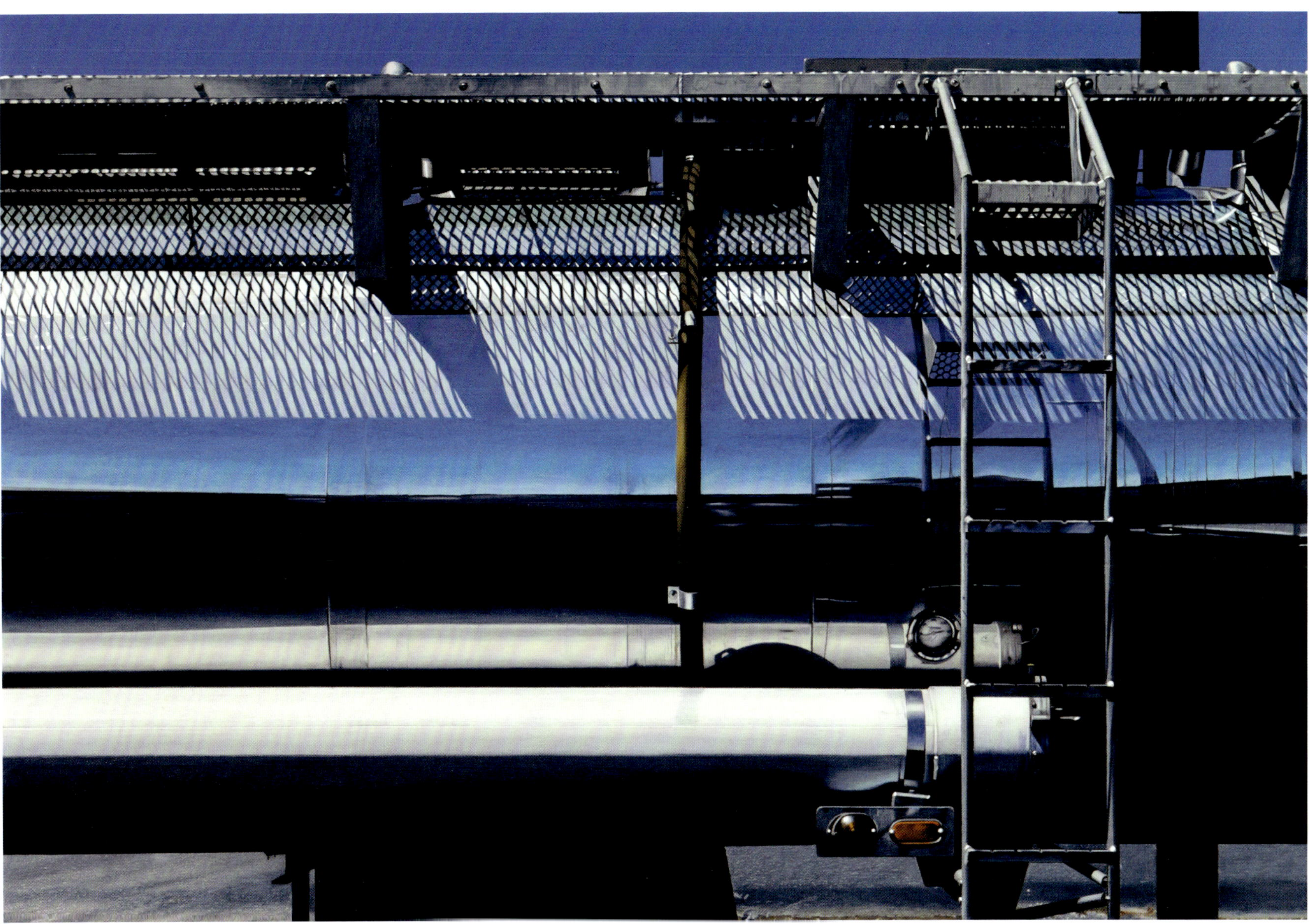

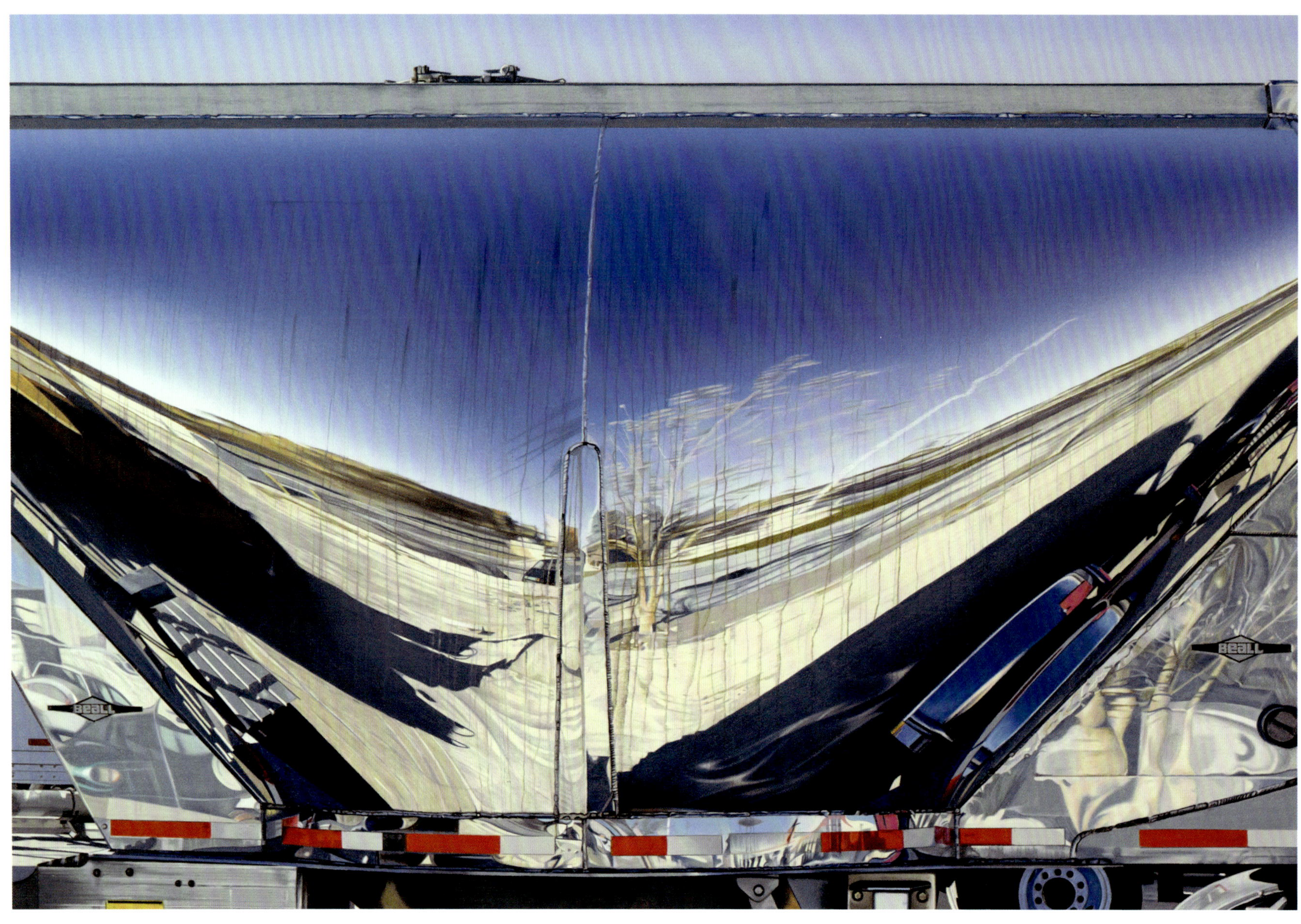

BEALL
BEALL

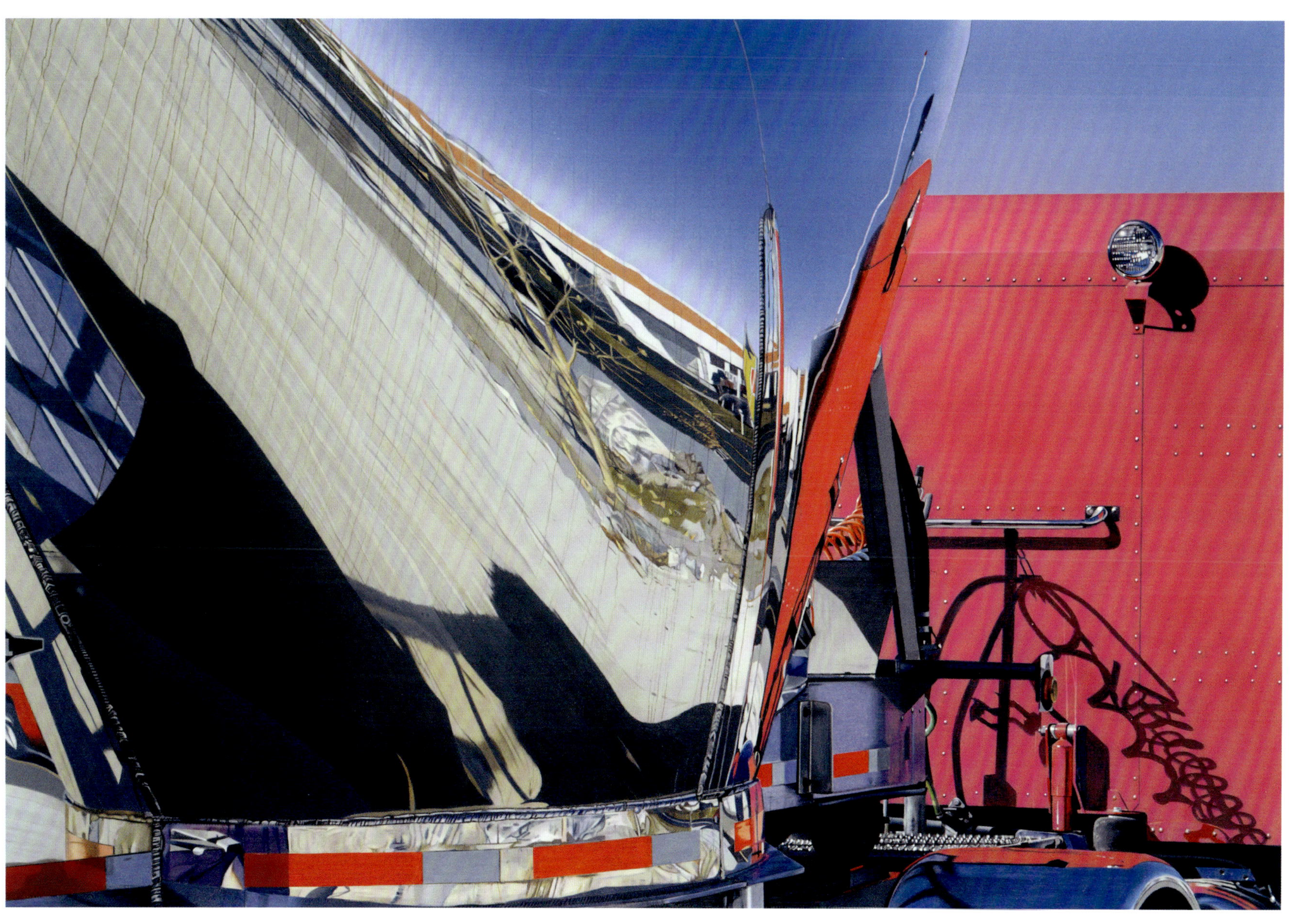

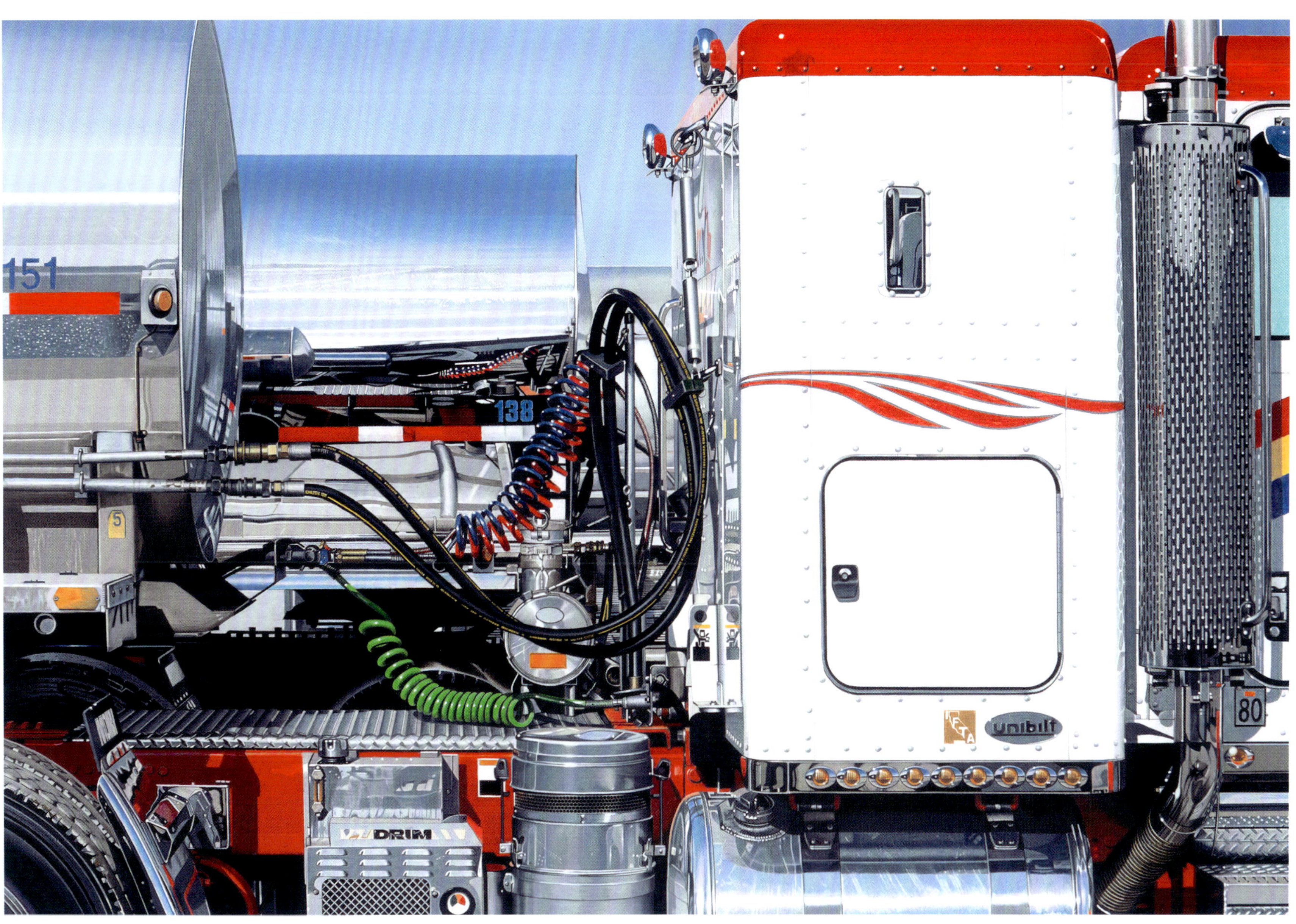

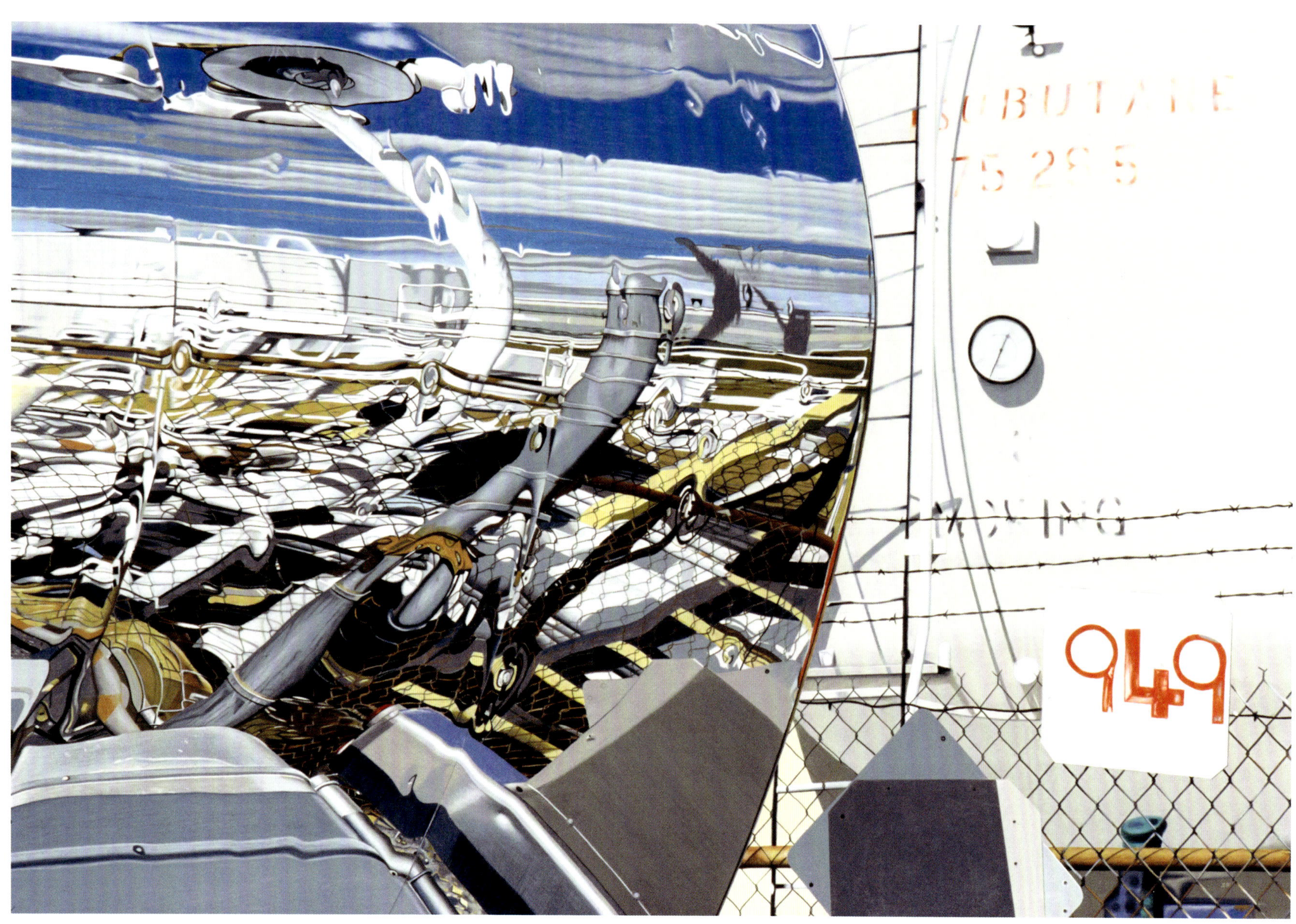

ISOBUTATE
75 29 5
SMOKING
949

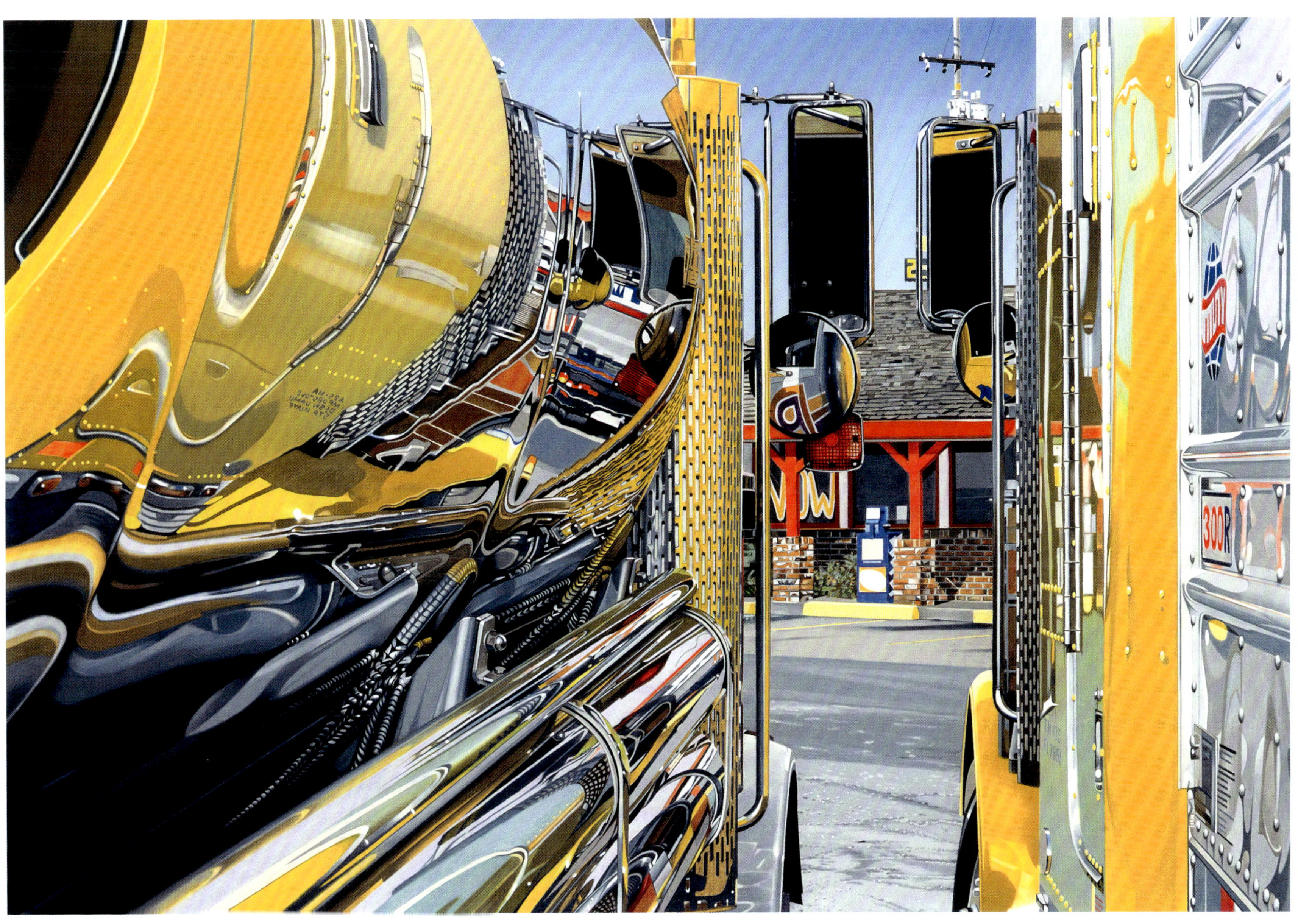

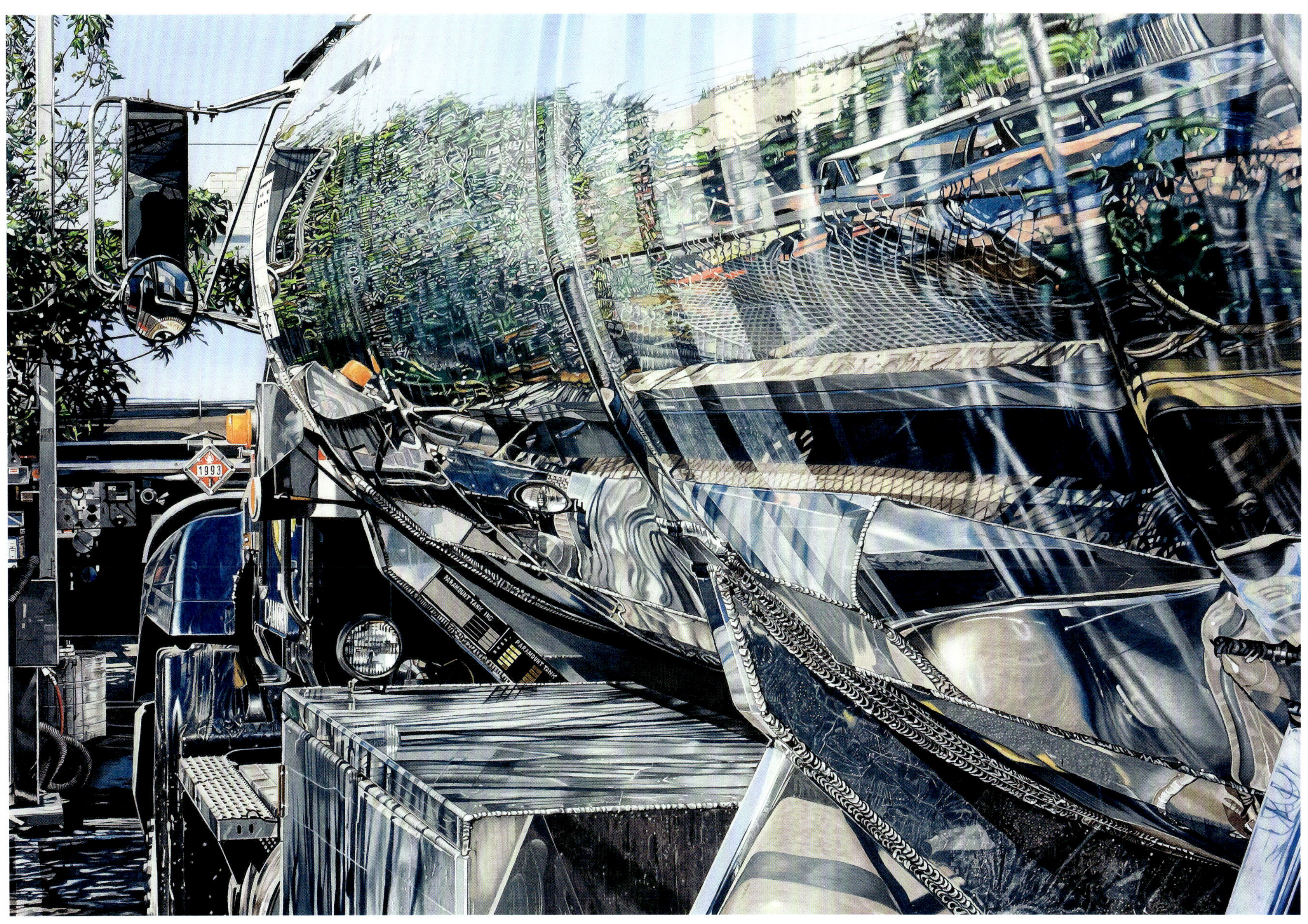

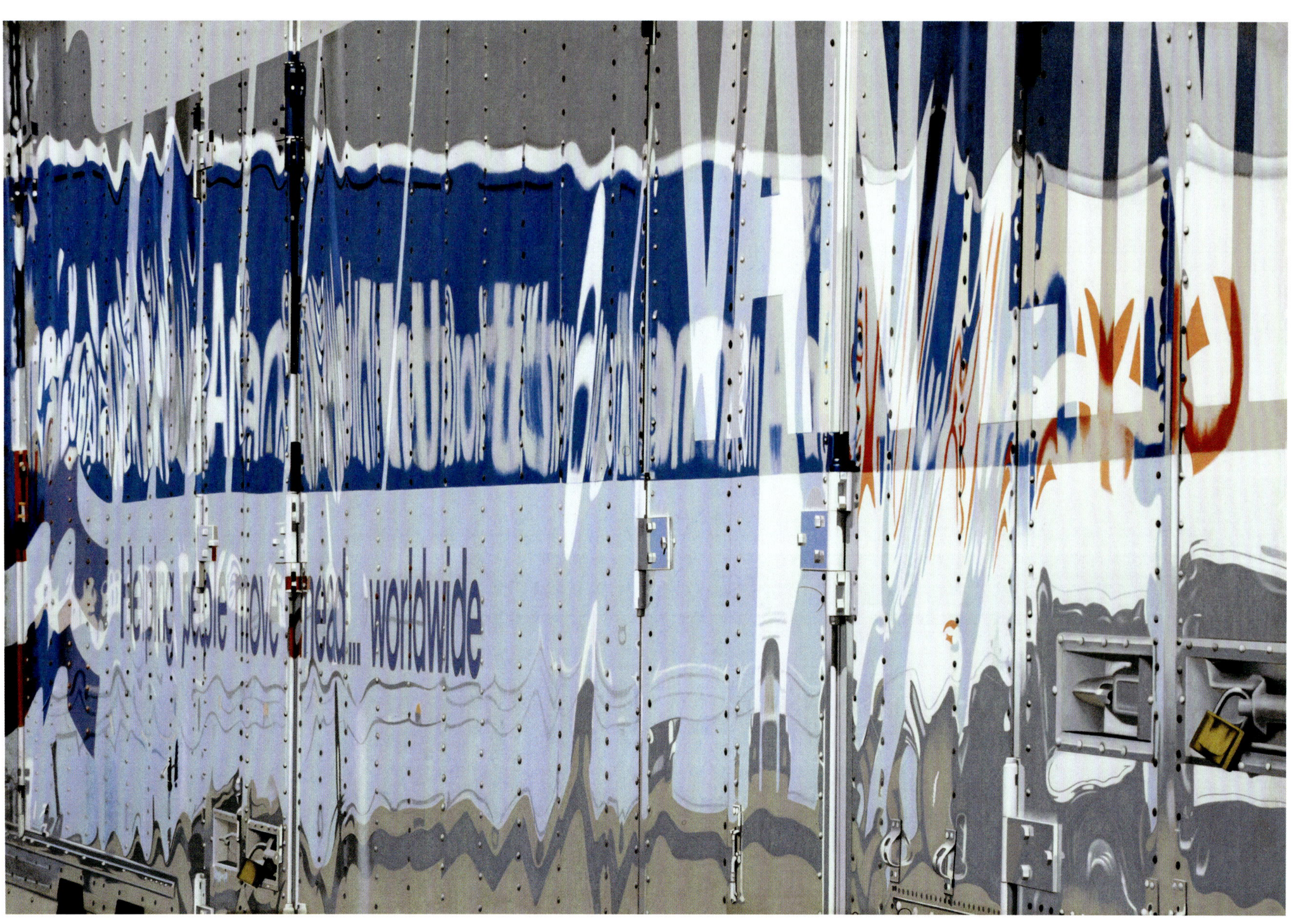
Helping people move ahead... worldwide

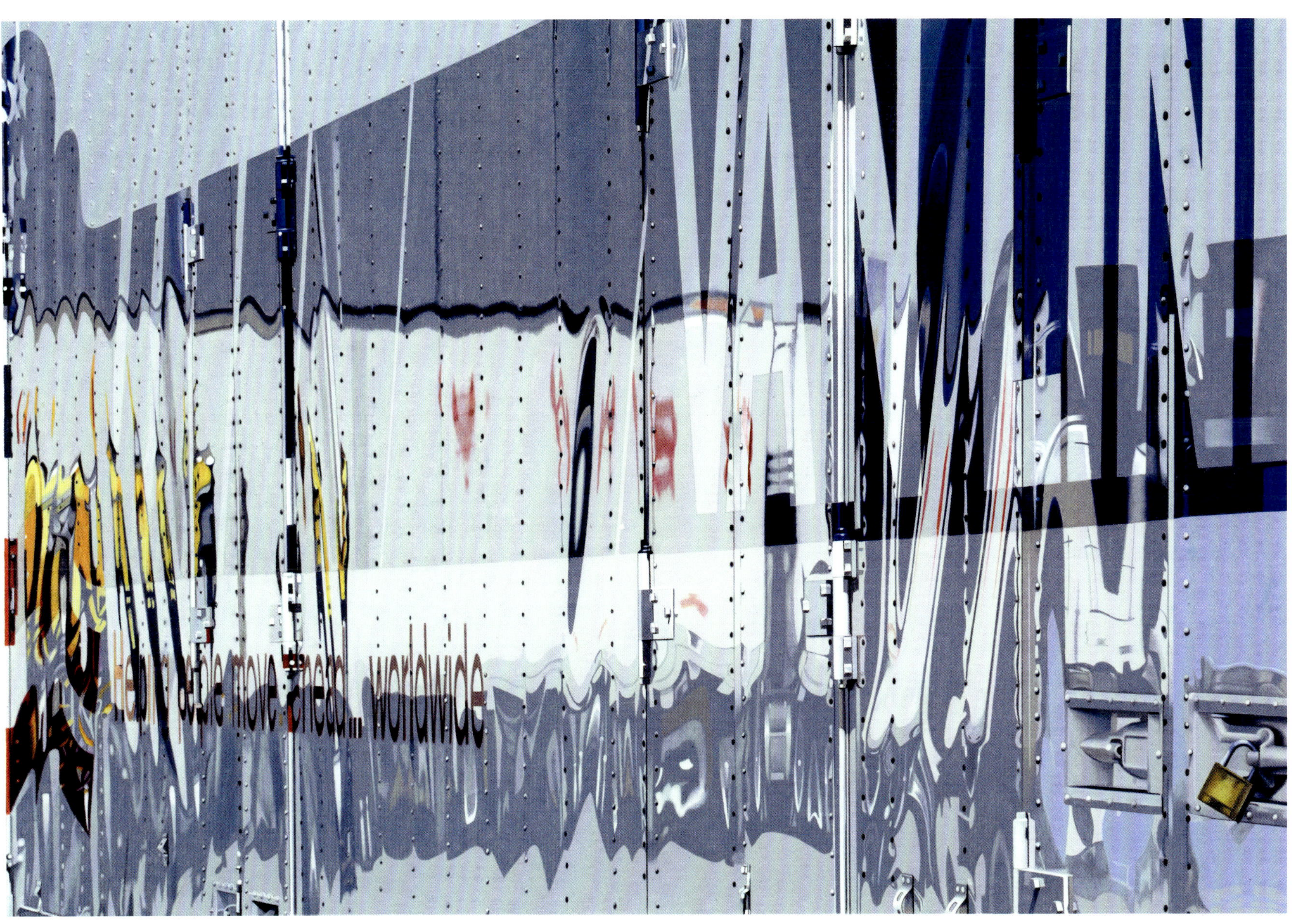

Helping people move ahead... worldwide

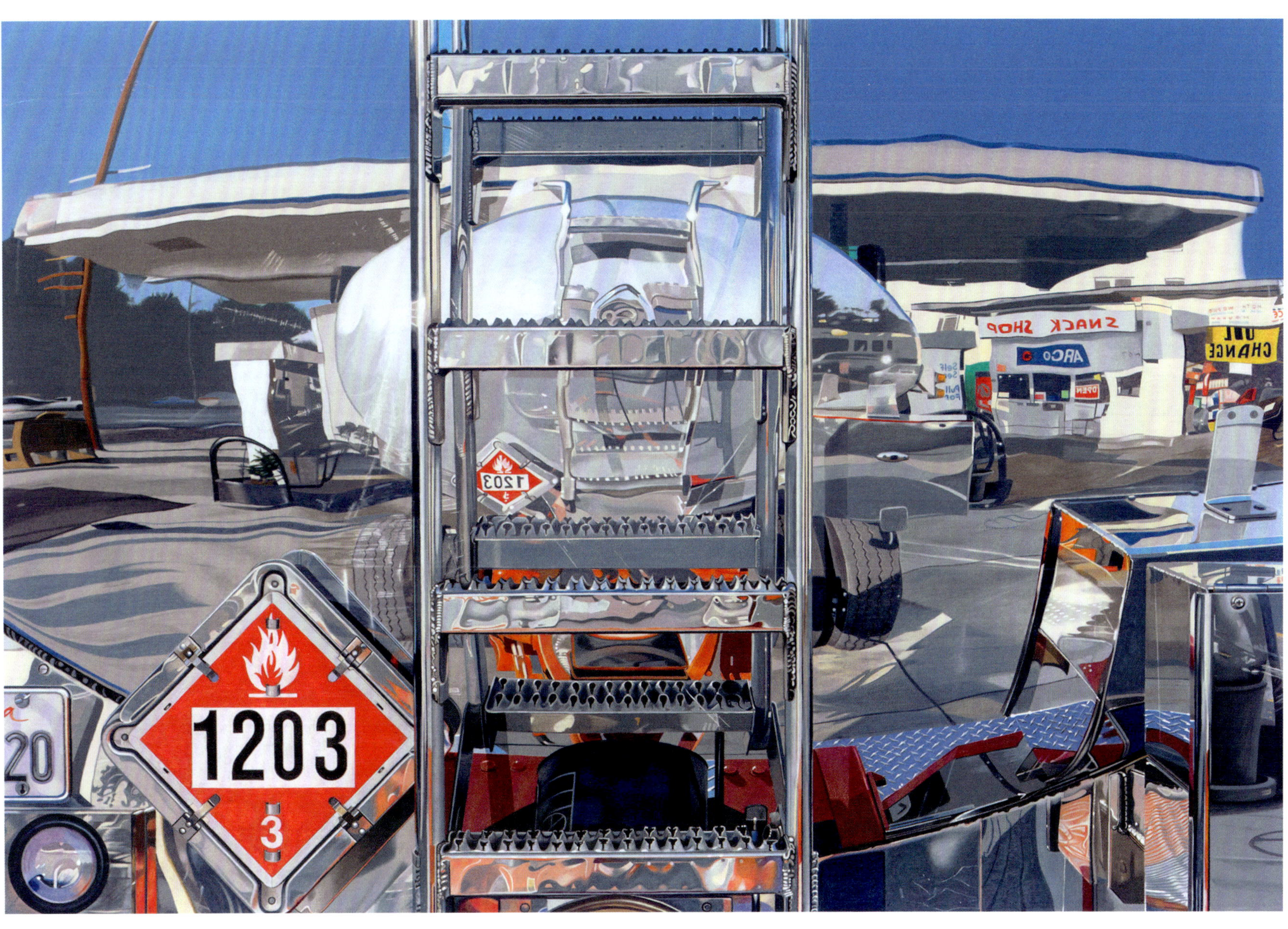

1203
3
1203
SNACK SHOP
ARCO
OIL CHANGE
20

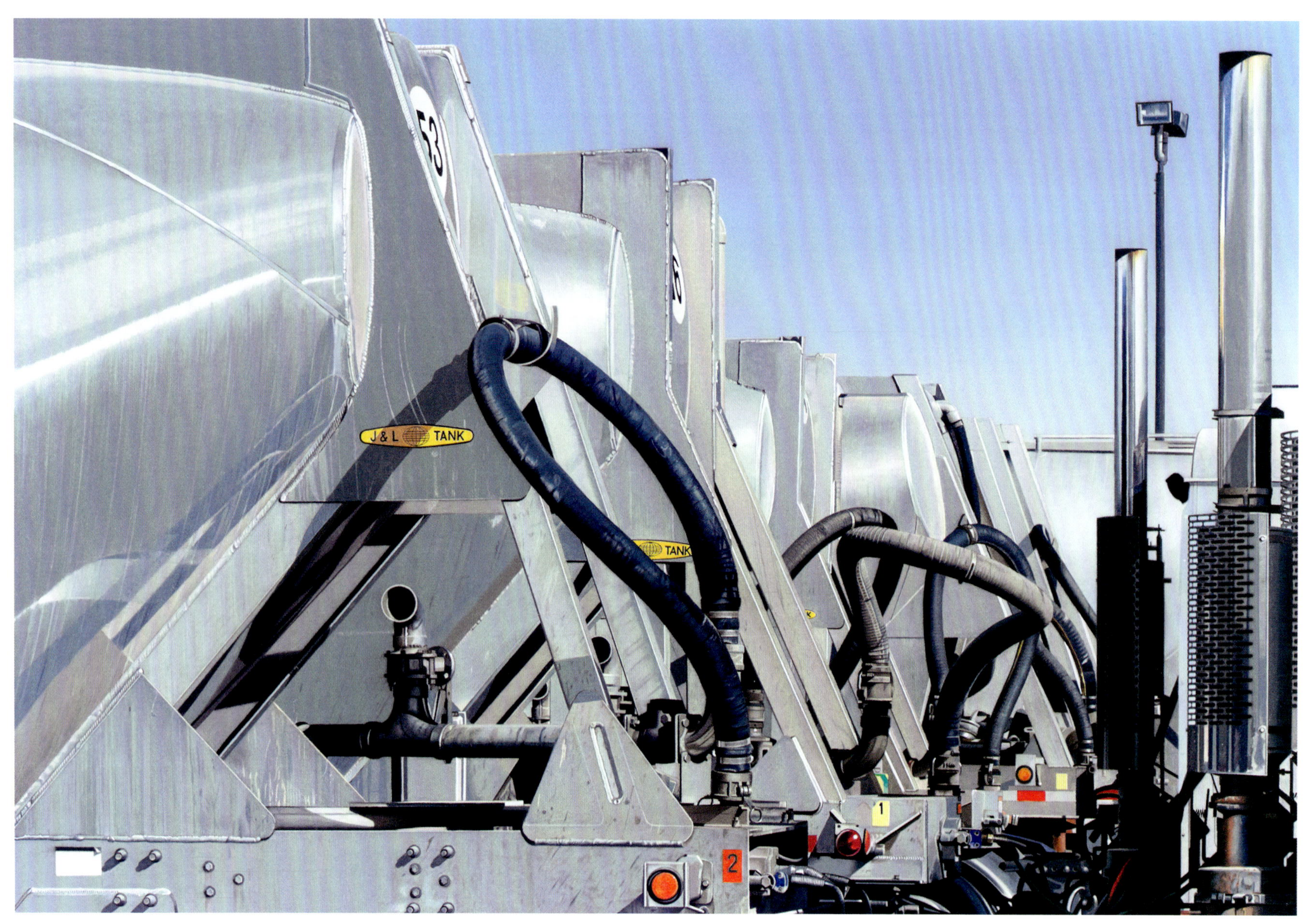

53
J & L TANK
TANK
2
1

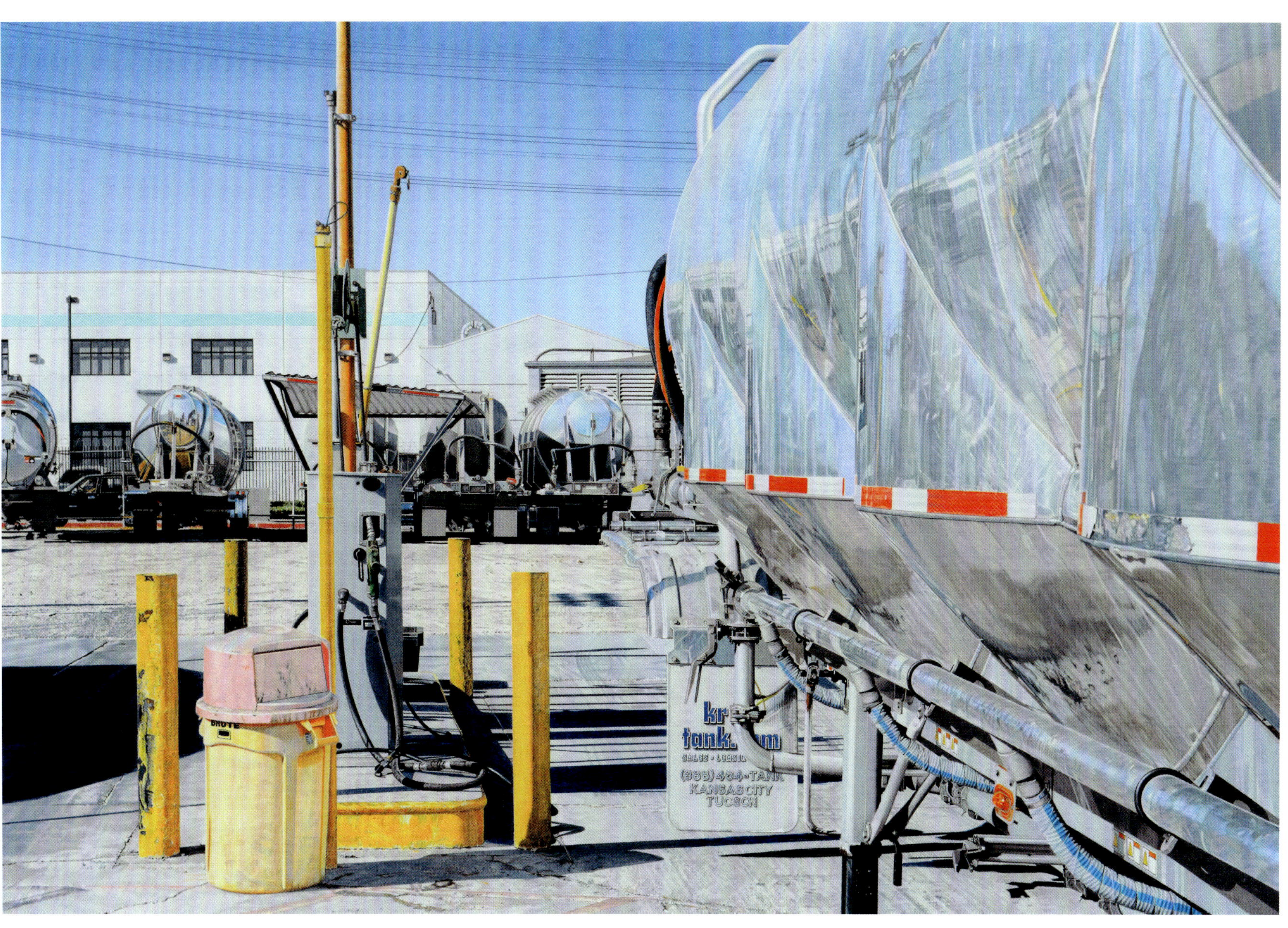

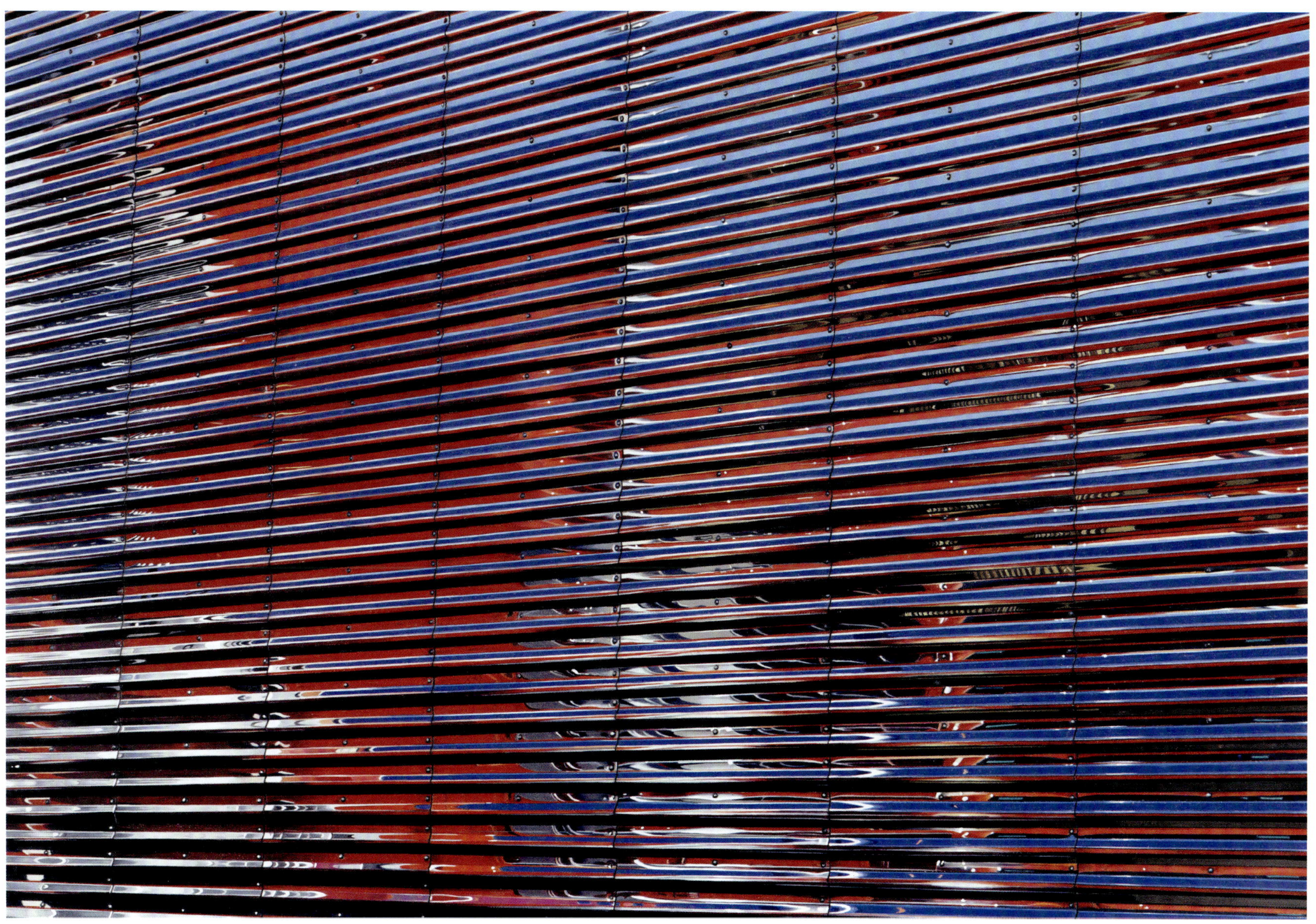

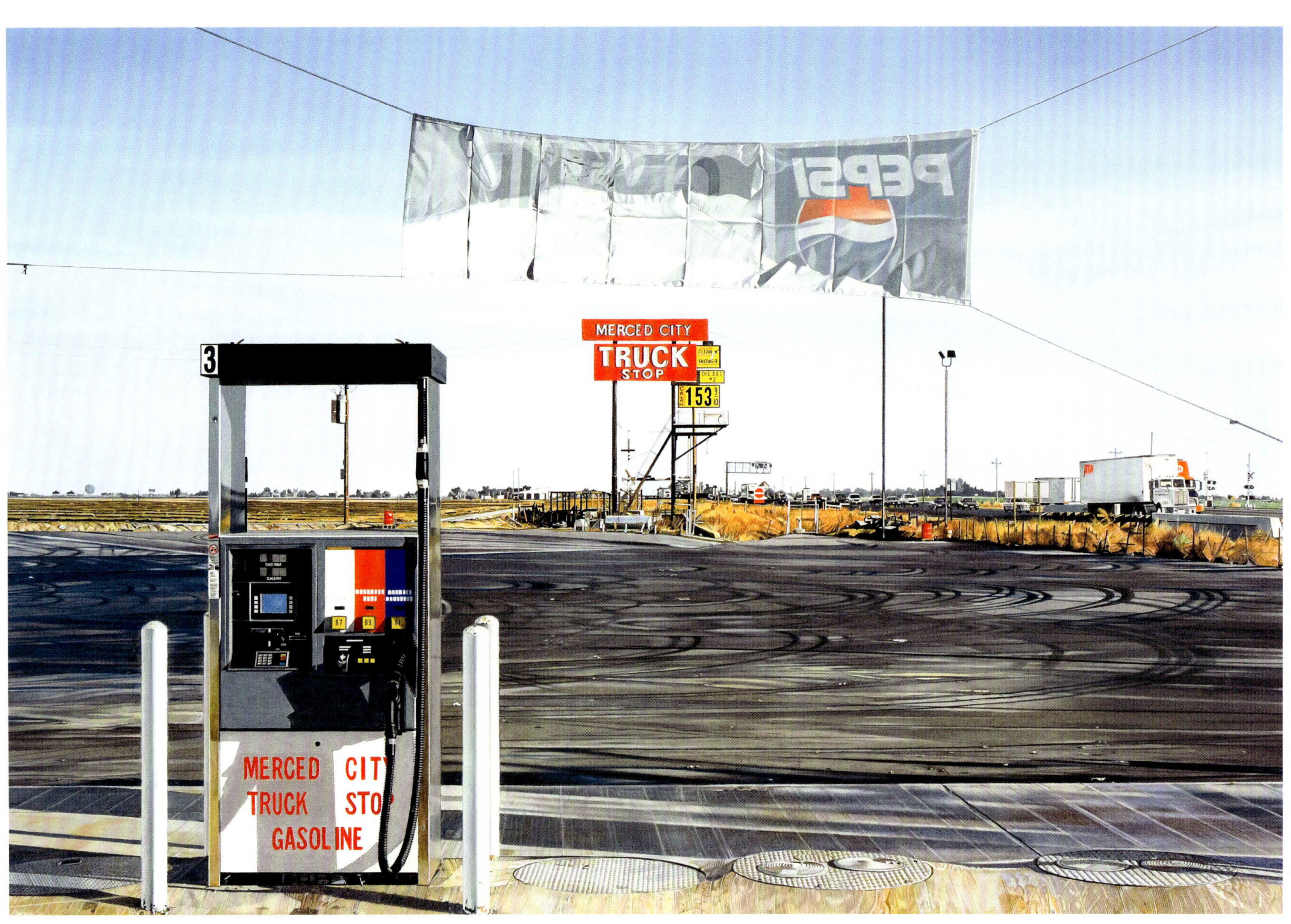
PEPSI
MERCED CITY
TRUCK
STOP
153
3
MERCED CITY
TRUCK STOP
GASOLINE

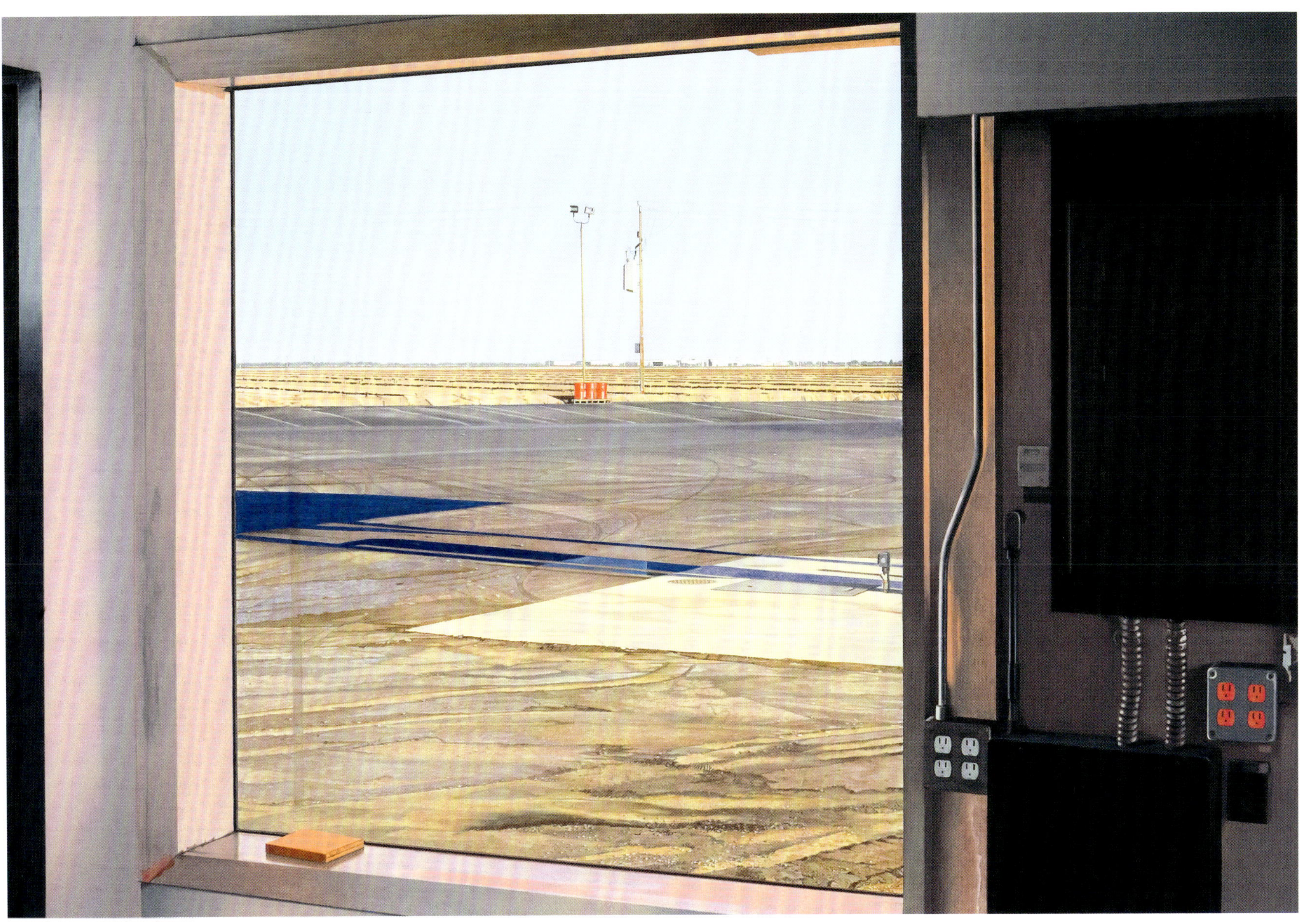

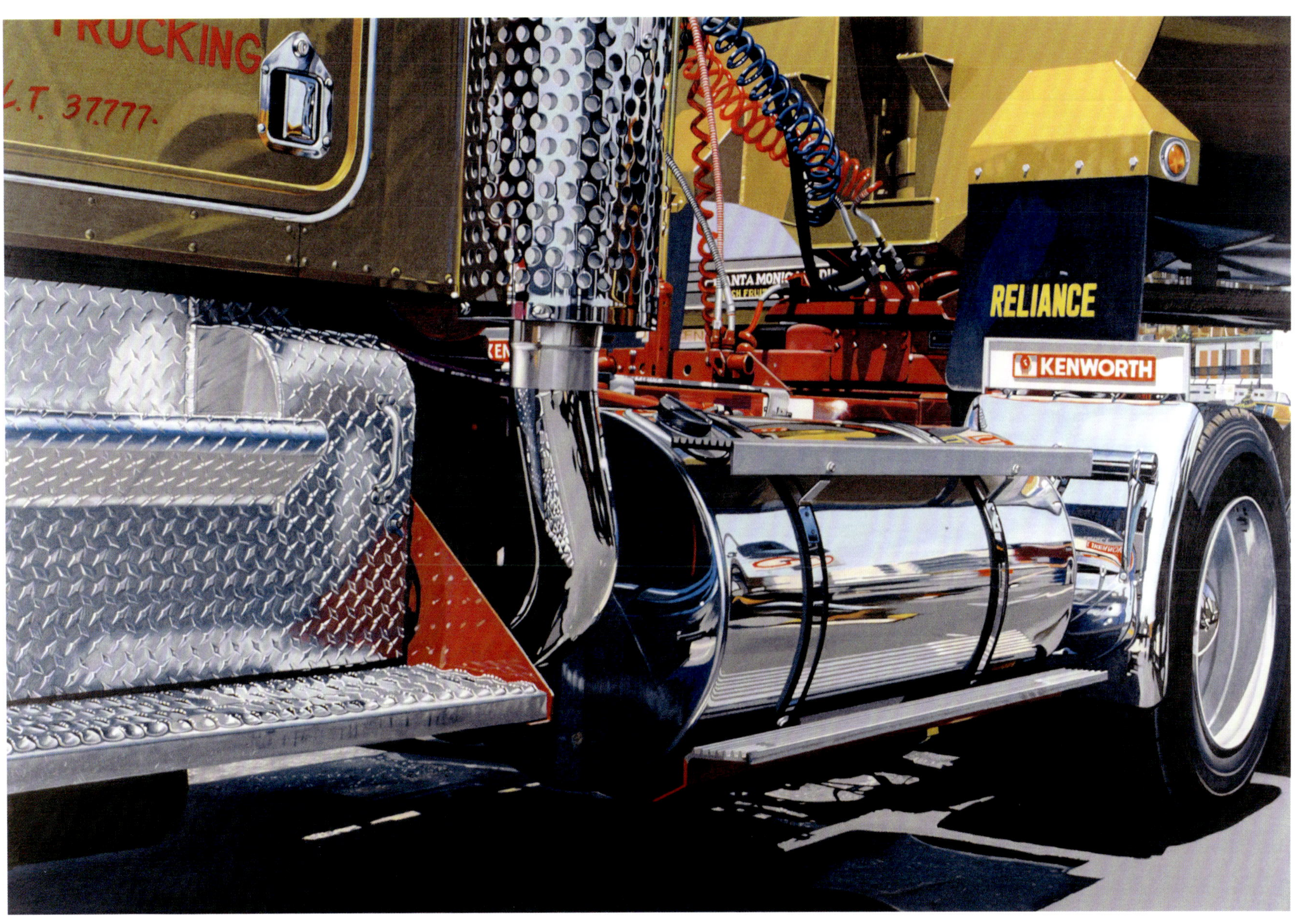
TRUCKING
L.T. 37,777.
RELIANCE
KENWORTH

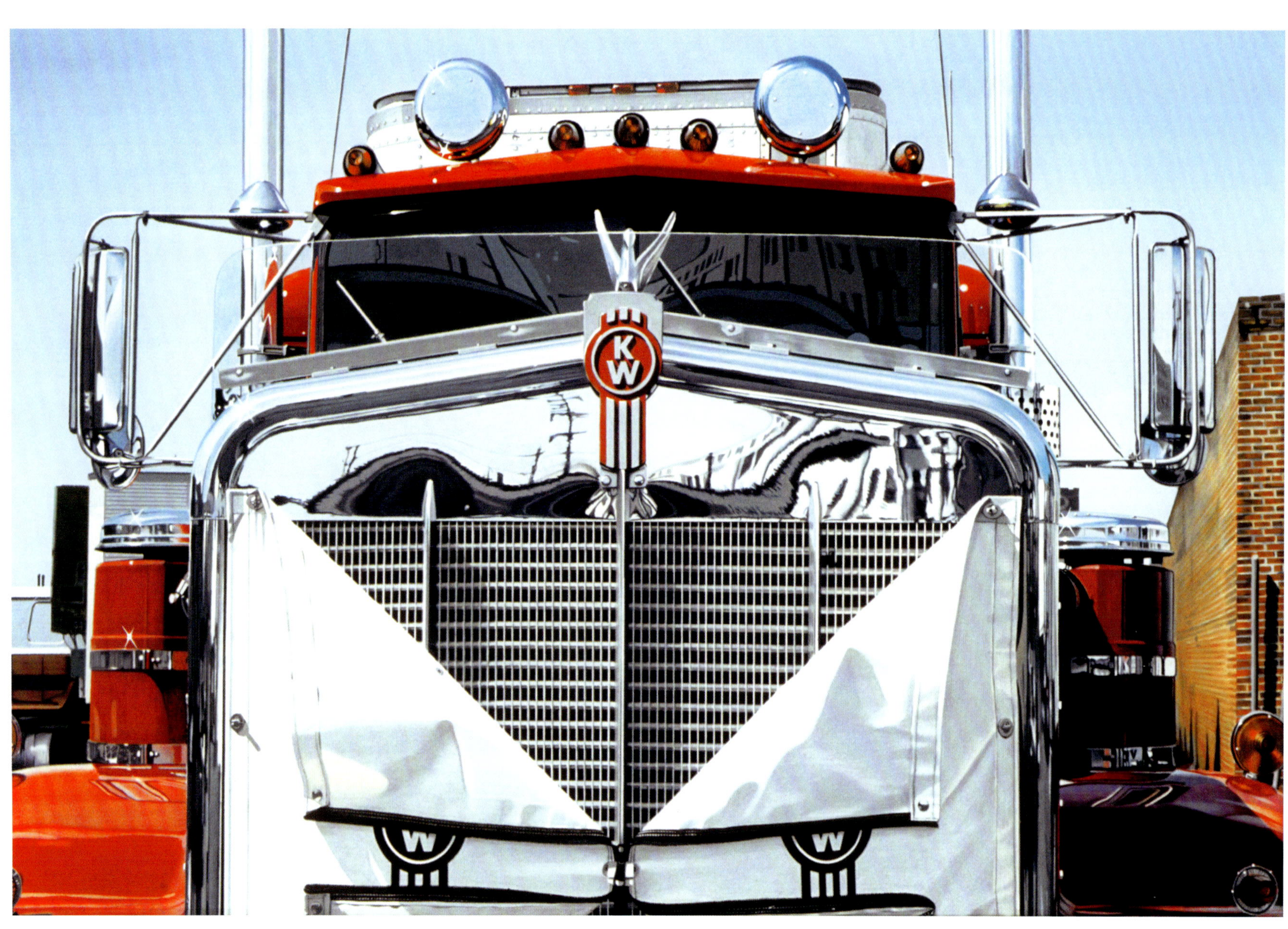

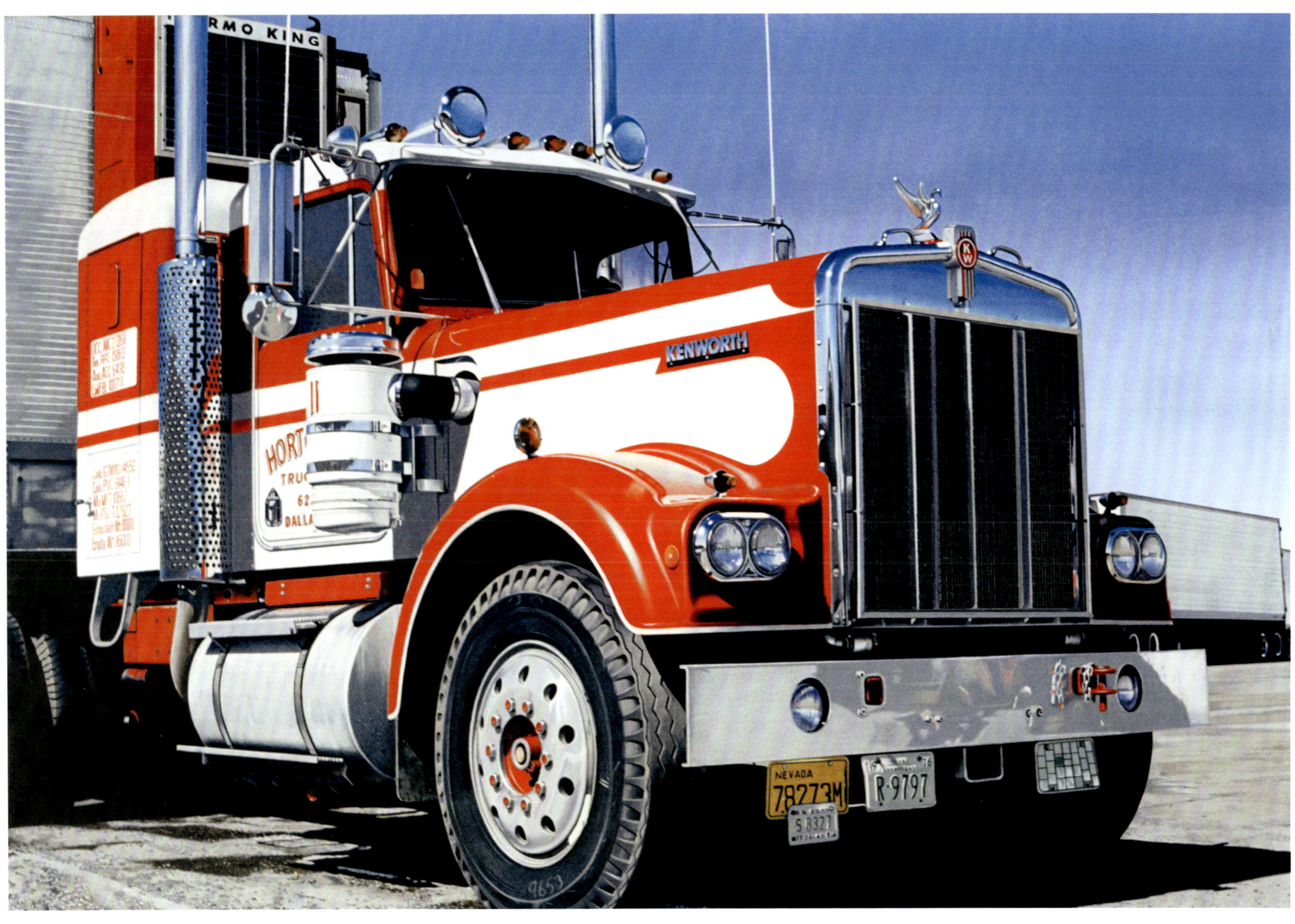

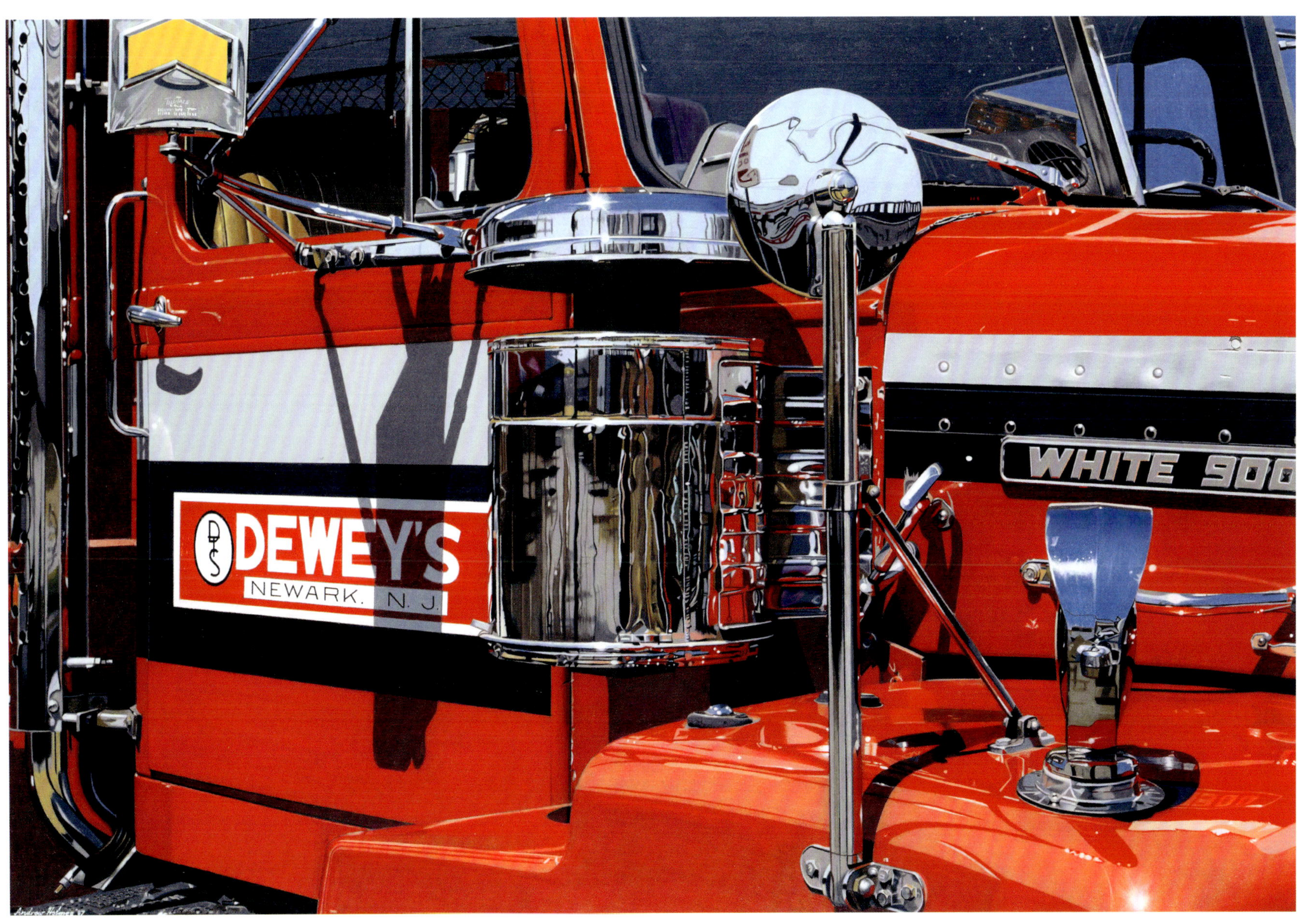
DEWEY'S
NEWARK. N. J.
WHITE 900

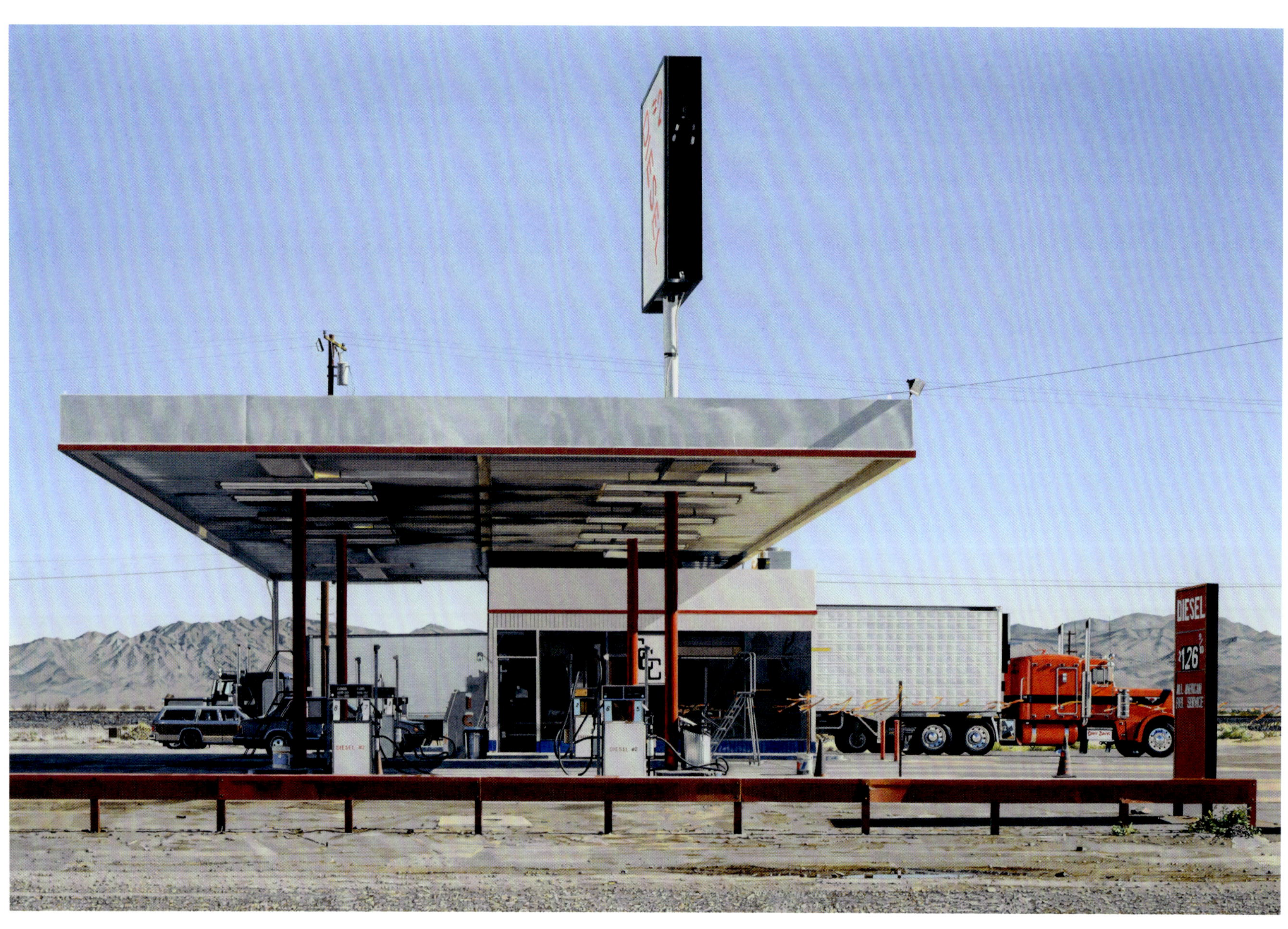

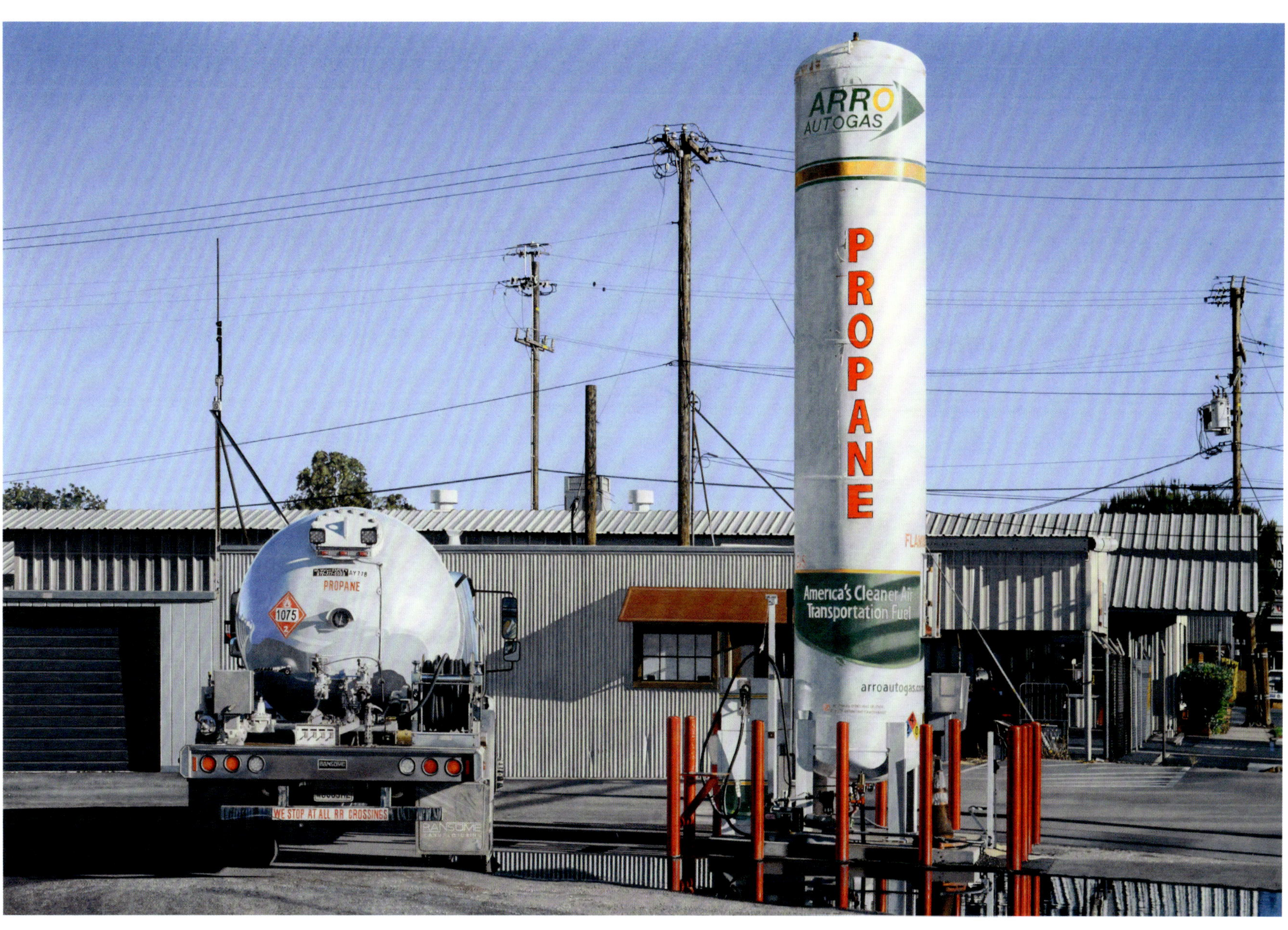

ARRO
AUTOGAS
PROPANE
America's Cleaner Air
Transportation Fuel
arroautogas.com
PROPANE
1075
WE STOP AT ALL RR CROSSINGS
RANSOME

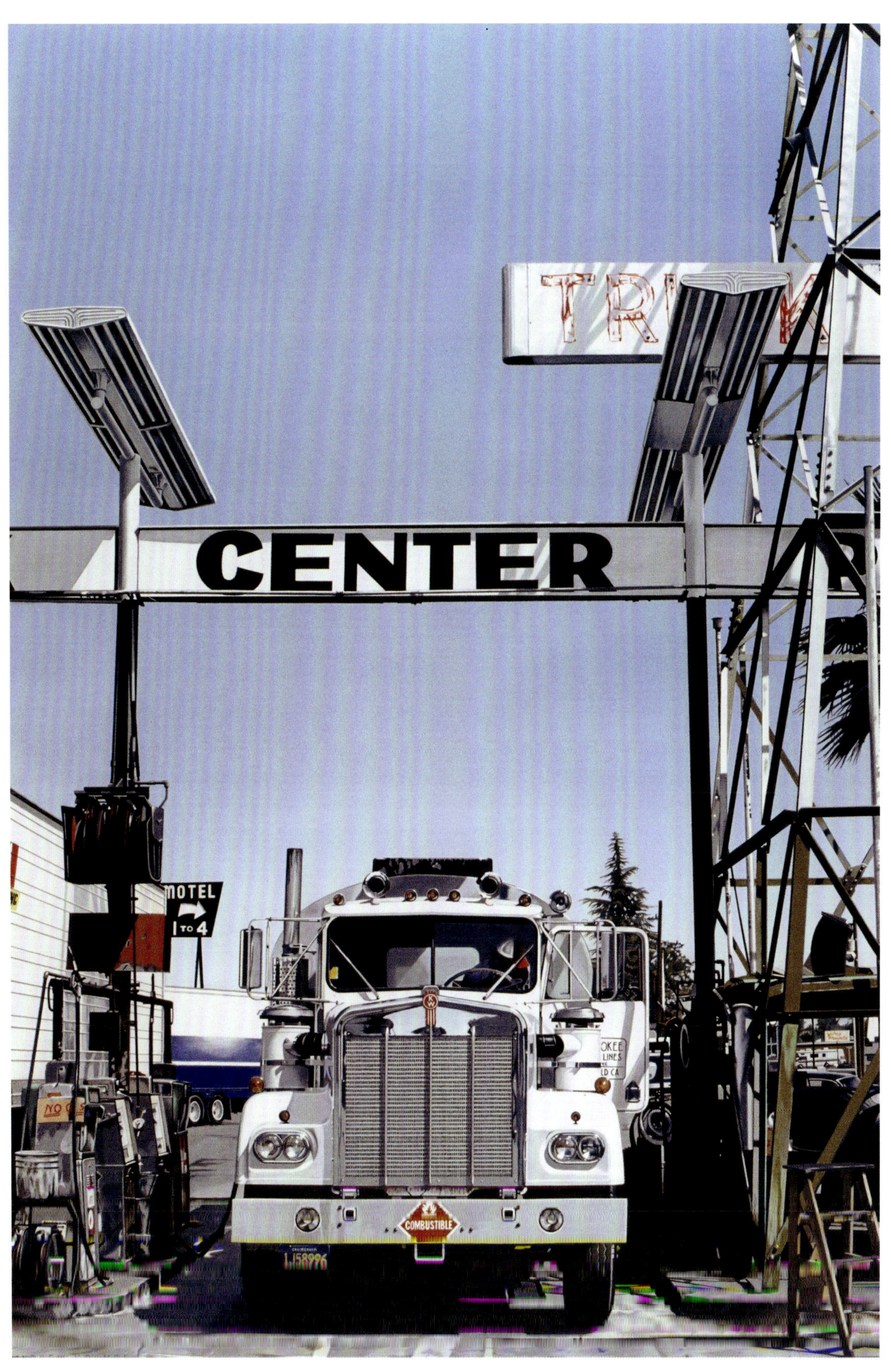

TR M
CENTER
MOTEL
TO 4
COMBUSTIBLE
OKEE
LINES
LD CA
1J58996

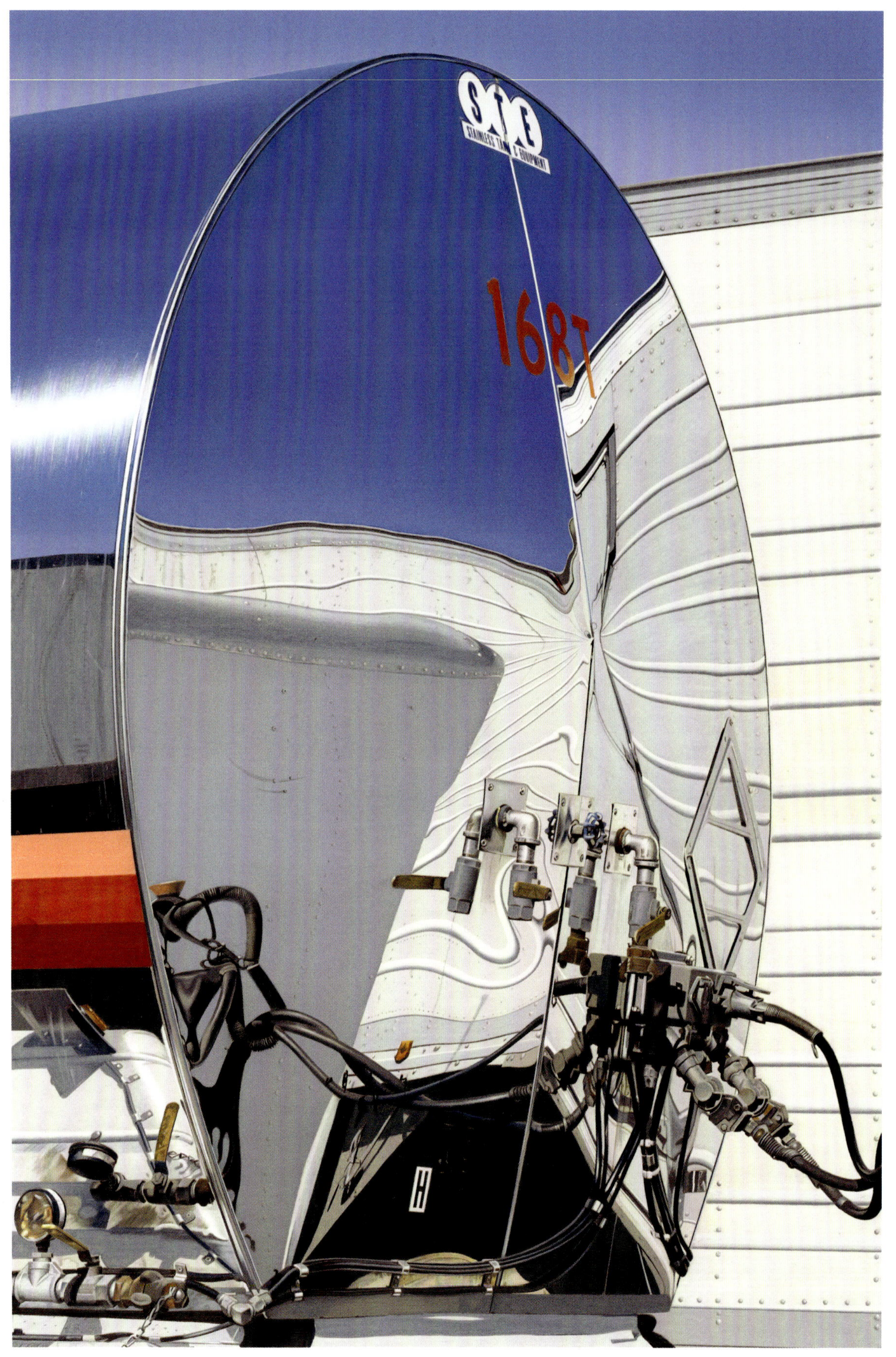


168T

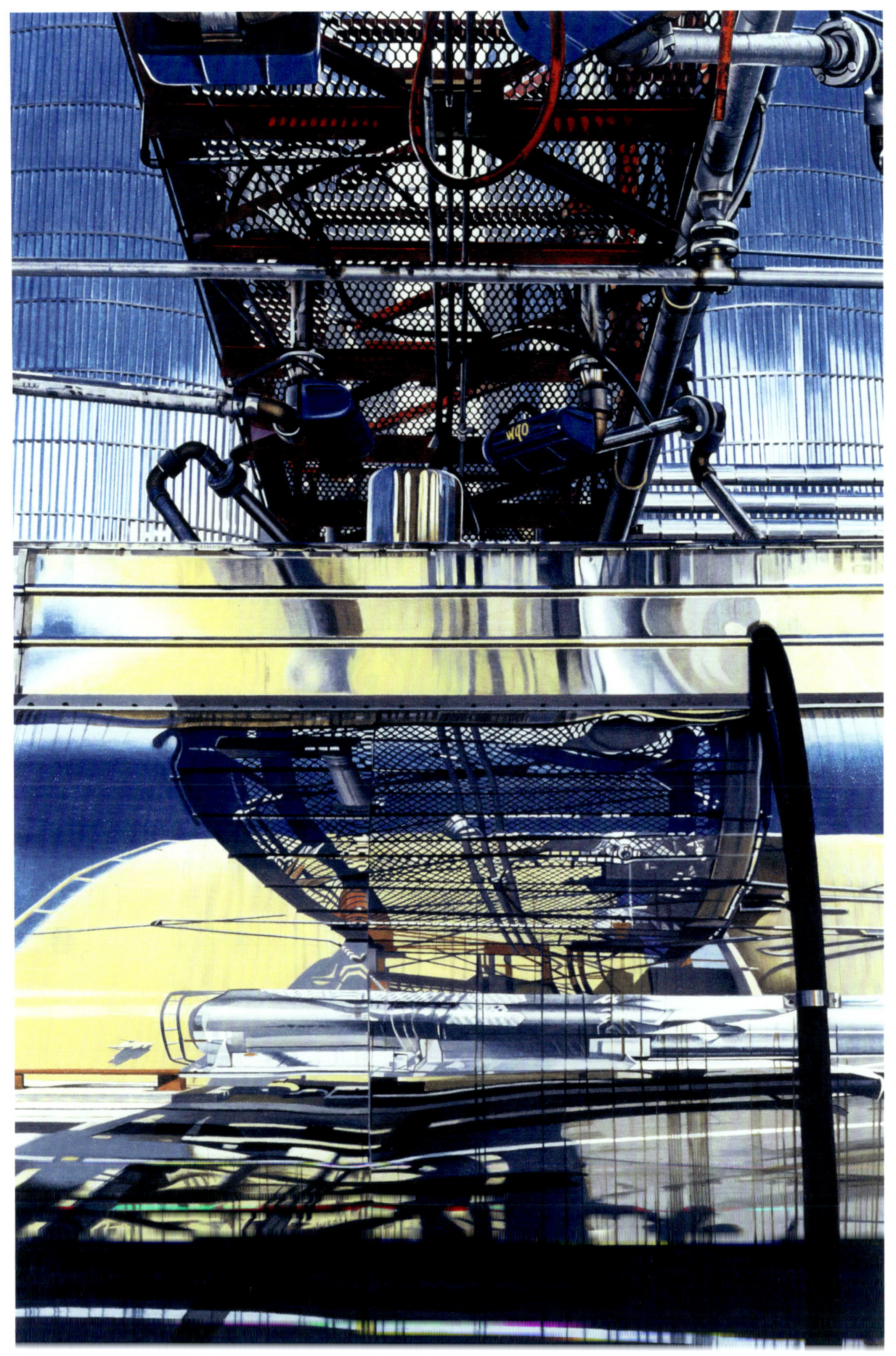

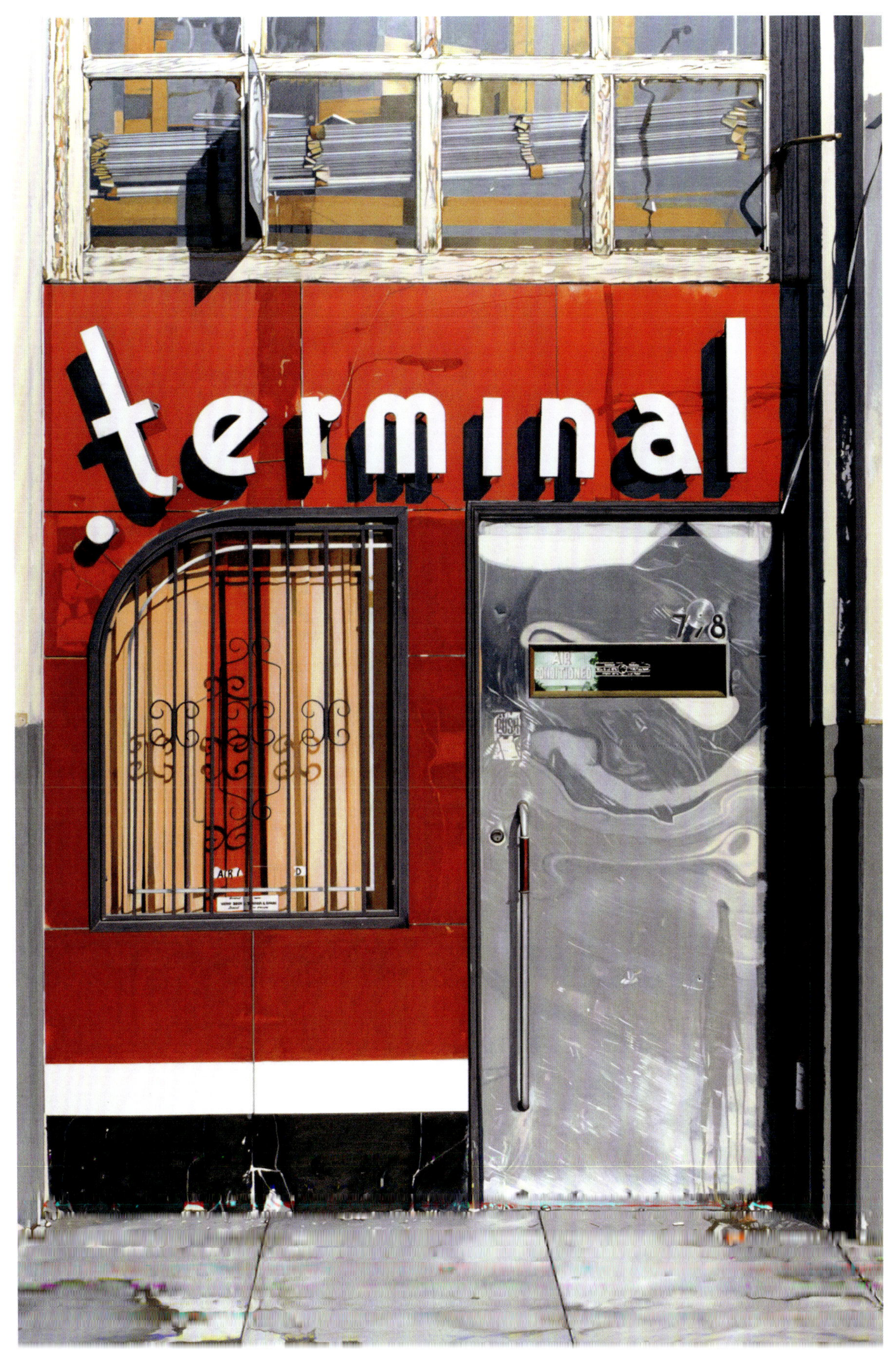

.terminal
178

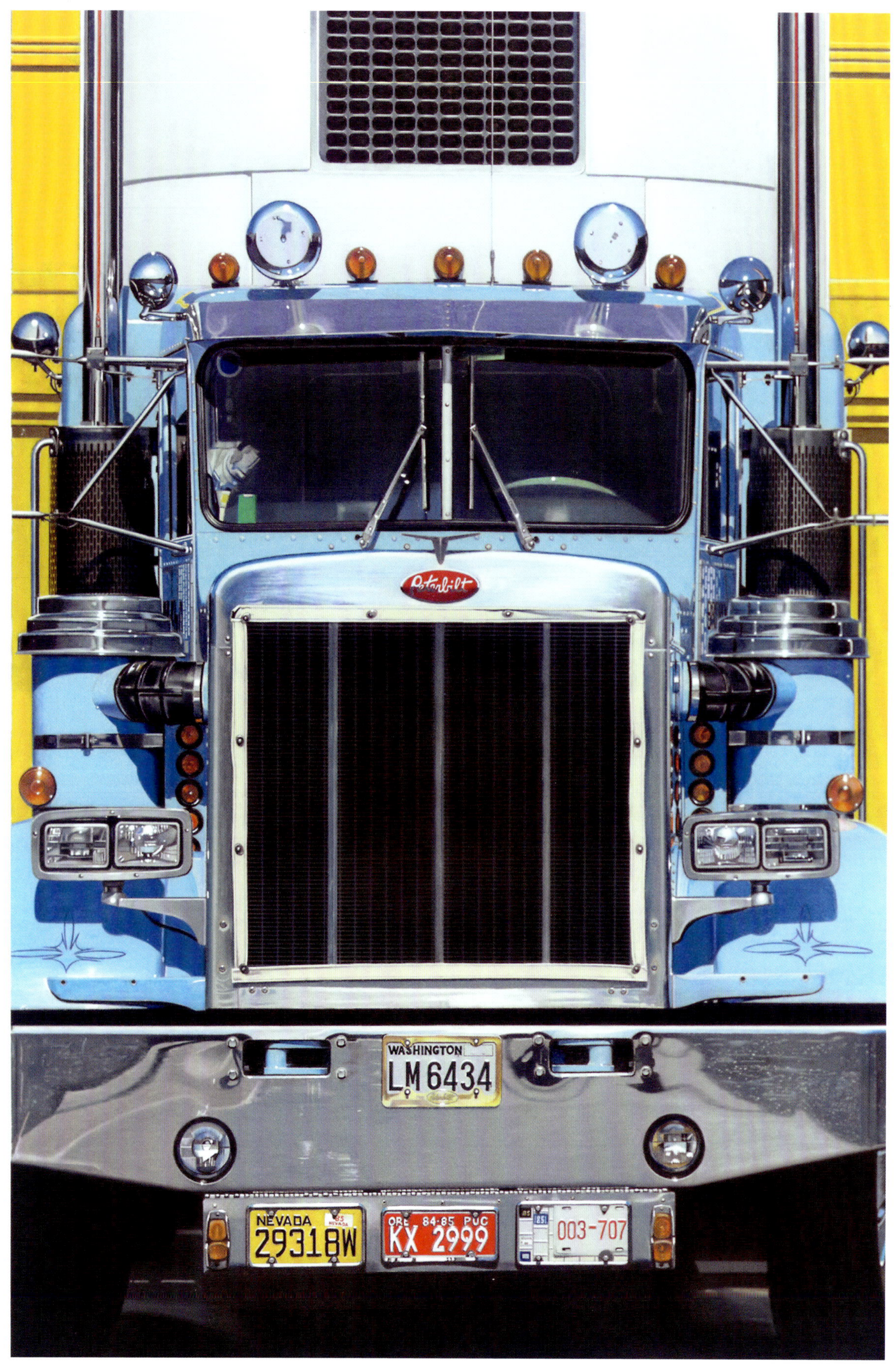

Peterbilt
WASHINGTON
LM 6434
NEVADA
29318W
OR 84-85 PUC
KX 2999
003-707

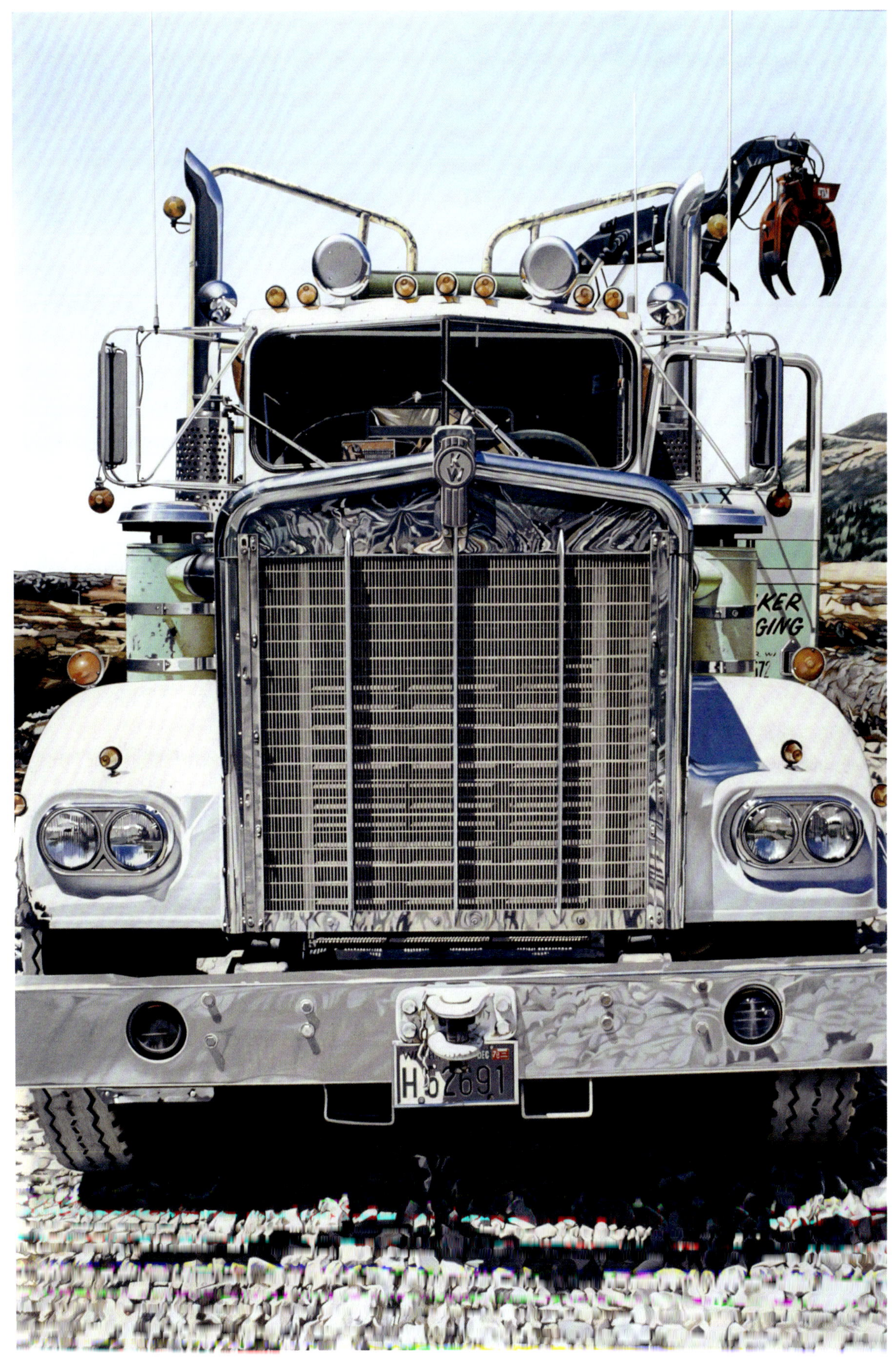

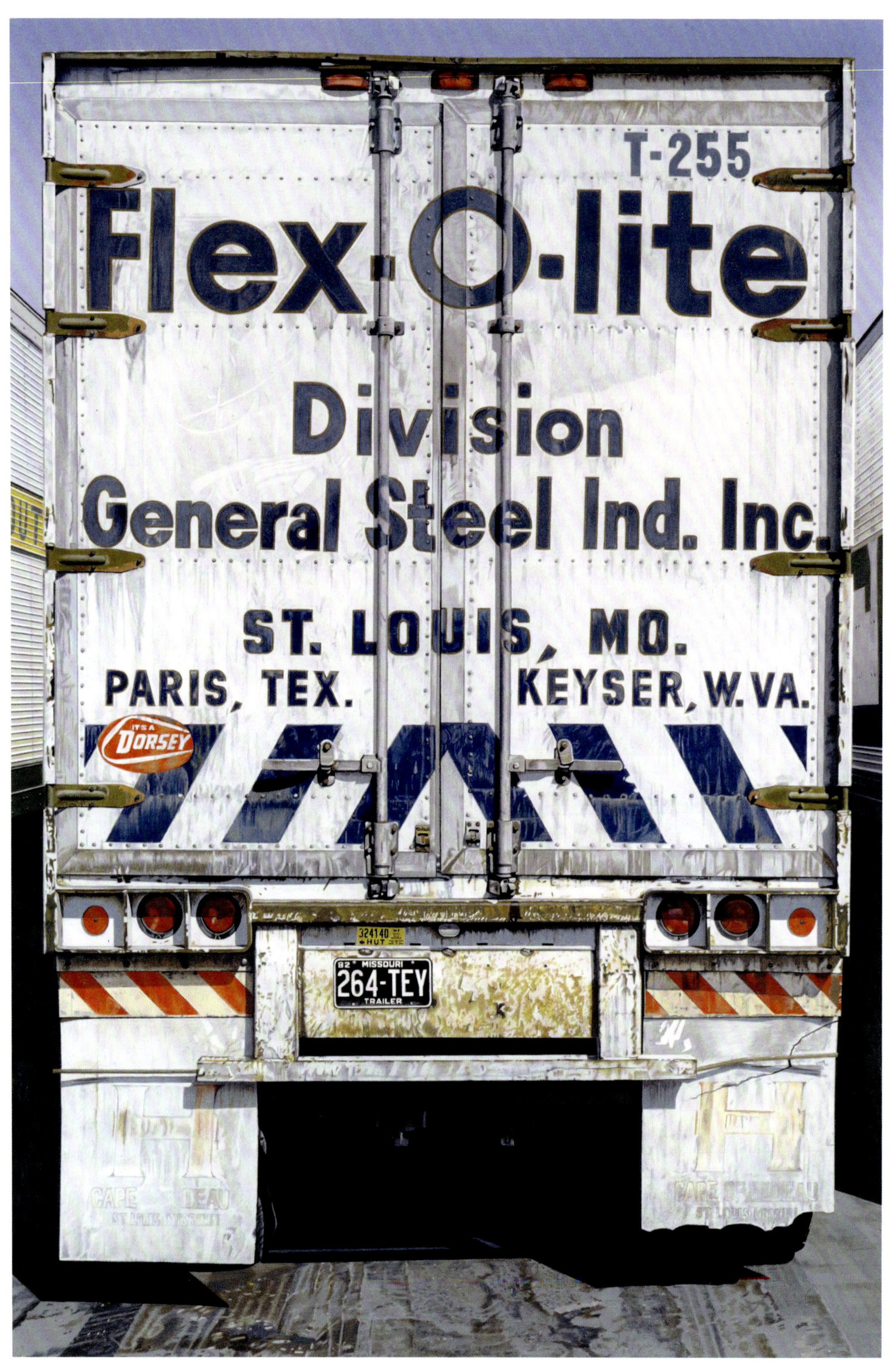
T-255
Flex-O-lite
Division
General Steel Ind. Inc.
ST. LOUIS, MO.
PARIS, TEX.        KEYSER, W. VA.
IT'S A DORSEY
82 MISSOURI
264-TEY
TRAILER

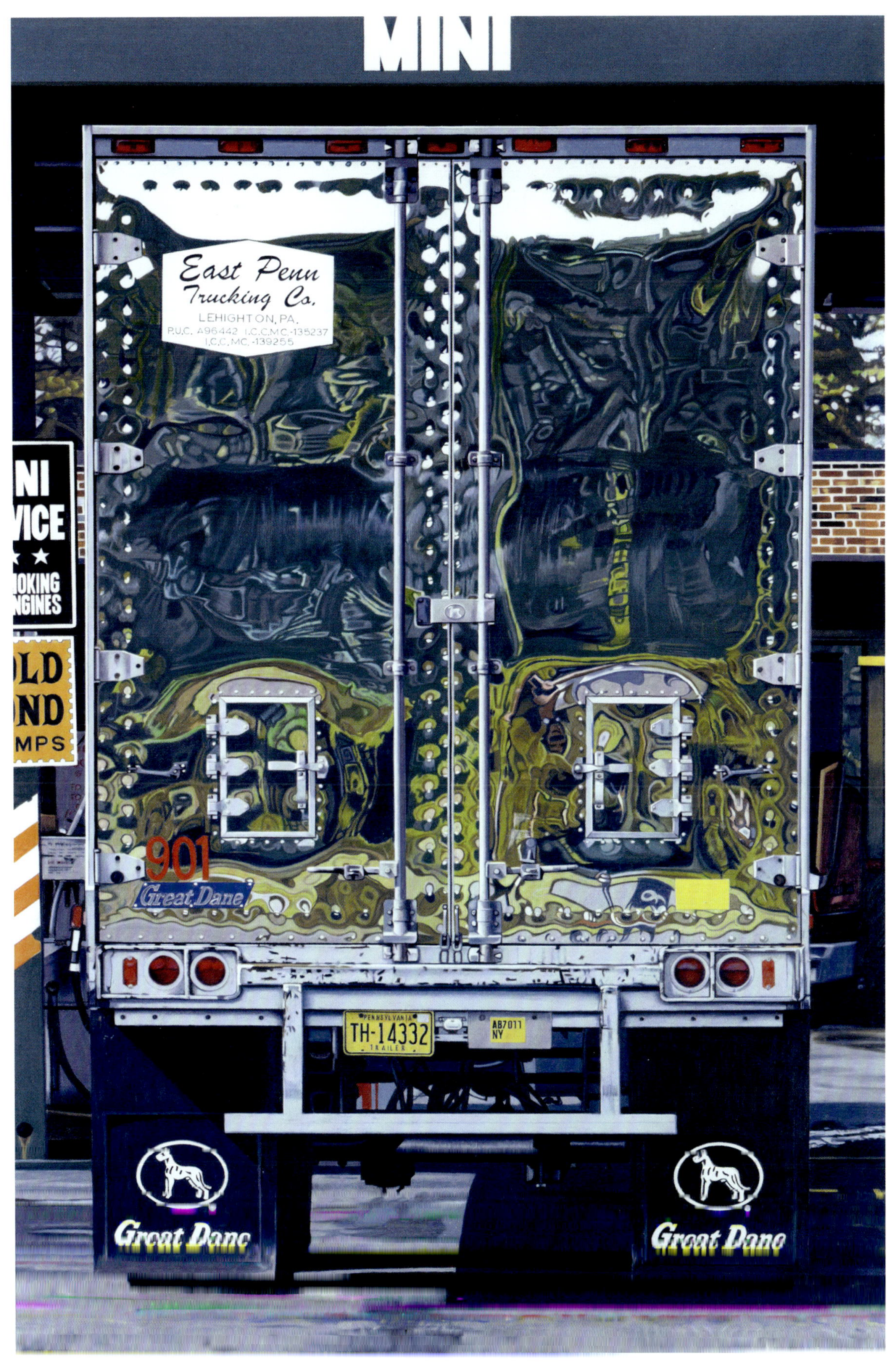

MINI
East Penn
Trucking Co.
LEHIGHTON, PA.
901
Great Dane
TH-14332
AB7011
NY
Great Dane
Great Dane

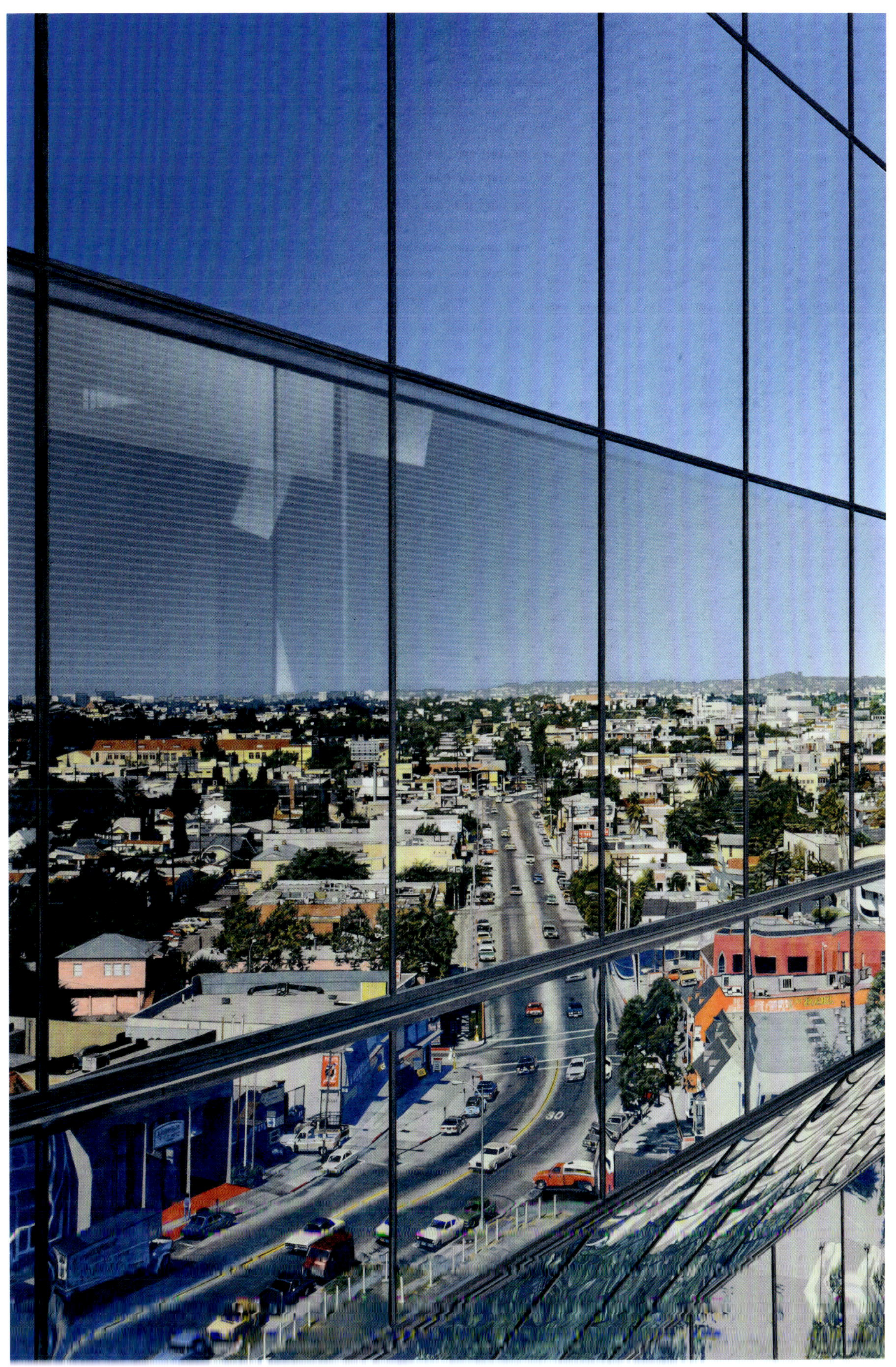

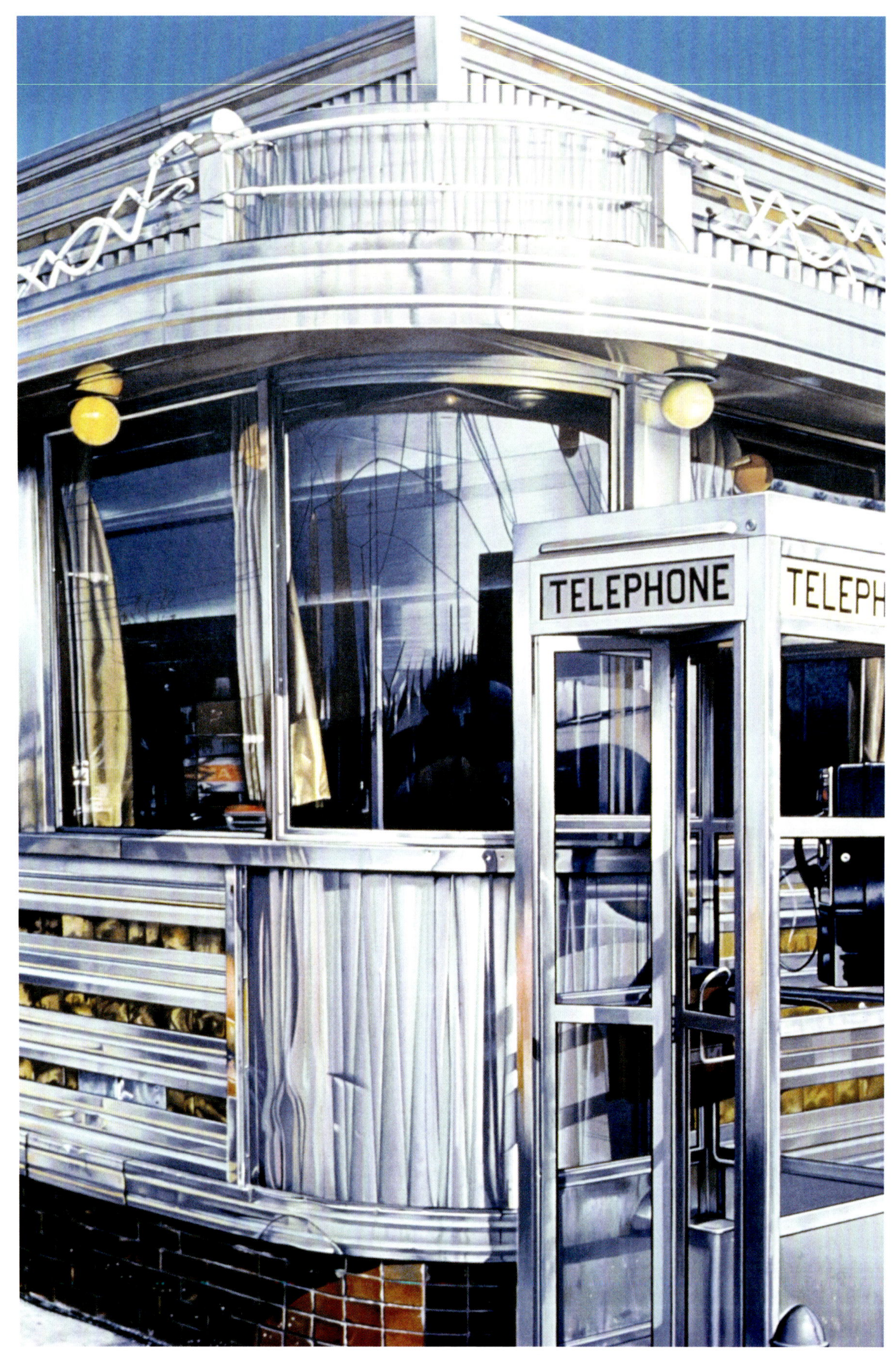

TELEPHONE
TELEPH

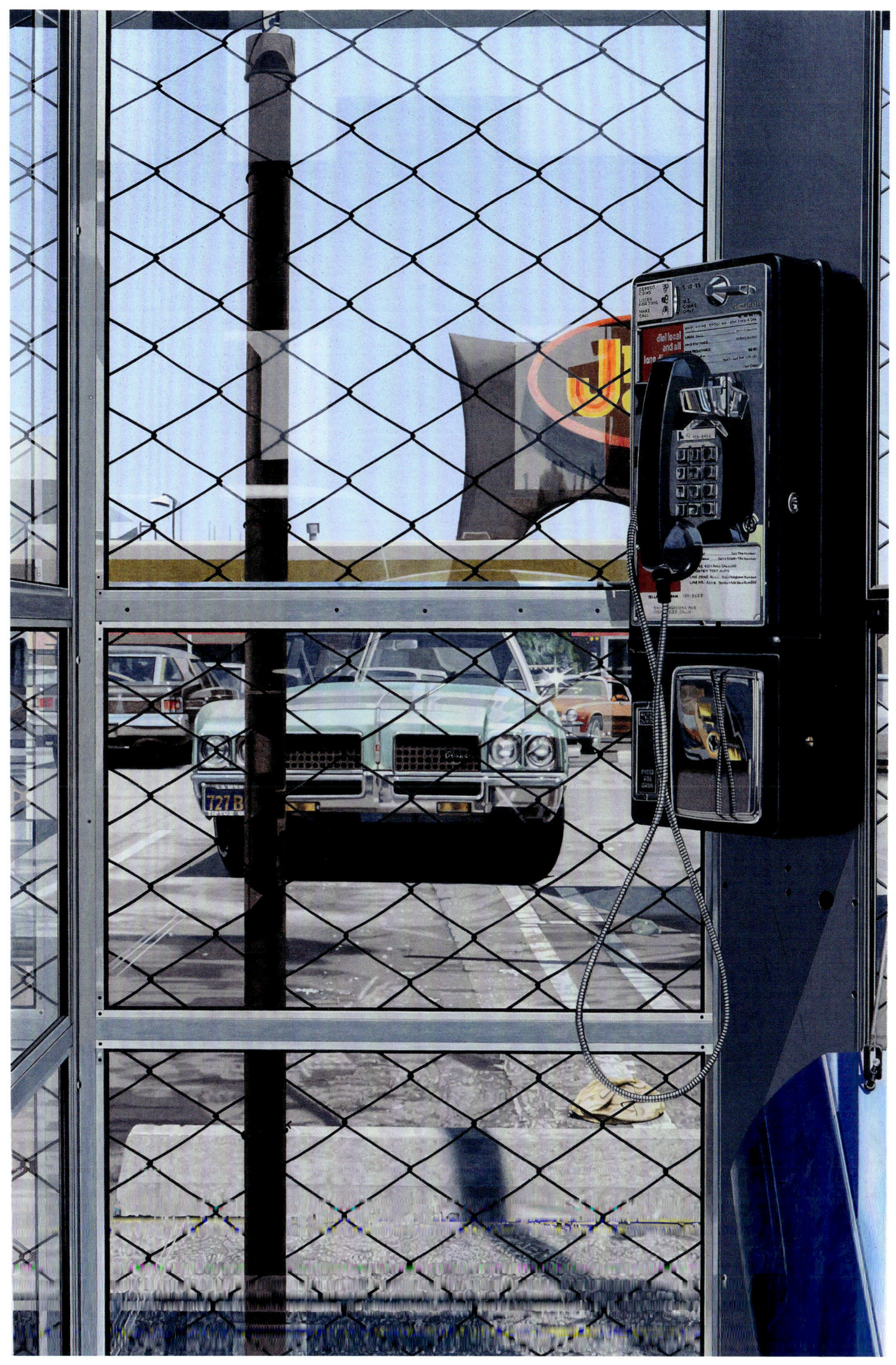

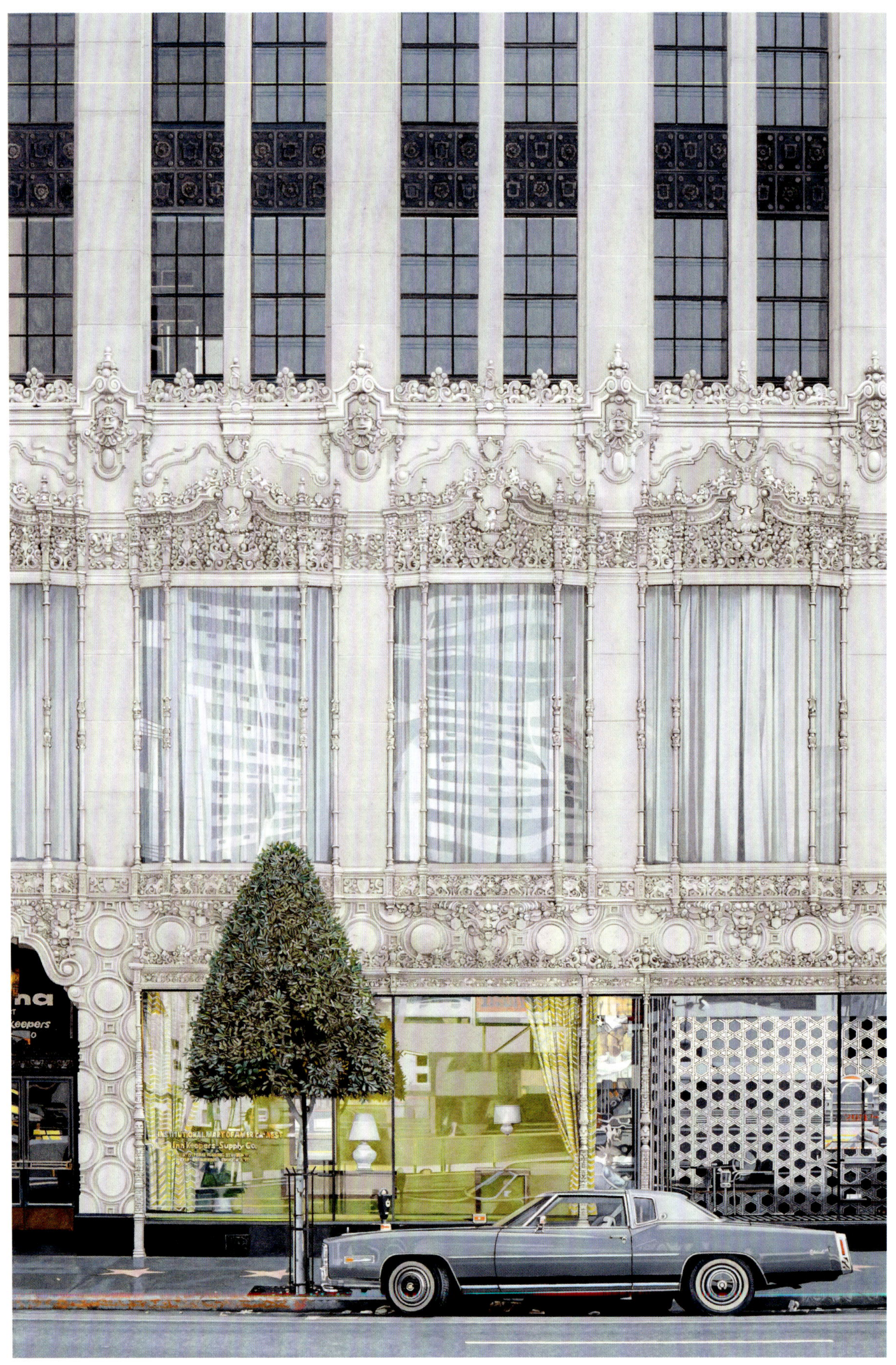

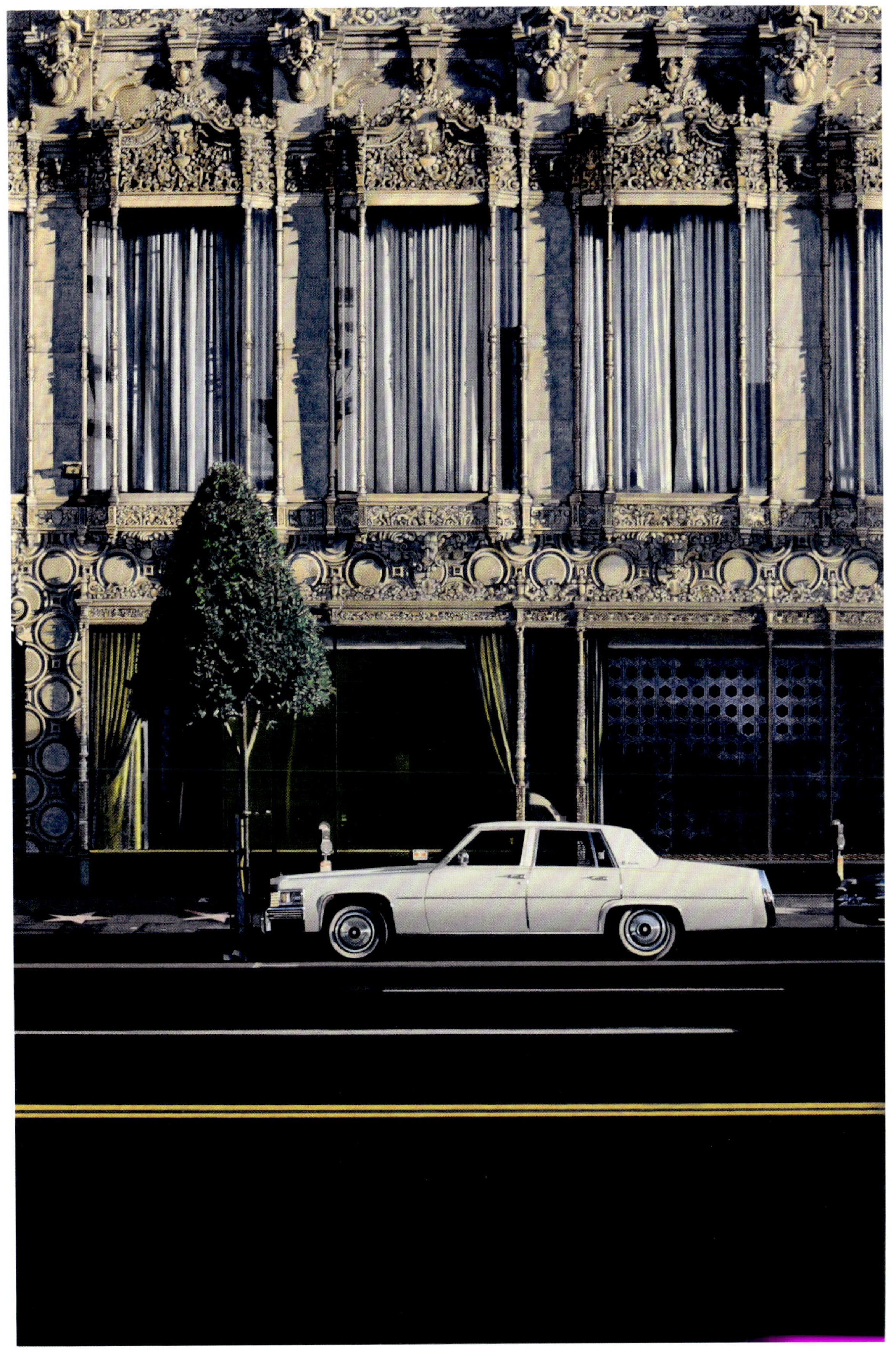

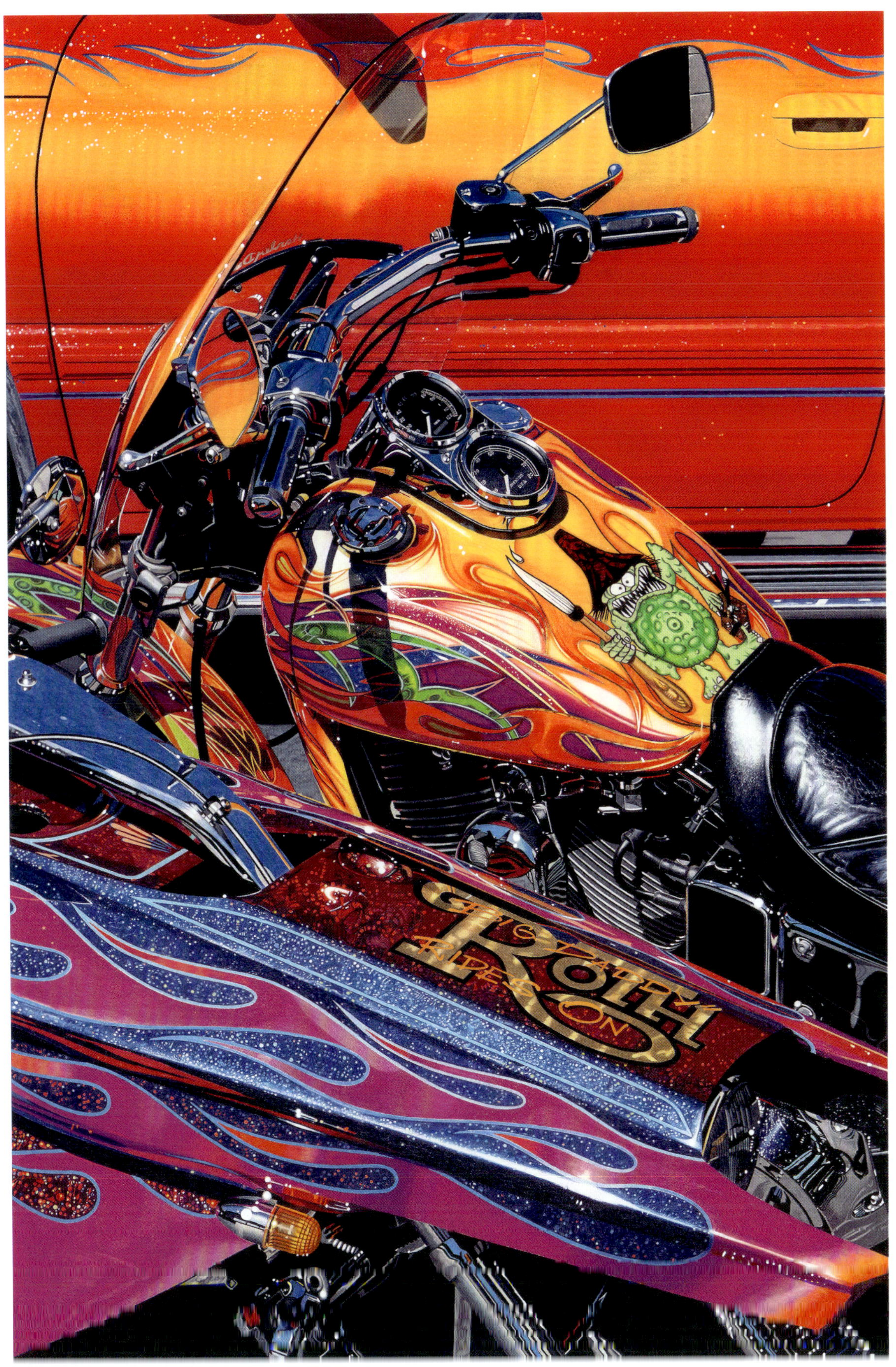

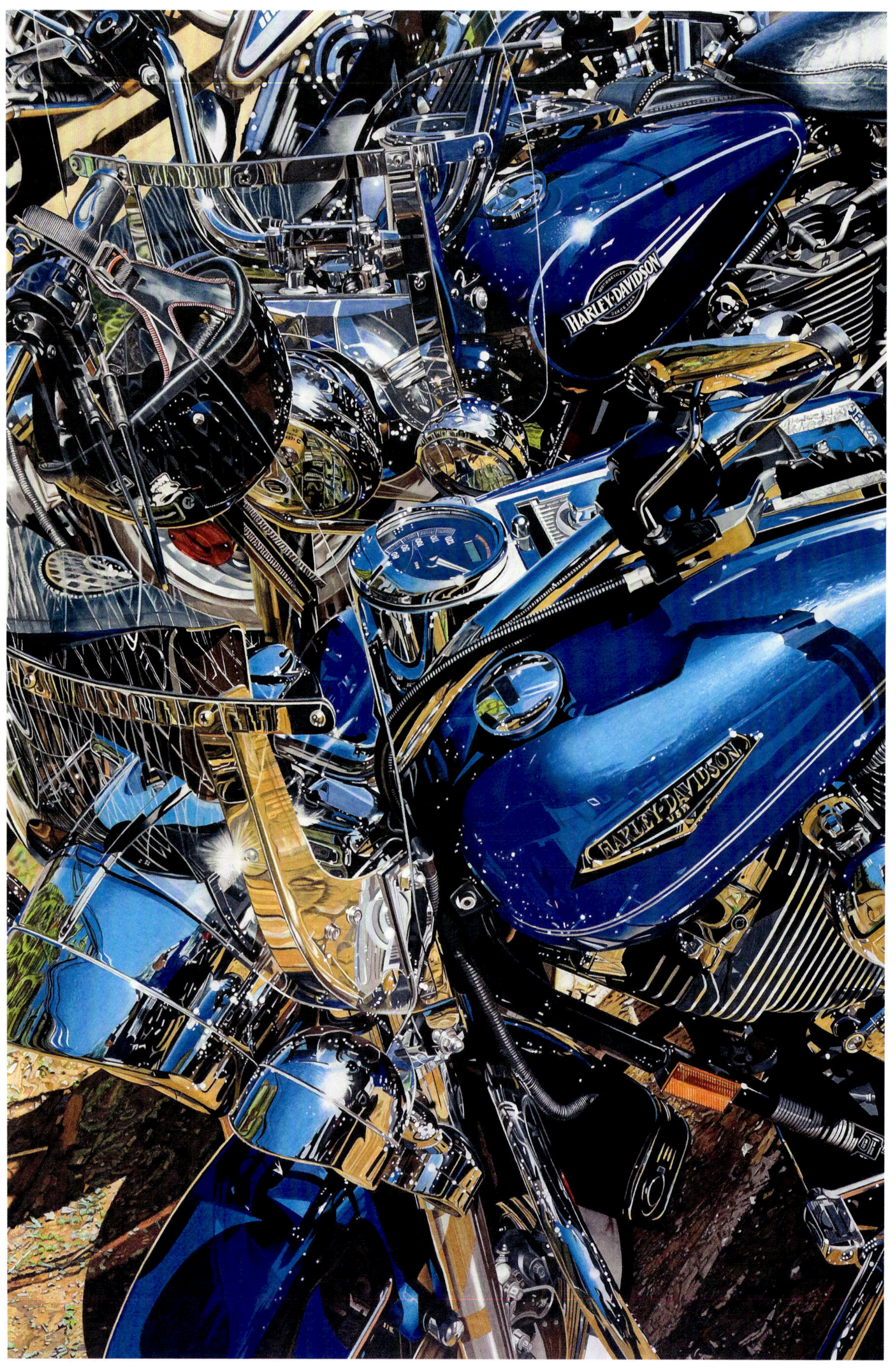

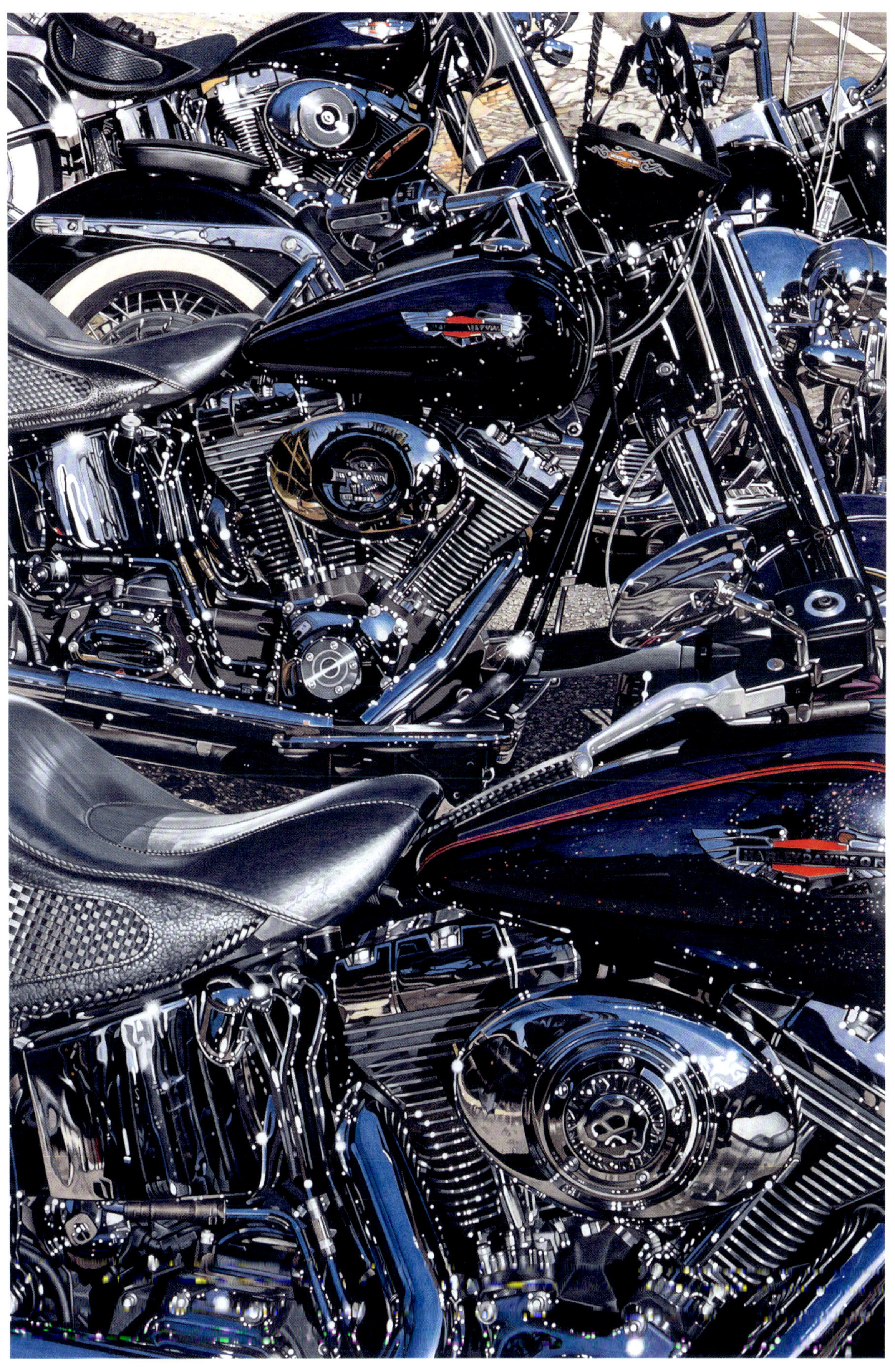

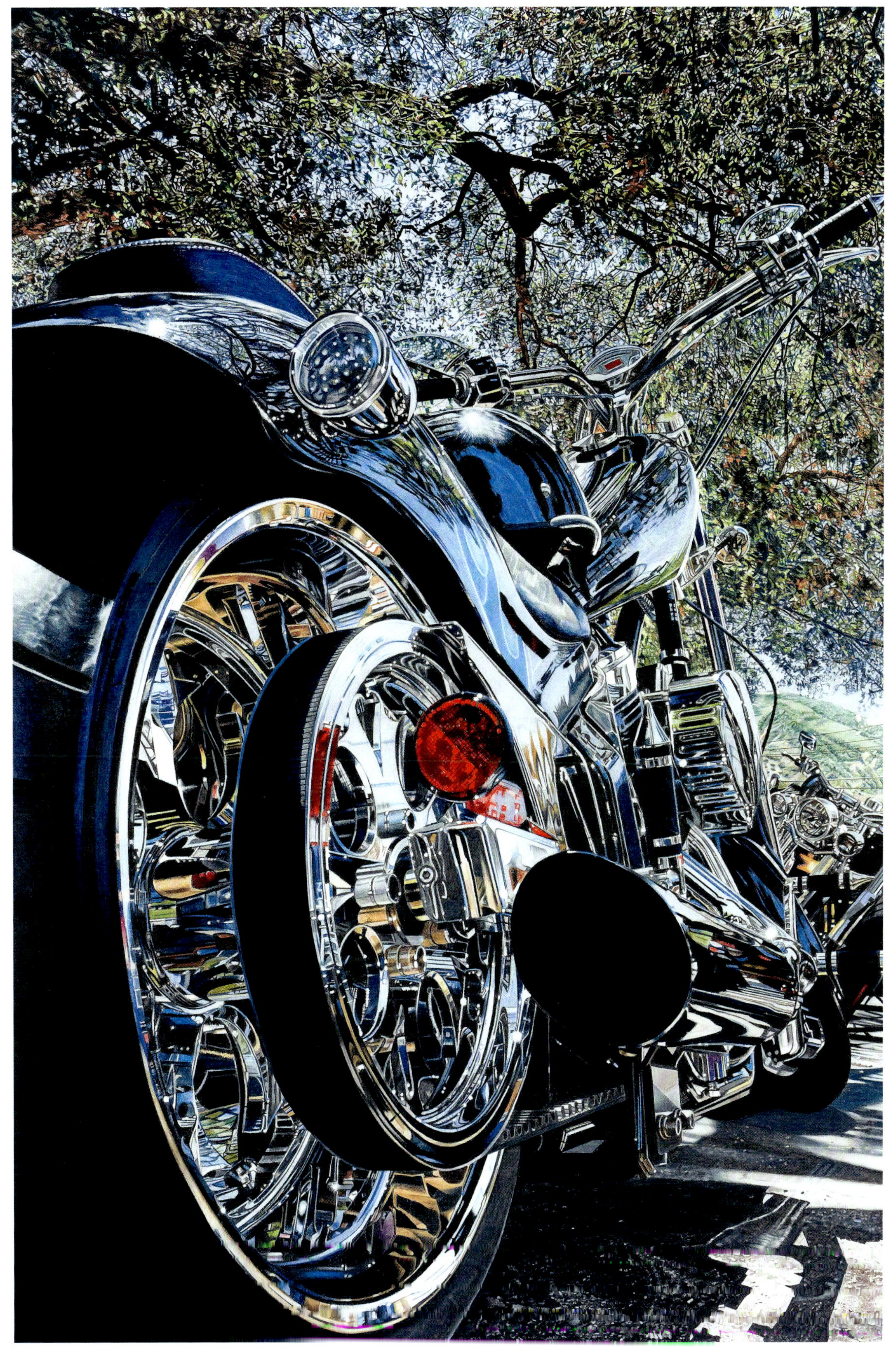

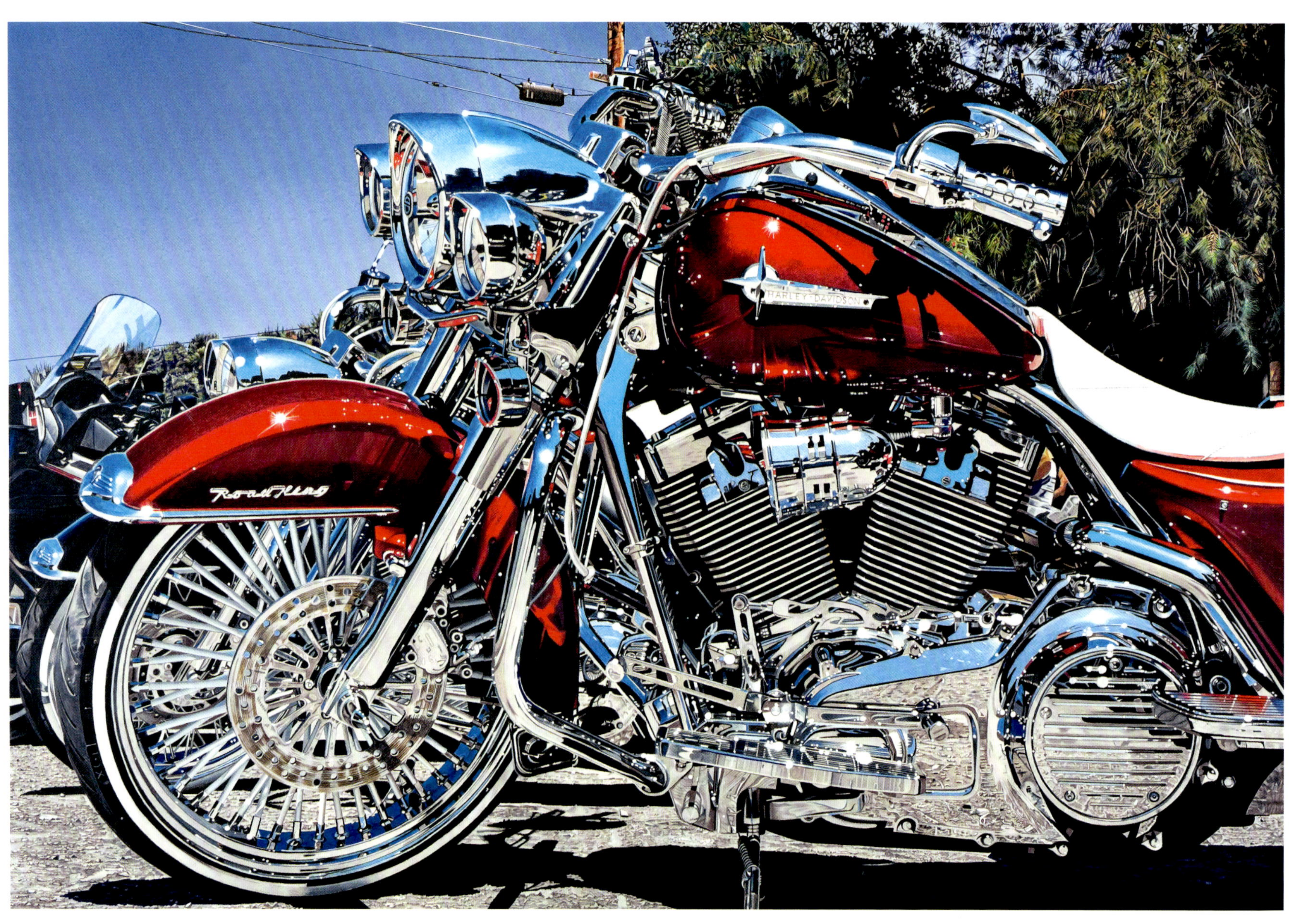

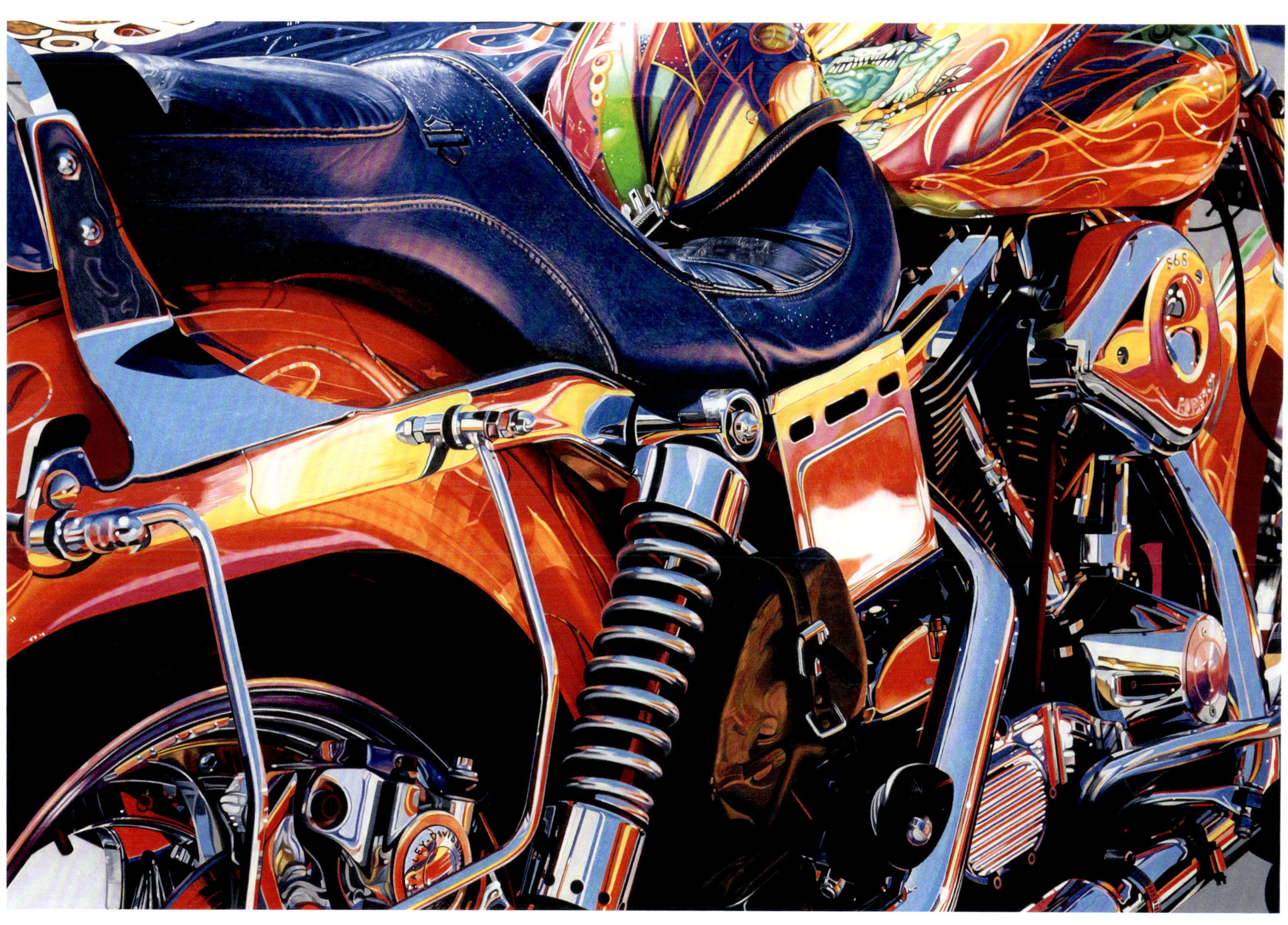

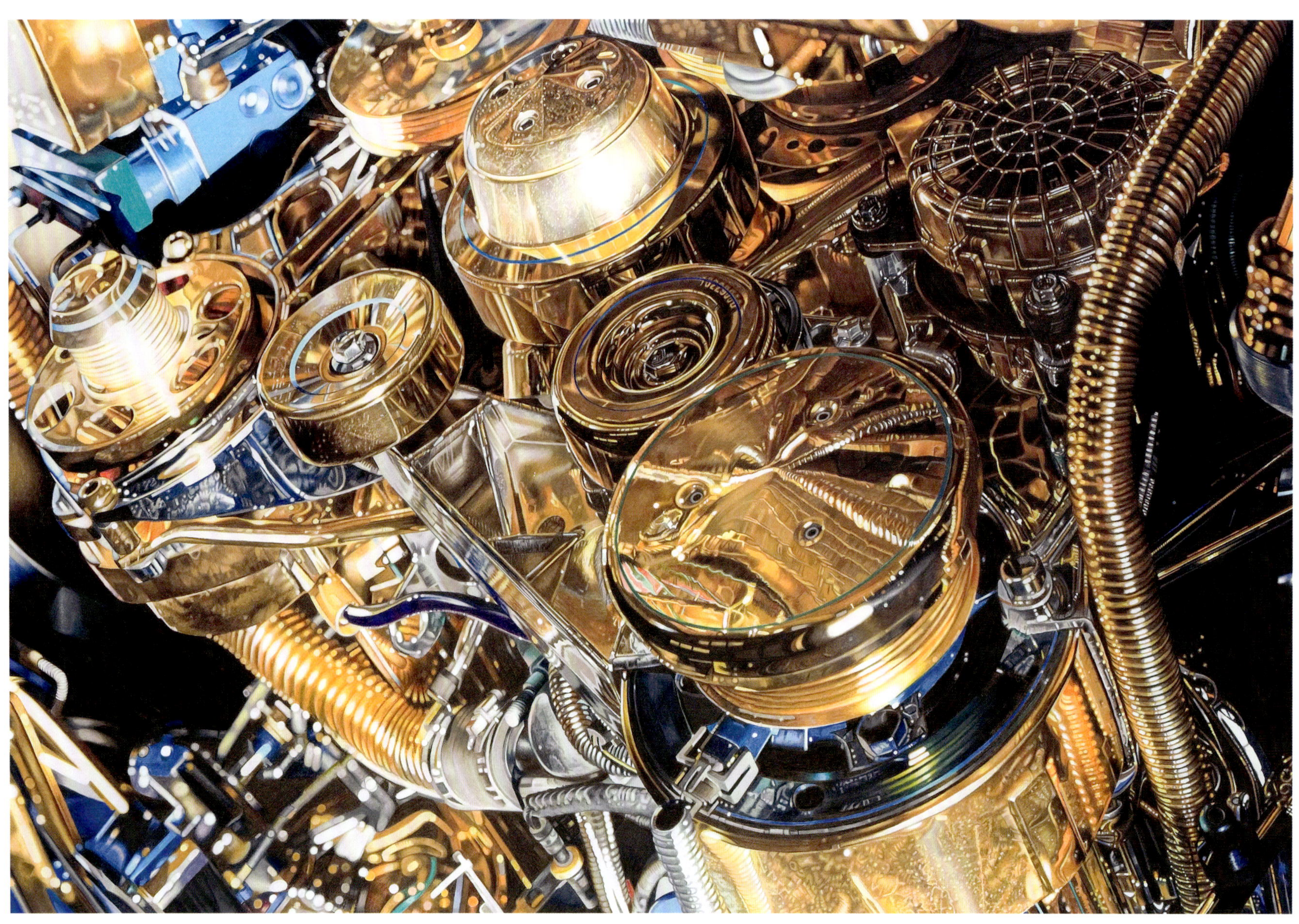

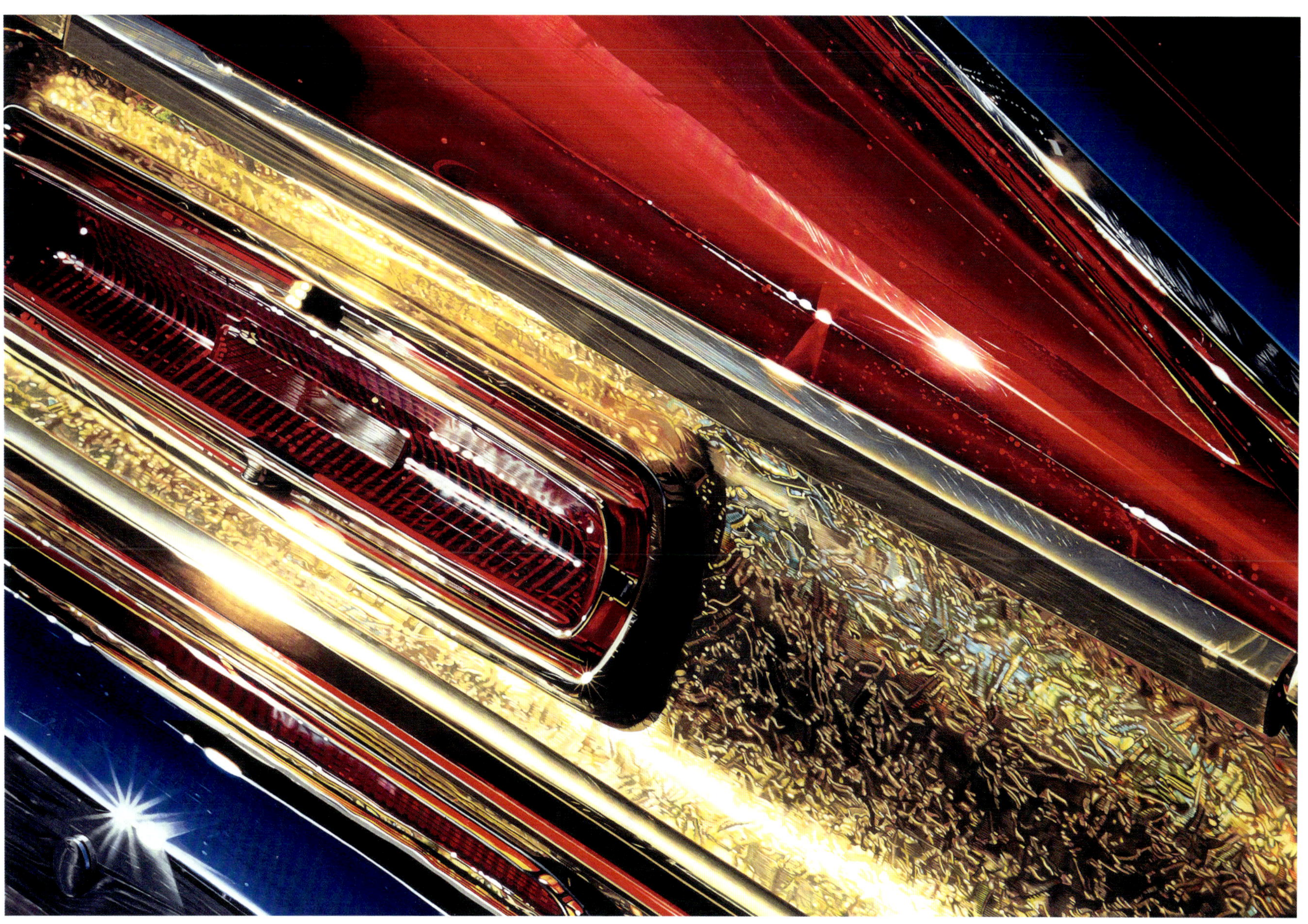

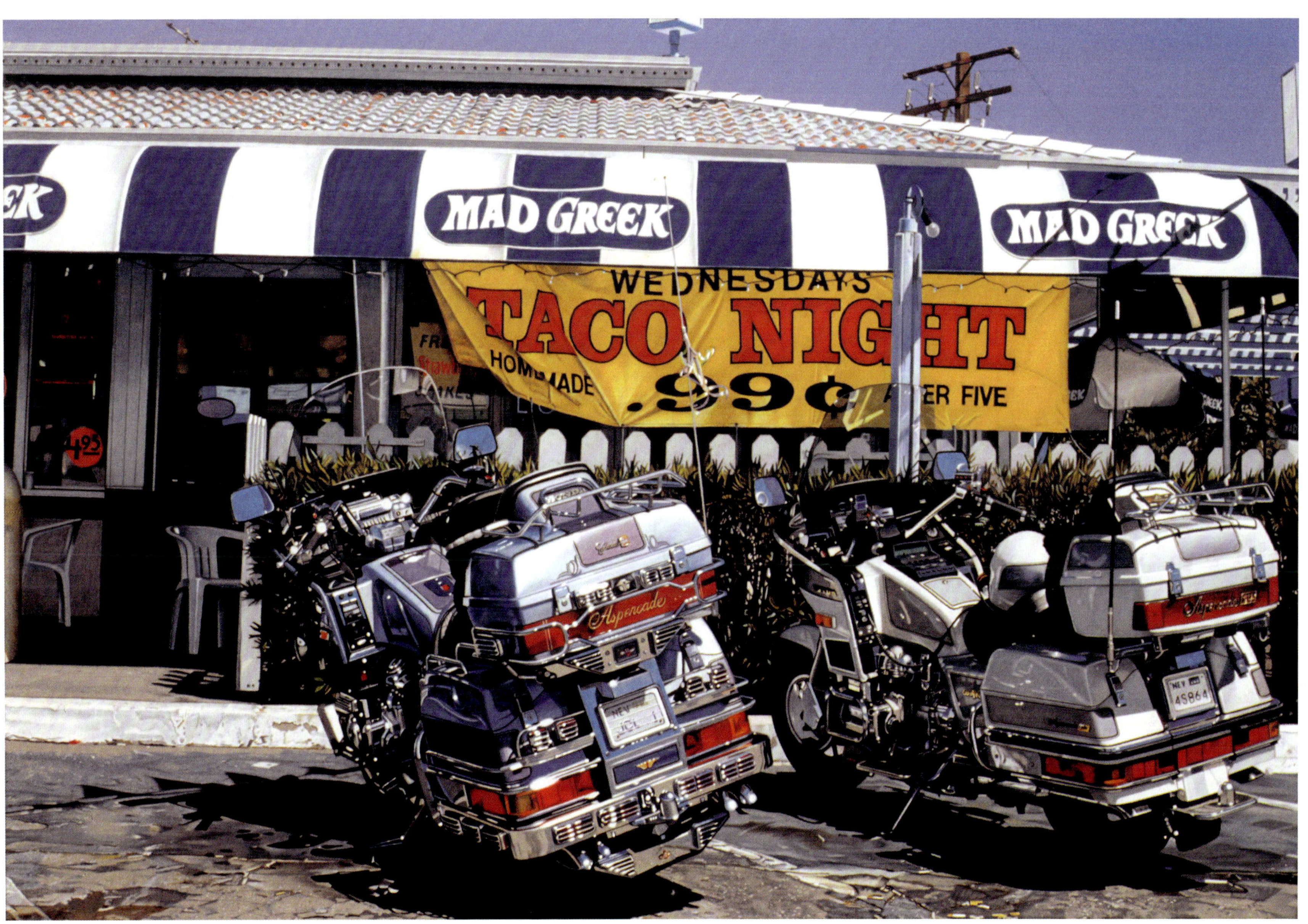

MAD GREEK
MAD GREEK
WEDNESDAYS
TACO NIGHT
HOMEMADE
.99¢ AFTER FIVE

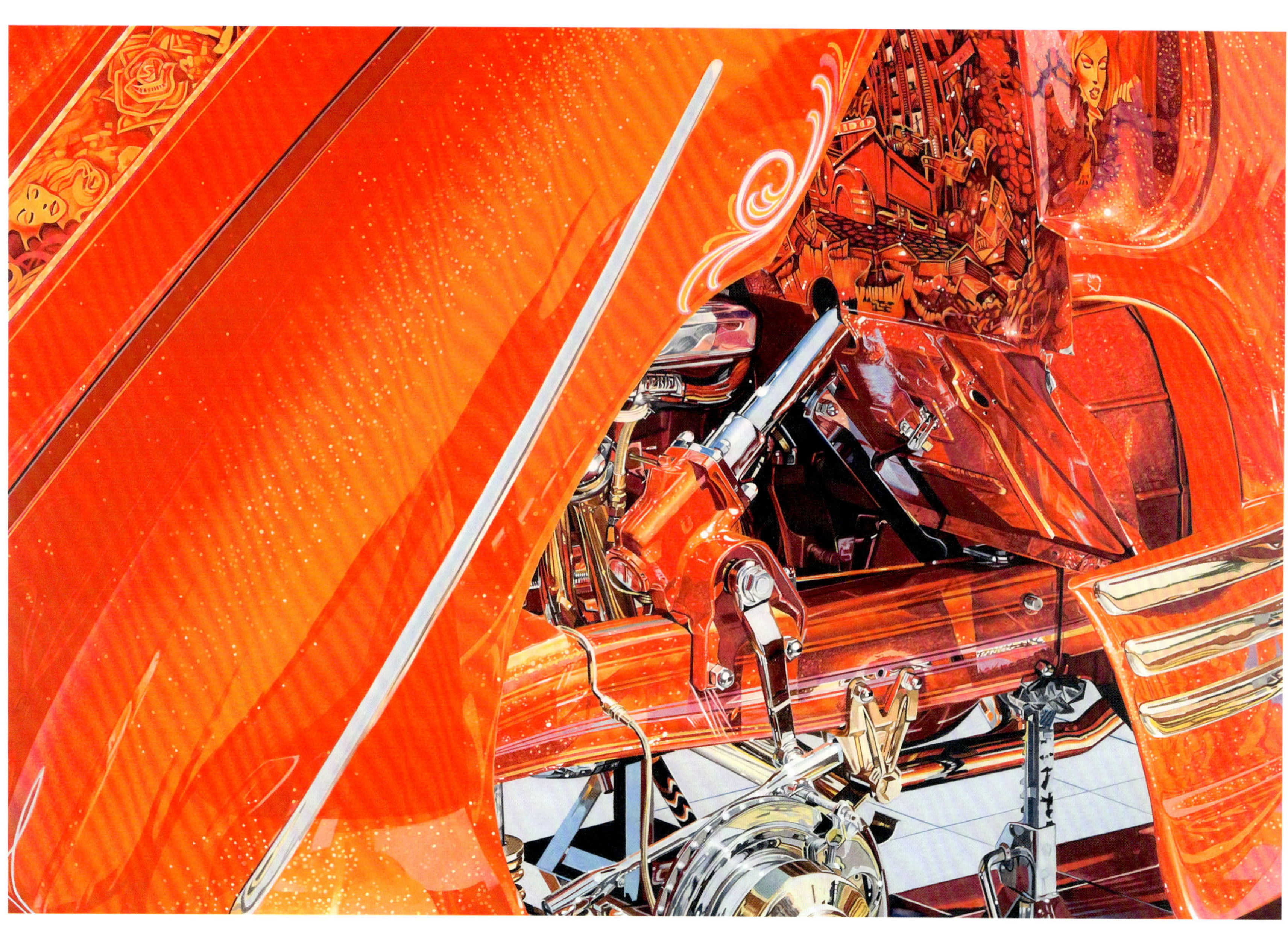

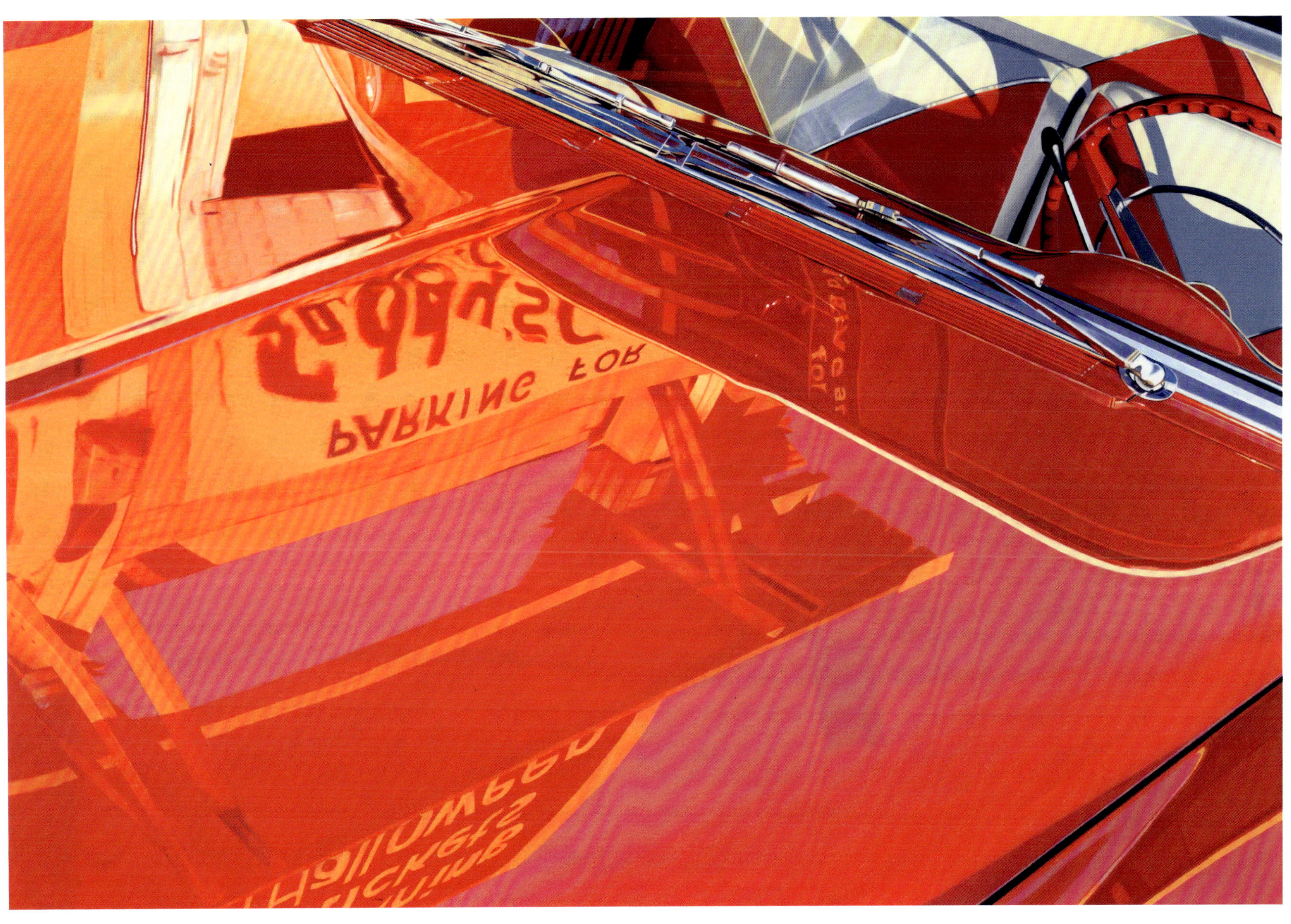

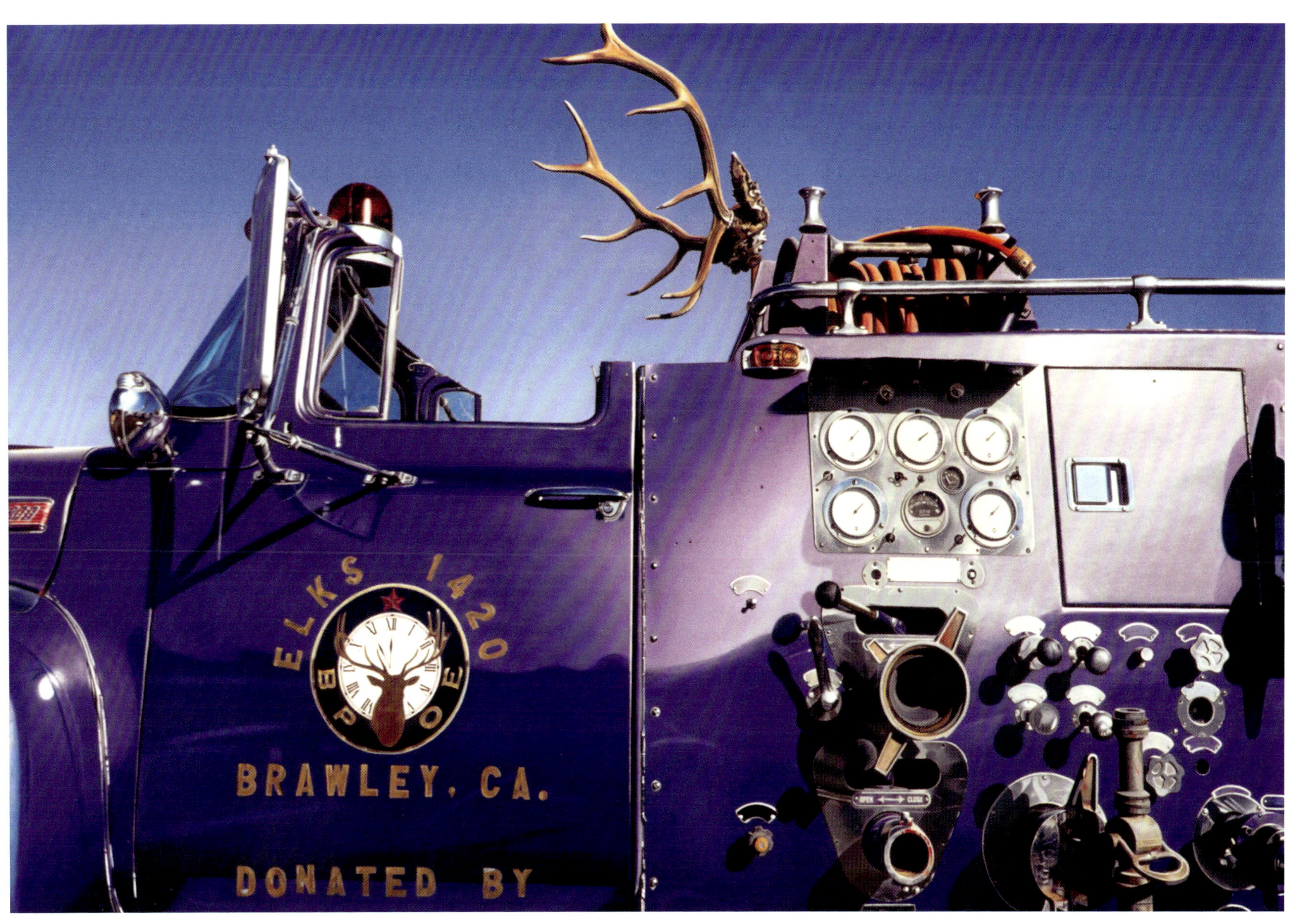
ELKS 1420
BPOE
BRAWLEY, CA.
DONATED BY

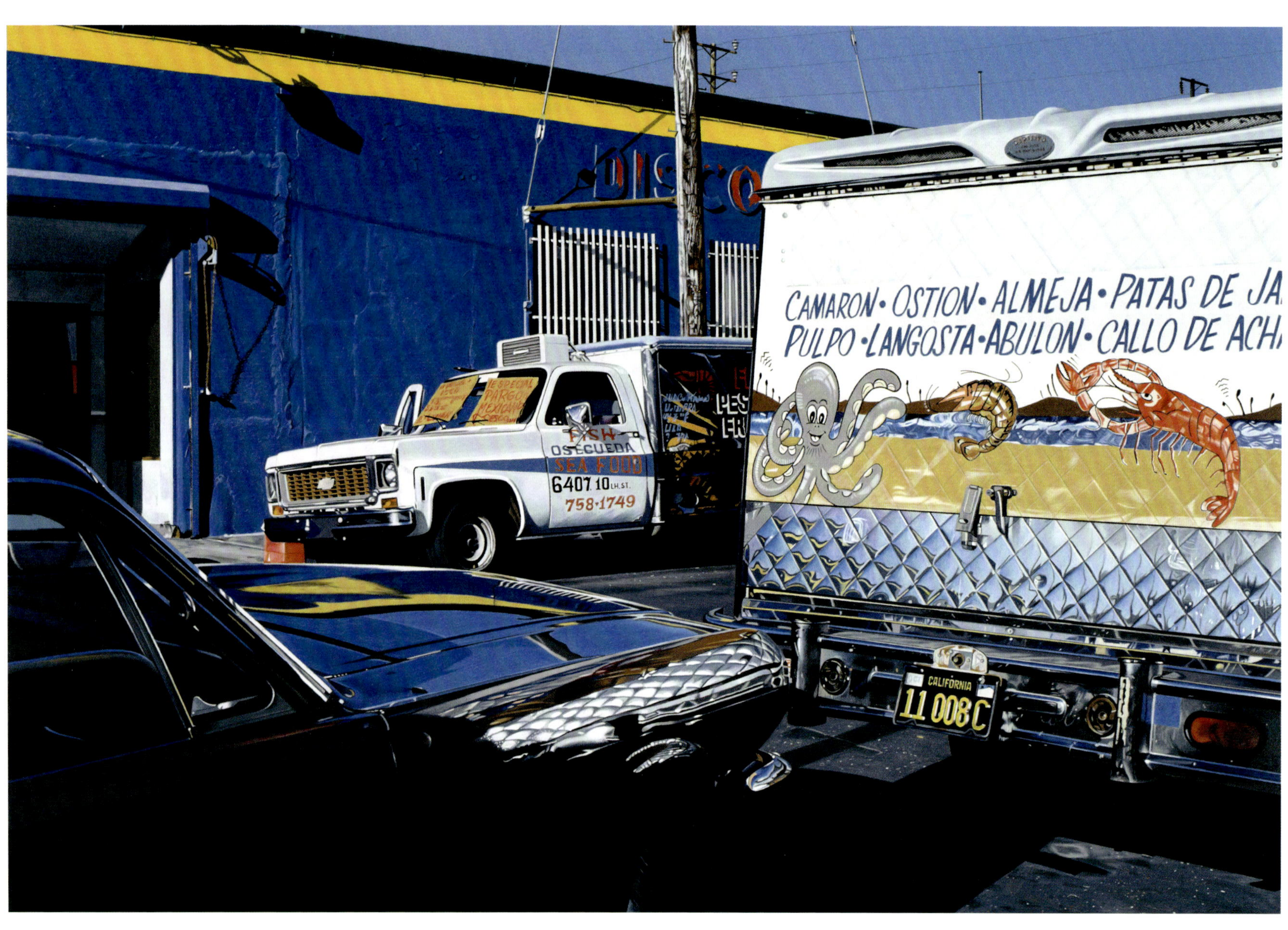
CAMARON · OSTION · ALMEJA · PATAS DE JA
PULPO · LANGOSTA · ABULON · CALLO DE ACH
FISH
OSEGUEDA
SEA FOOD
6407 10 LH. ST.
758-1749
CALIFORNIA
11 008 C

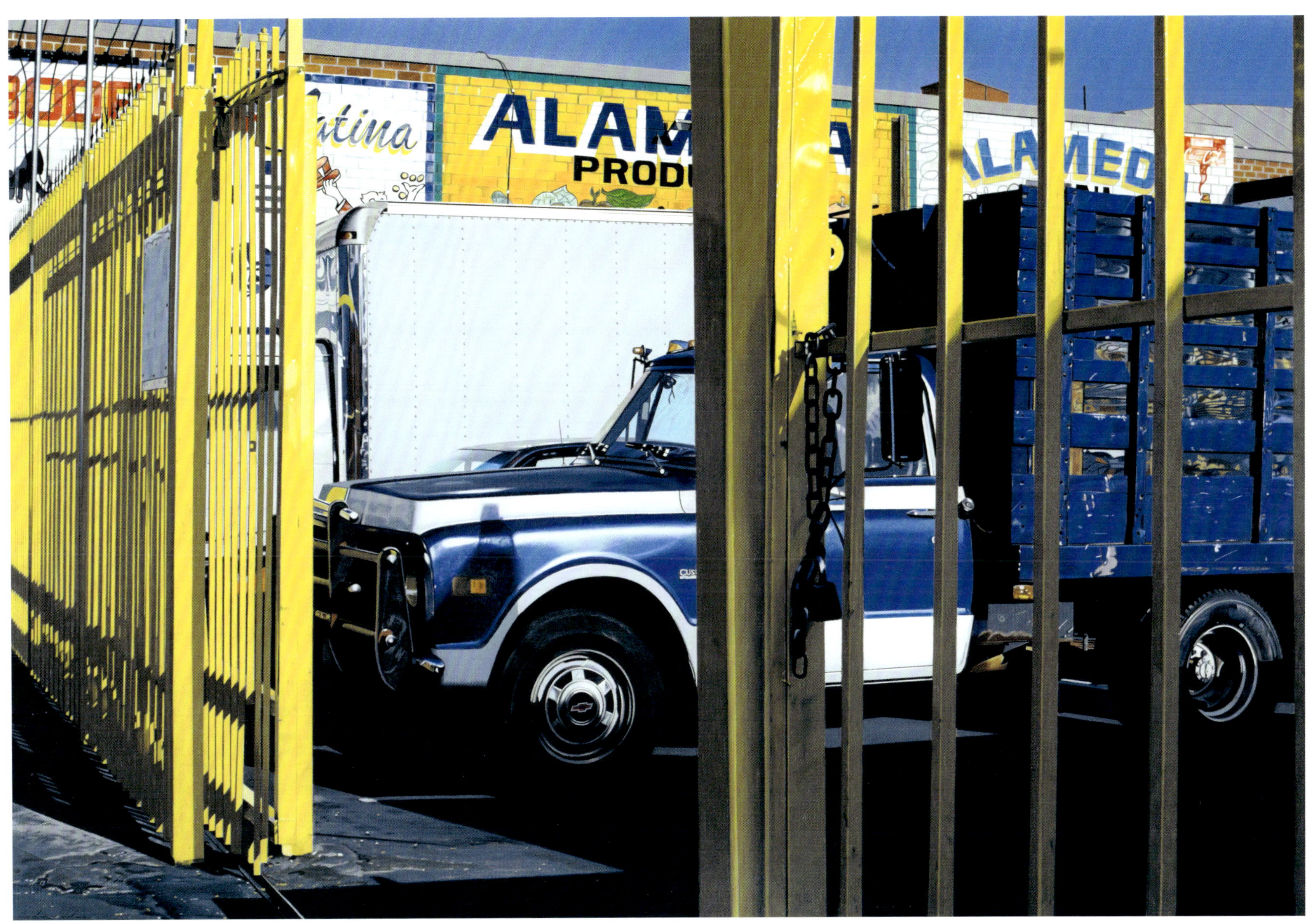
atina
ALAM
PROD
ALAMED

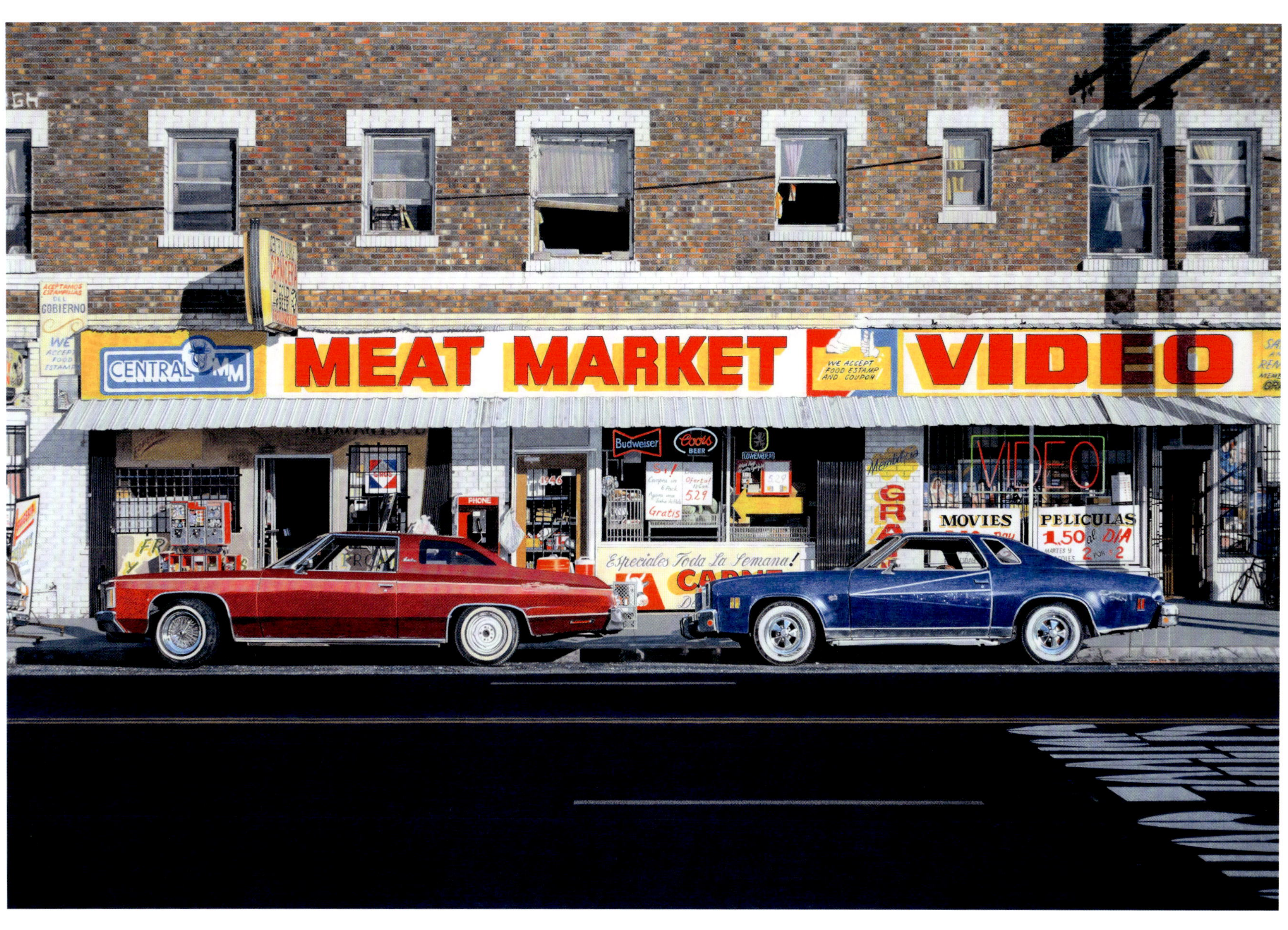
CENTRAL 10MM
MEAT MARKET
VIDEO
WE ACCEPT FOOD STAMP AND COUPON
Budweiser
Coors BEER
LÖWENBRÄU
VIDEO
MOVIES
PELICULAS
1.50 al DIA
Especiales Toda La Semana!
PHONE
WE ACCEPT FOOD STAMPS
DEL GOBIERNO

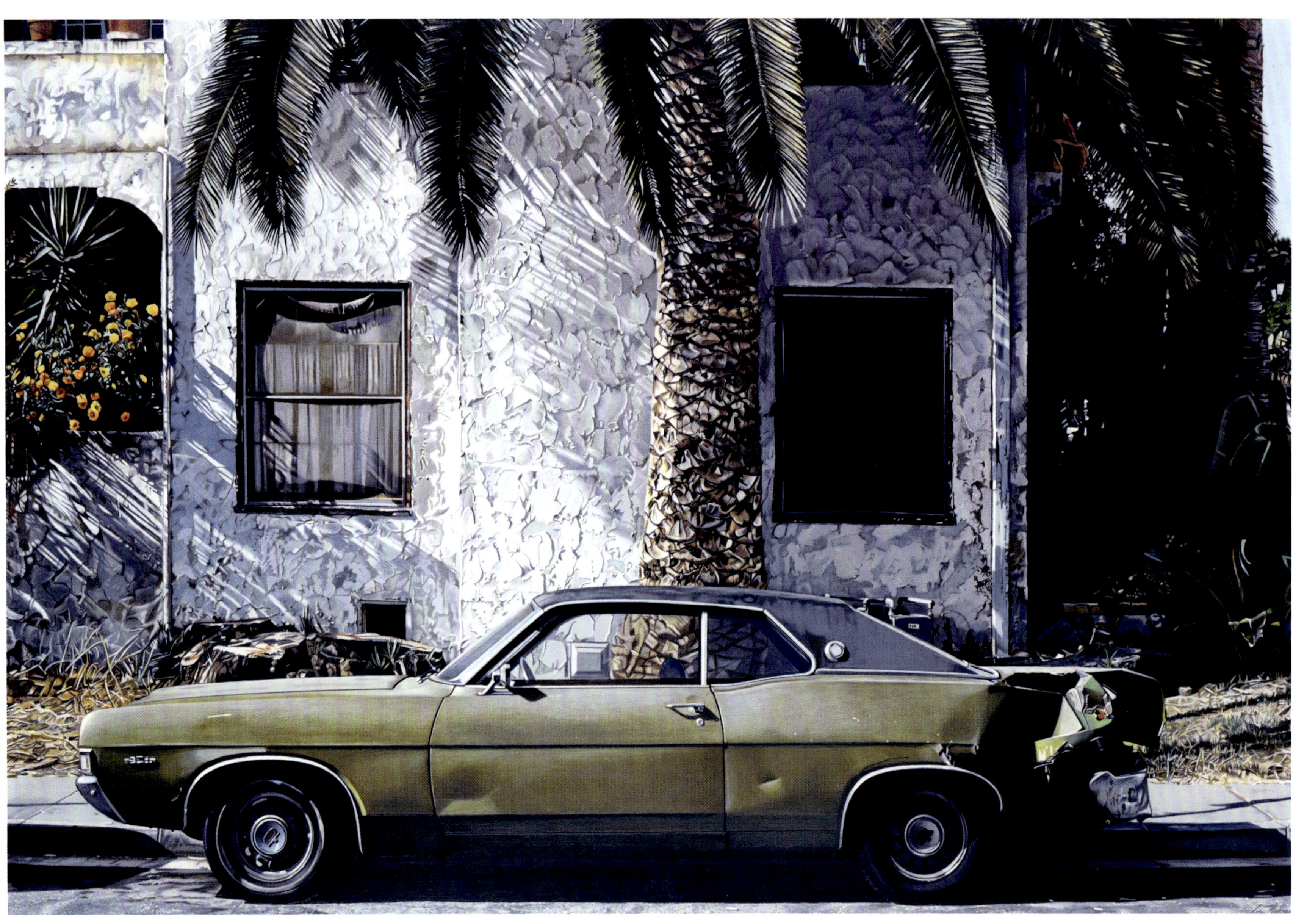

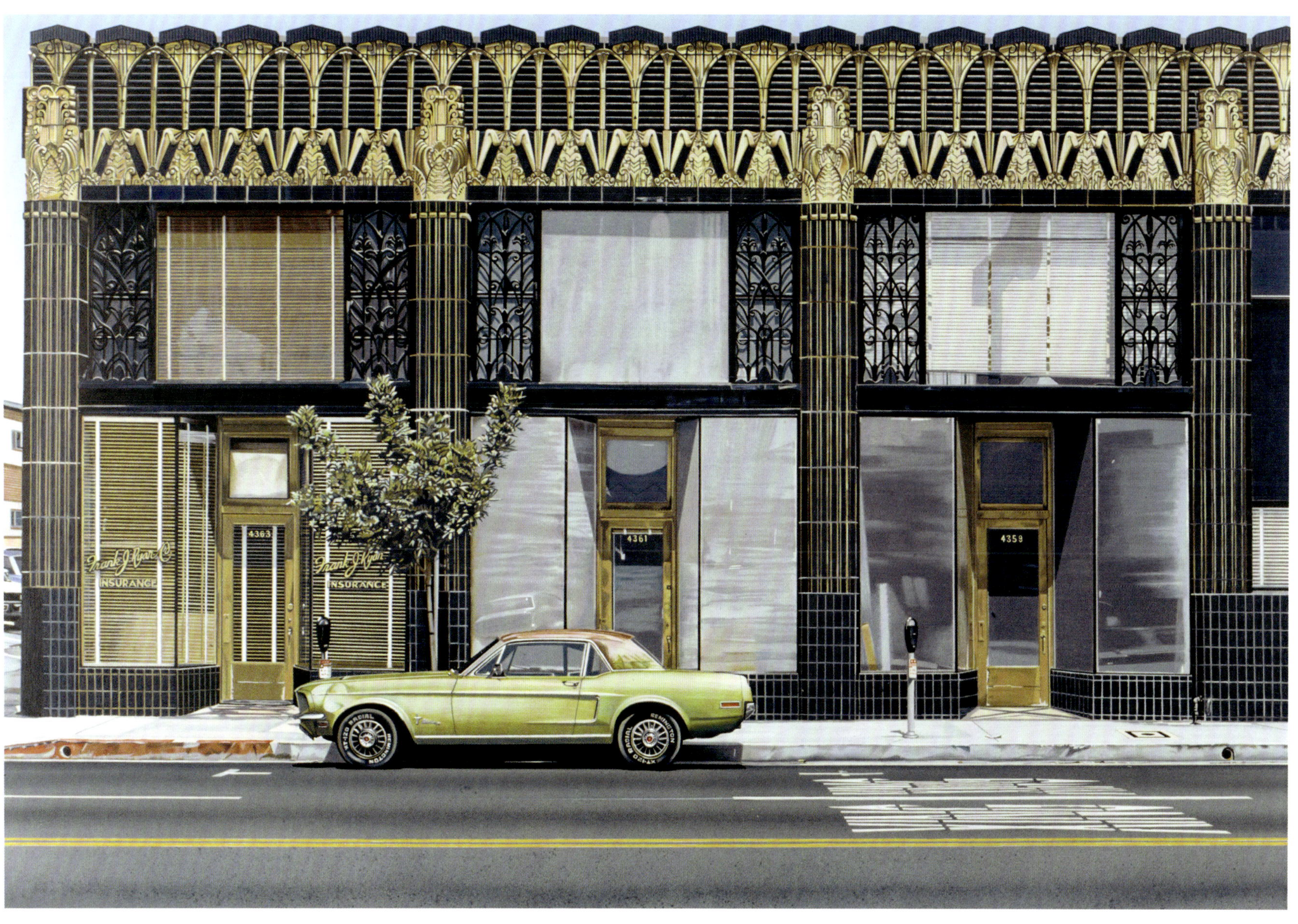

Frank J. Ryan Co.
INSURANCE
Frank J. Ryan
INSURANCE
4363
4361
4359

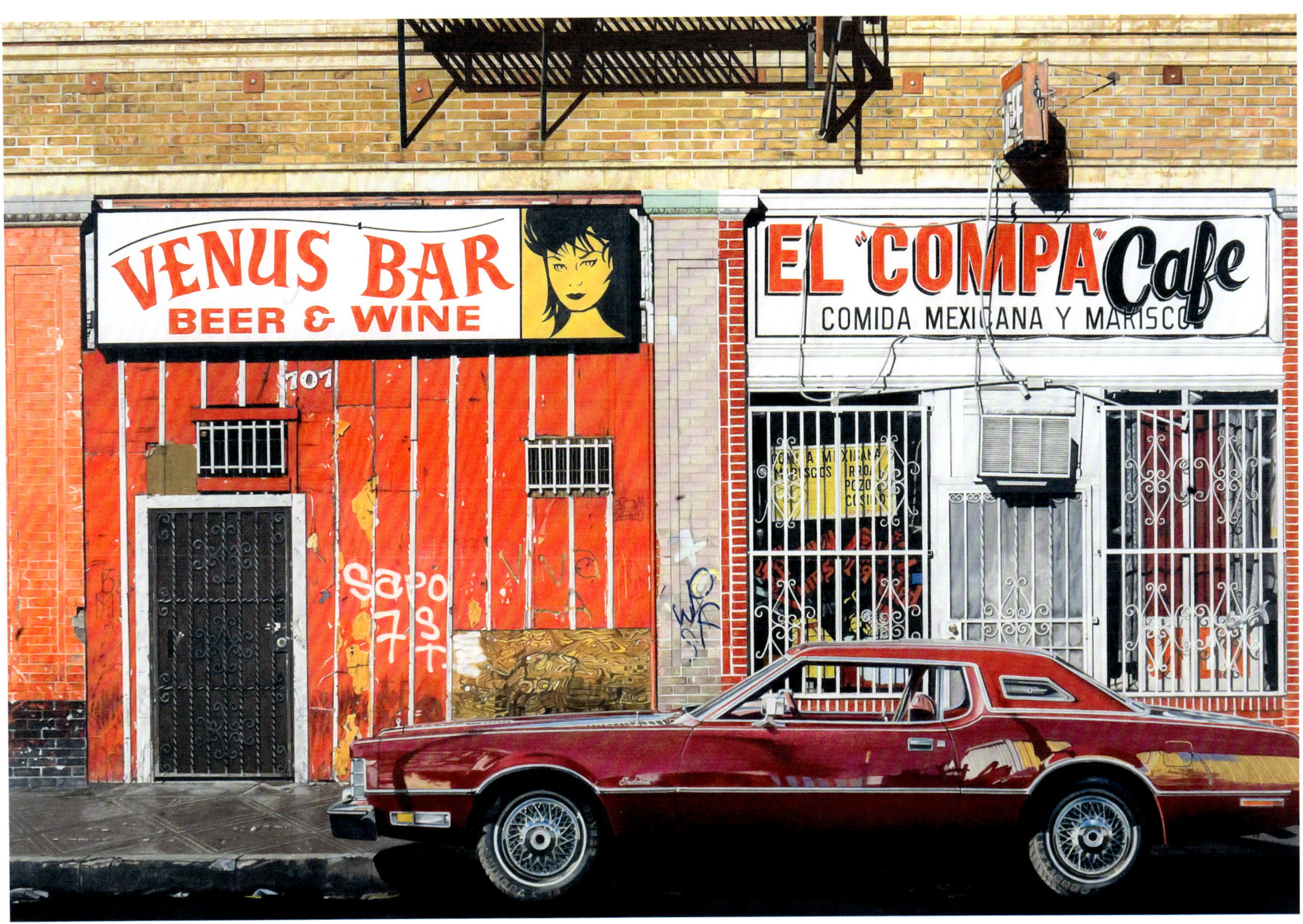

VENUS BAR
BEER & WINE
EL "COMPA" Cafe
COMIDA MEXICANA Y MARISCO
707
SAPO
7 ST

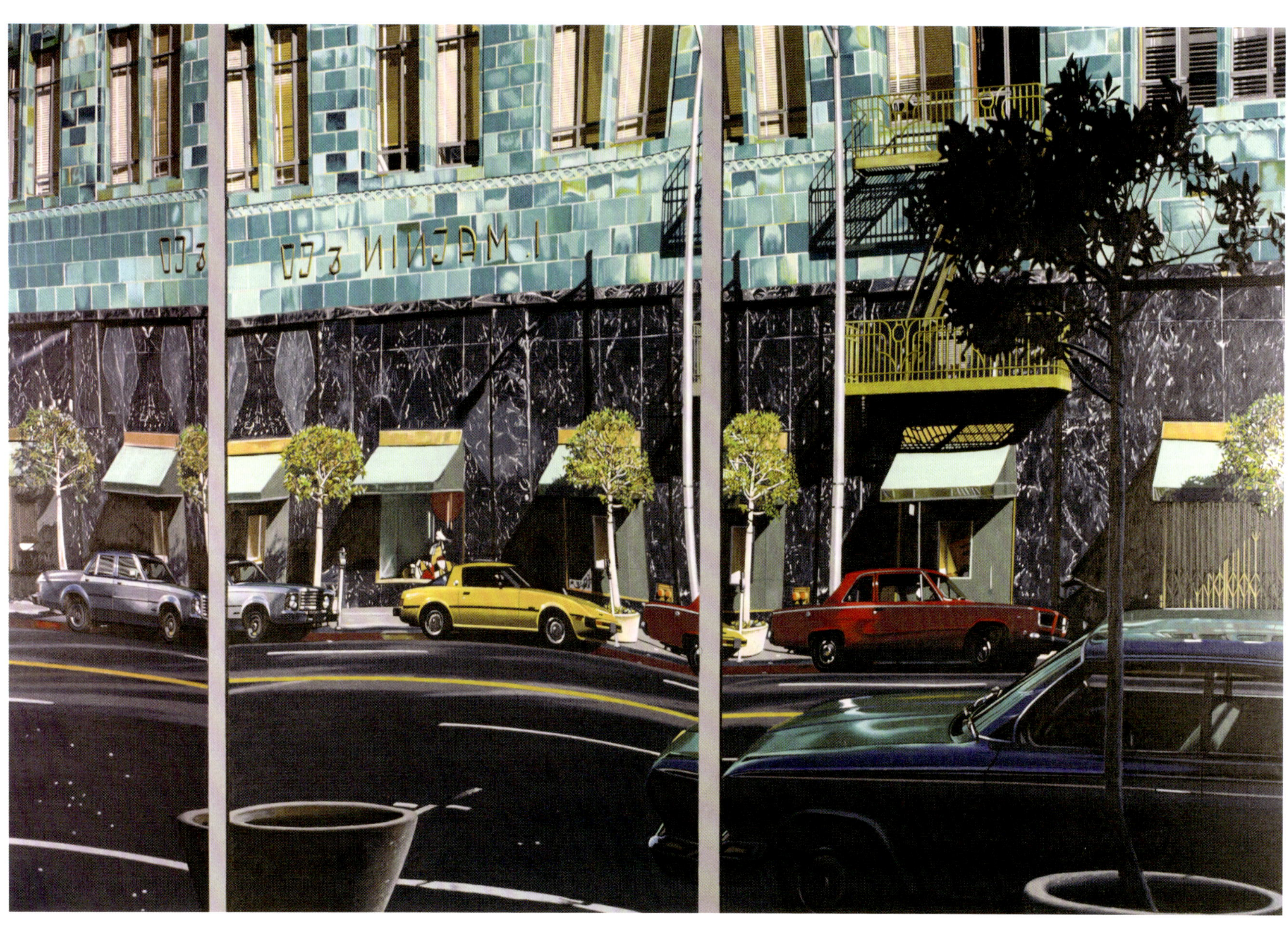

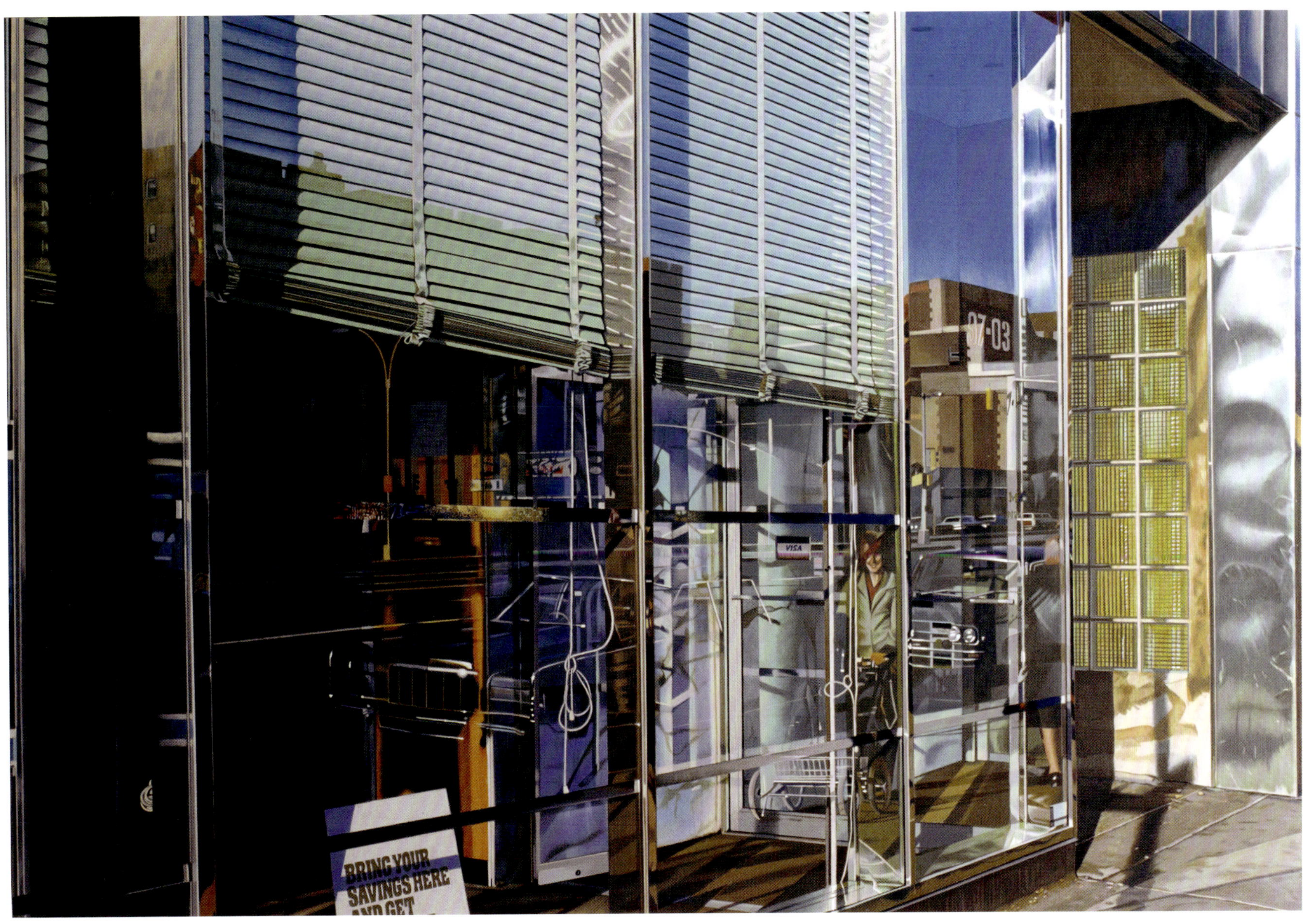


07-03
VISA
BRING YOUR
SAVINGS HERE
AND GET

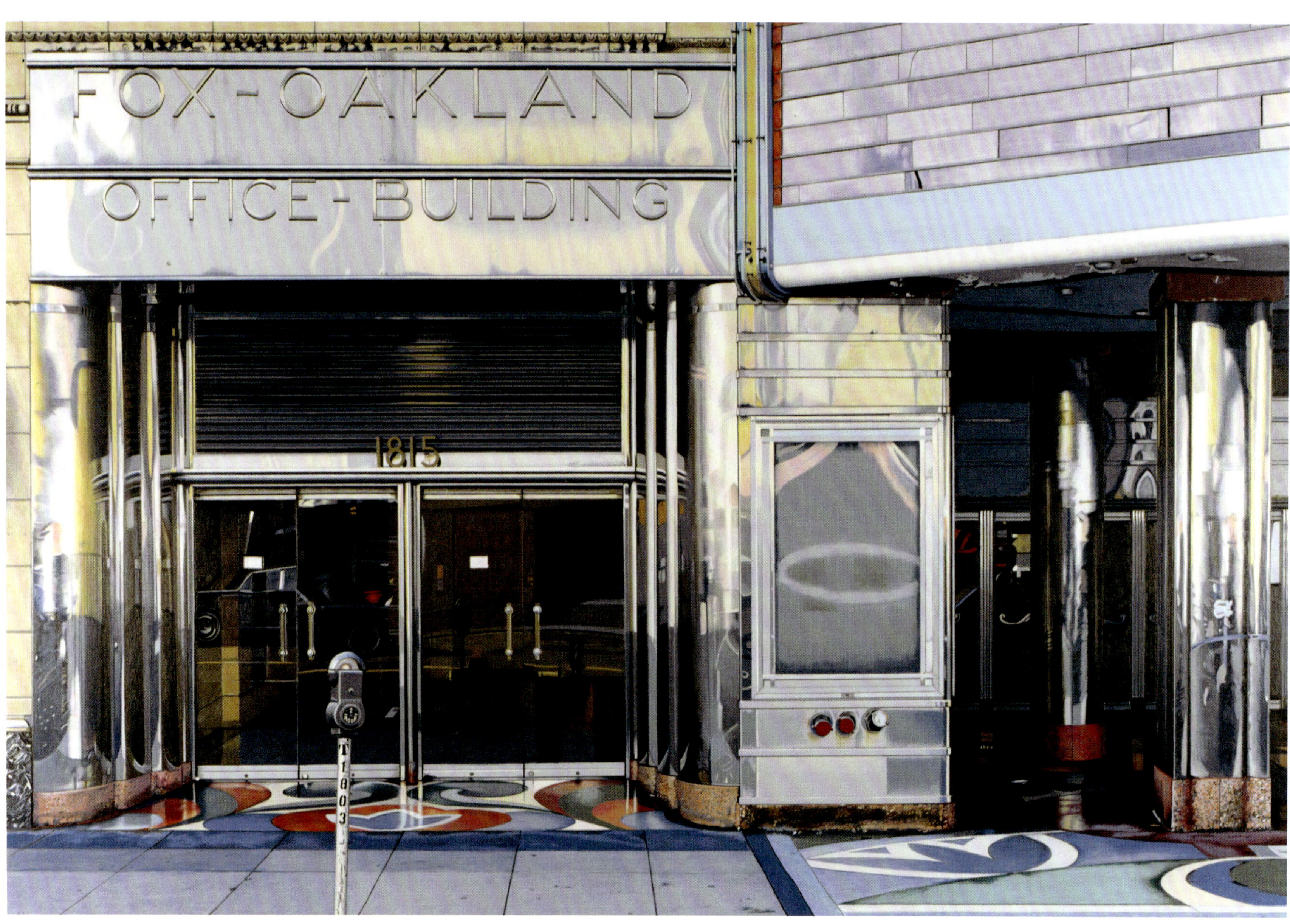

FOX · OAKLAND
OFFICE · BUILDING
1815

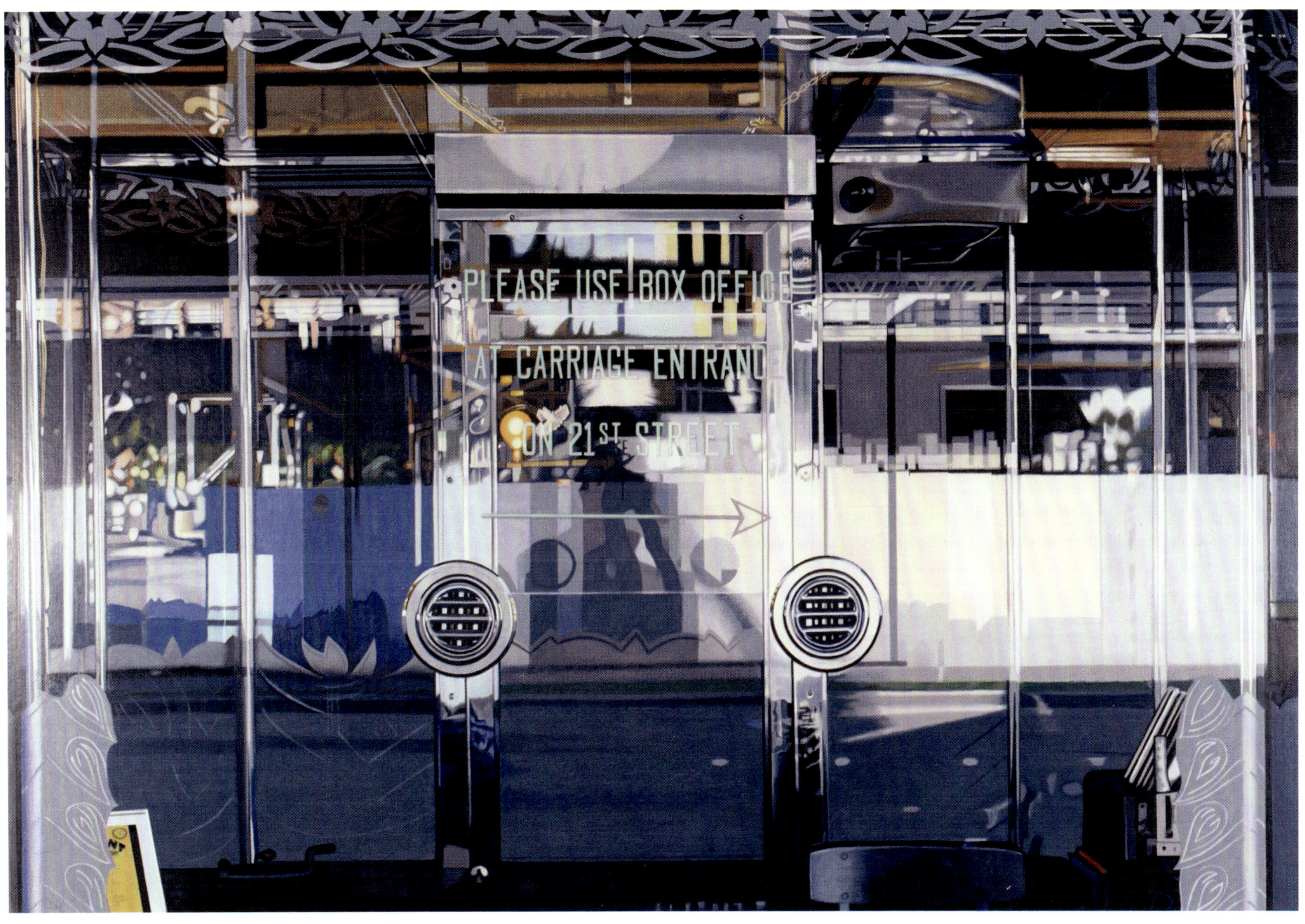
PLEASE USE BOX OFFICE
AT CARRIAGE ENTRANCE
ON 21ST STREET

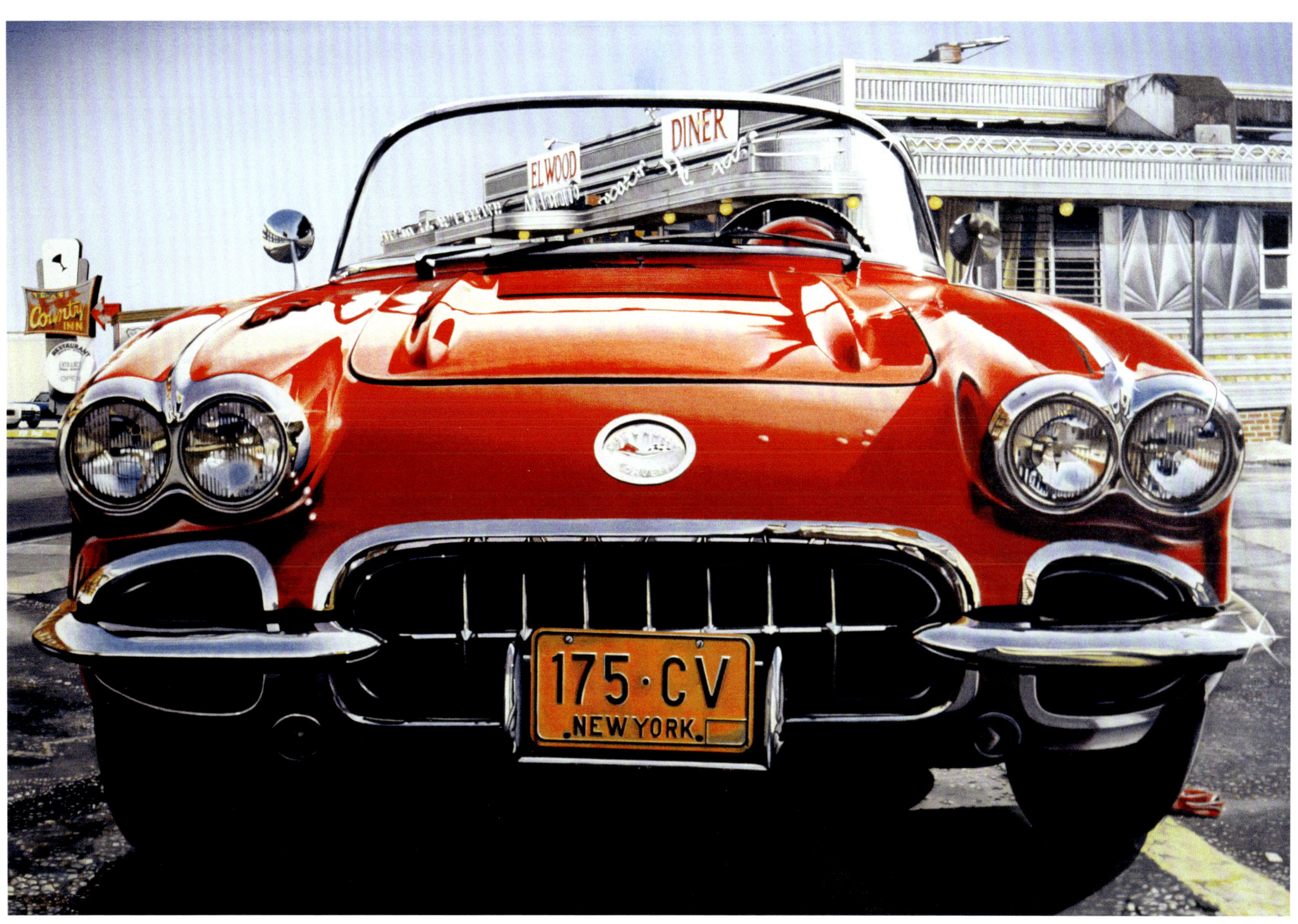

Country
INN
ELWOOD DINER
175·CV
NEW YORK

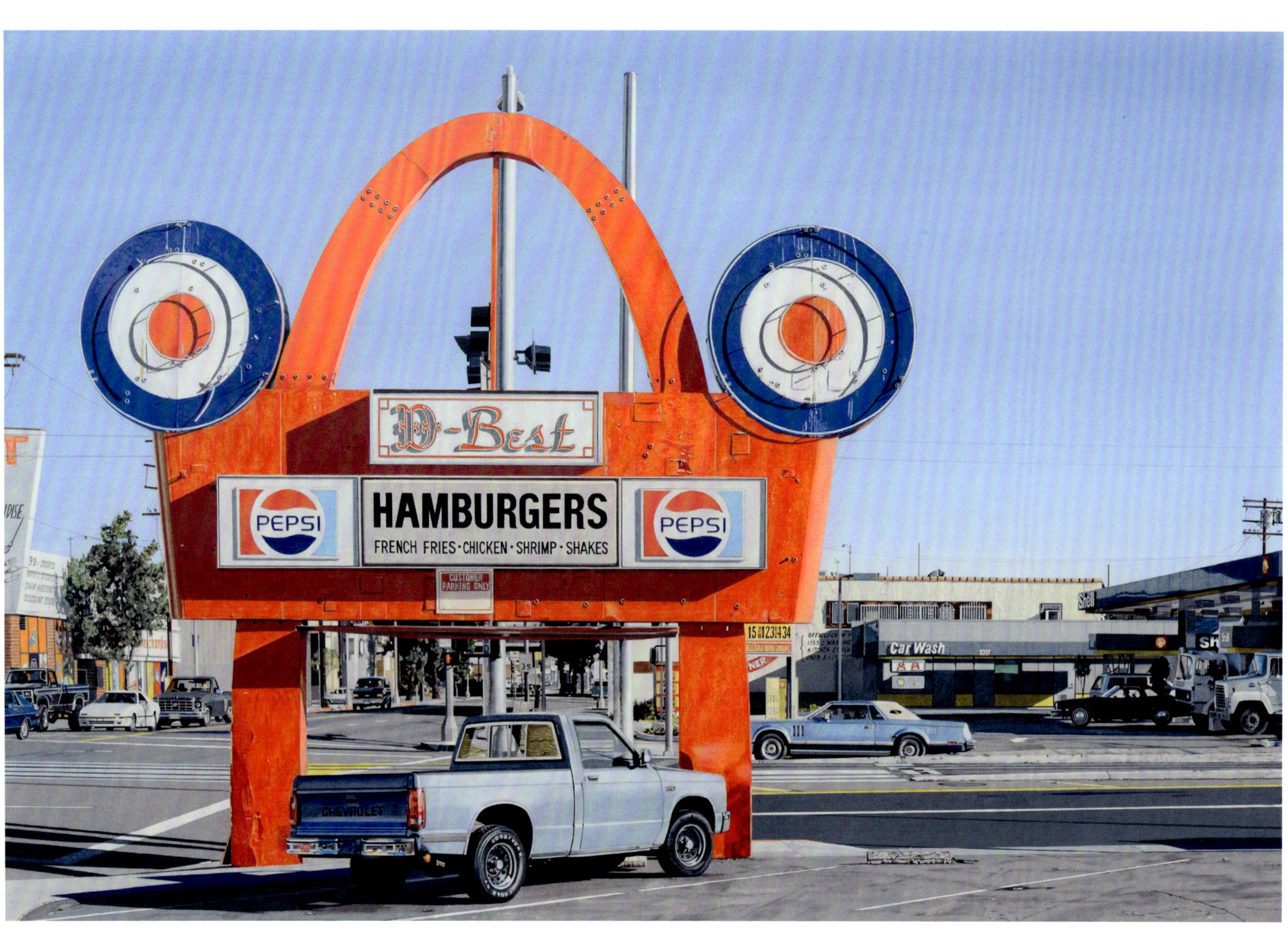
D-Best
HAMBURGERS
FRENCH FRIES · CHICKEN · SHRIMP · SHAKES
PEPSI
PEPSI
CUSTOMER PARKING ONLY
Car Wash
CHEVROLET

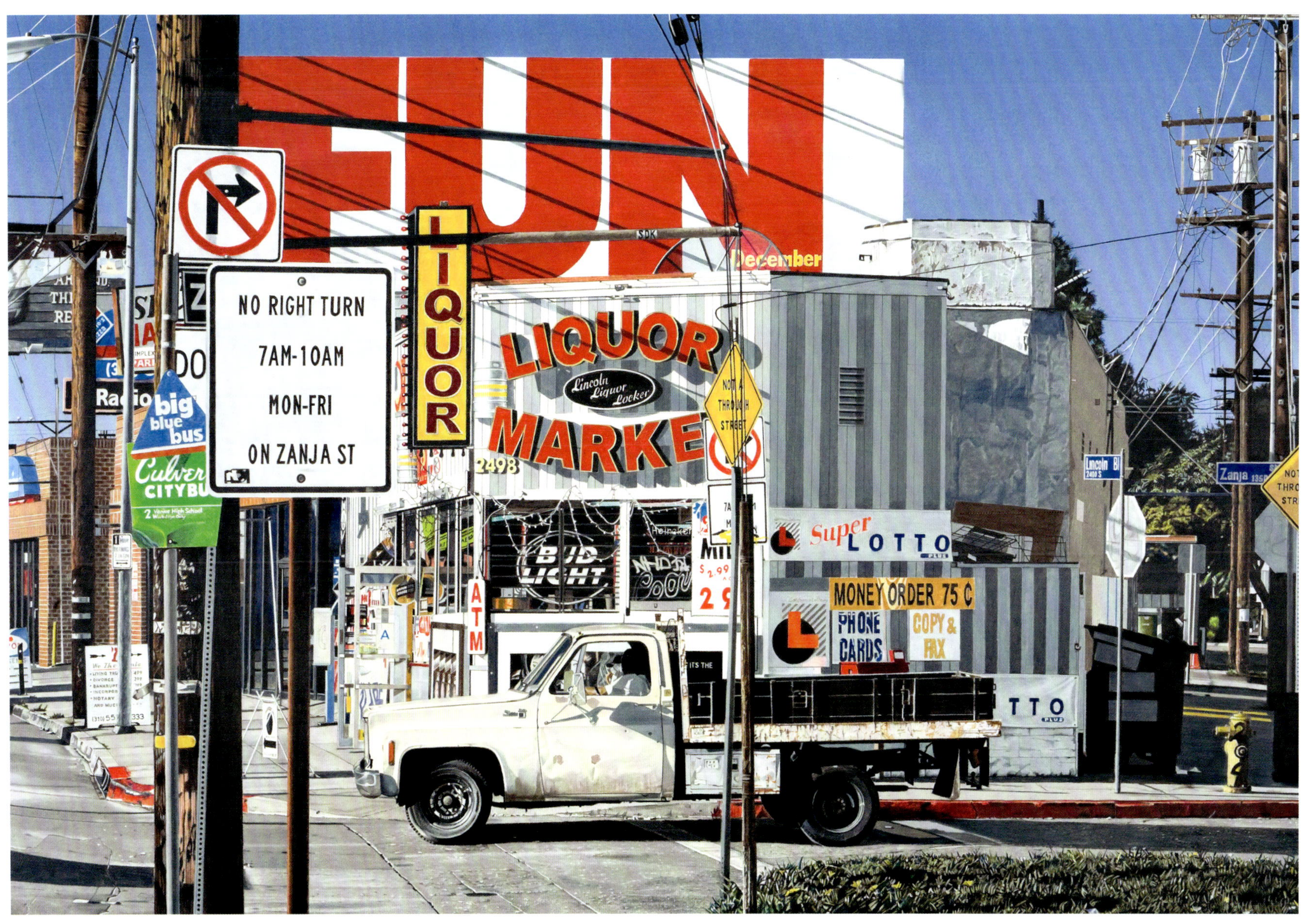

FUN
December
LIQUOR
NO RIGHT TURN
7AM-10AM
MON-FRI
ON ZANJA ST
LIQUOR
Lincoln Liquor Locker
MARKE
2498
big
blue
bus
Radio
Culver
CITYBU
BUD
LIGHT
ATM
Super LOTTO
MONEY ORDER 75 C
PHONE CARDS
COPY & FAX
TTO
Lincoln Bl
Zanja

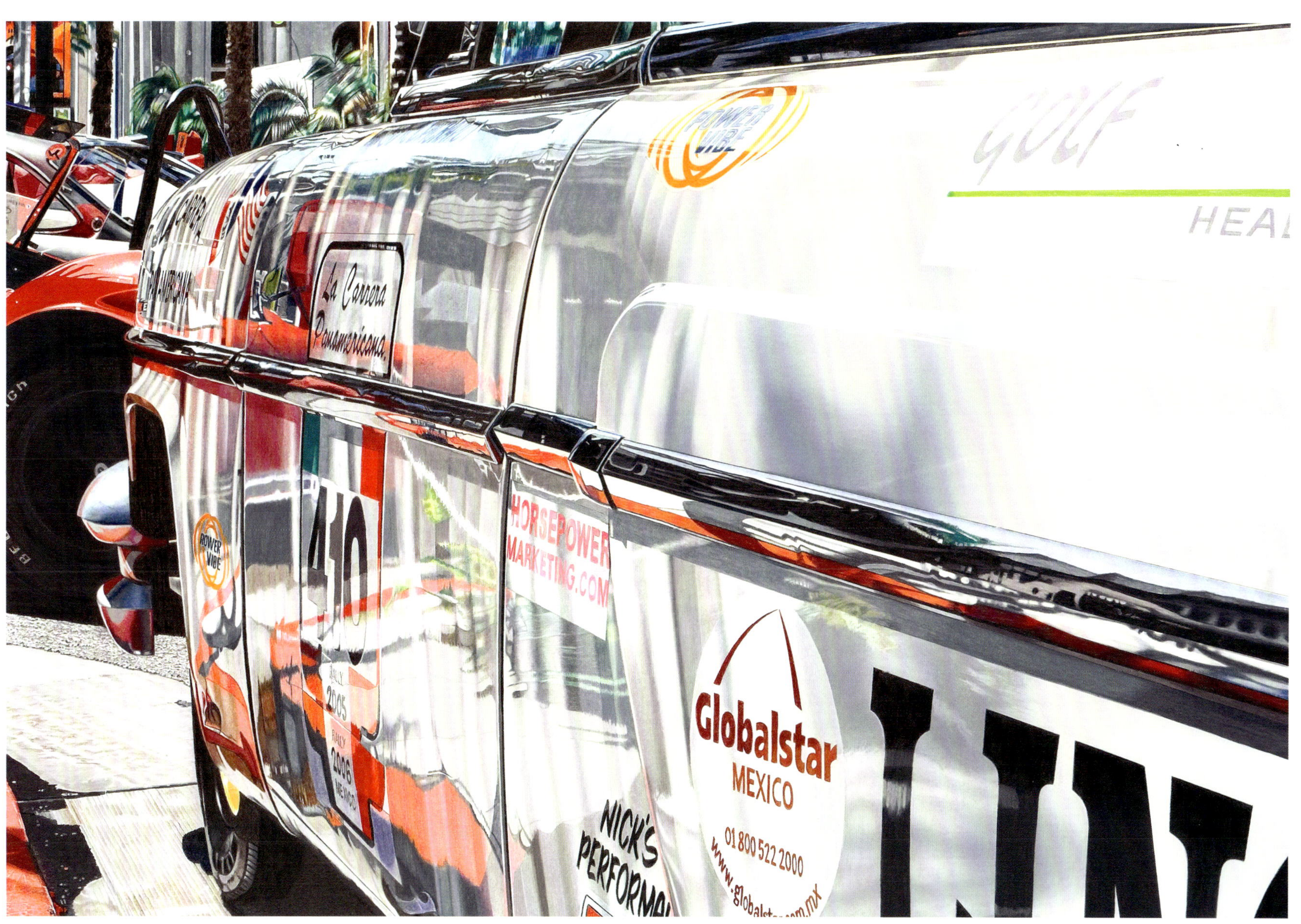
POWER VIBE
GOLF
HEAL
La Carrera Panamericana
410
POWER VIBE
HORSEPOWER
MARKETING.COM
Globalstar
MEXICO
01 800 522 2000
www.globalstar.com.mx
NICK'S
PERFORMA

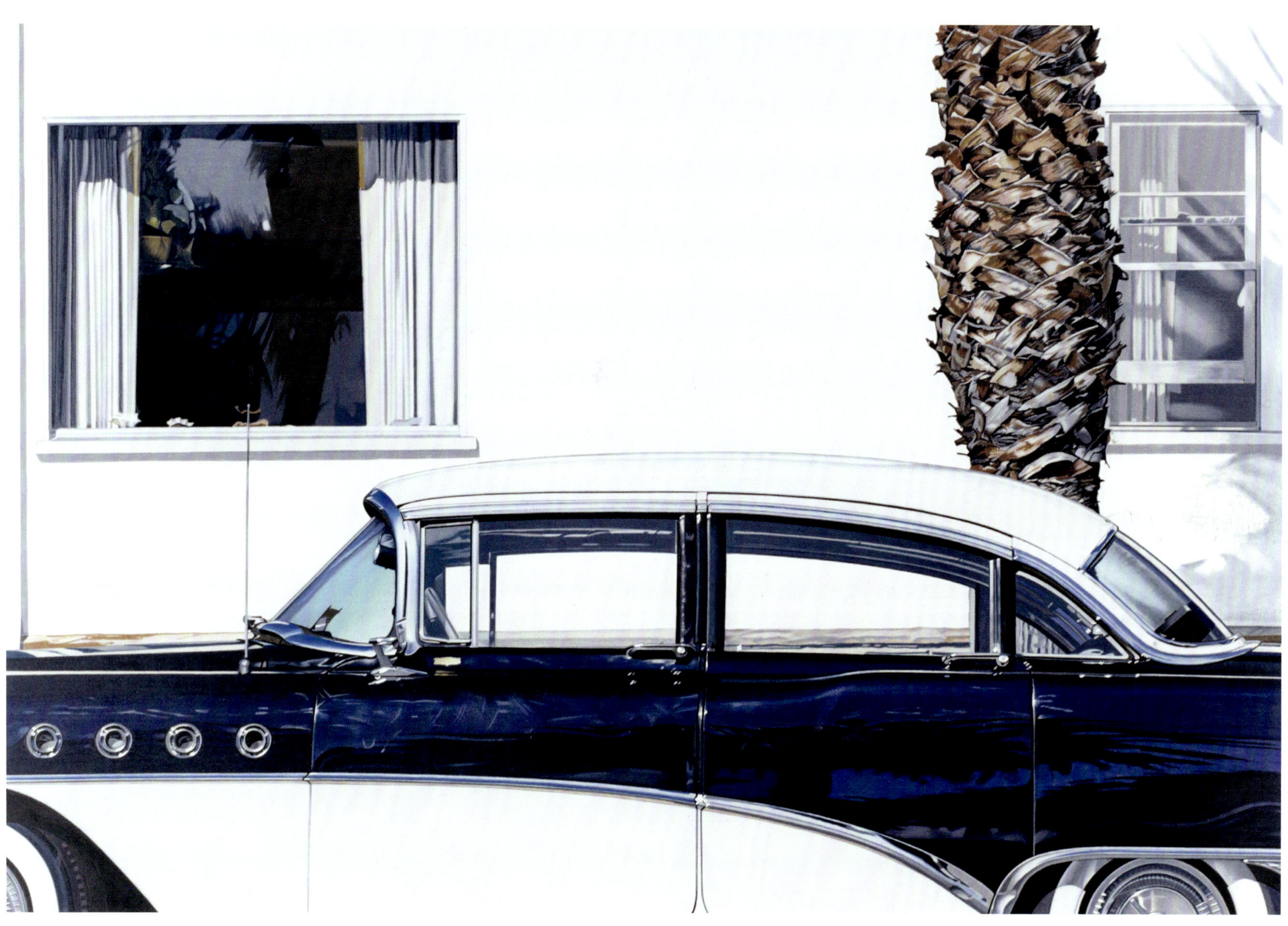

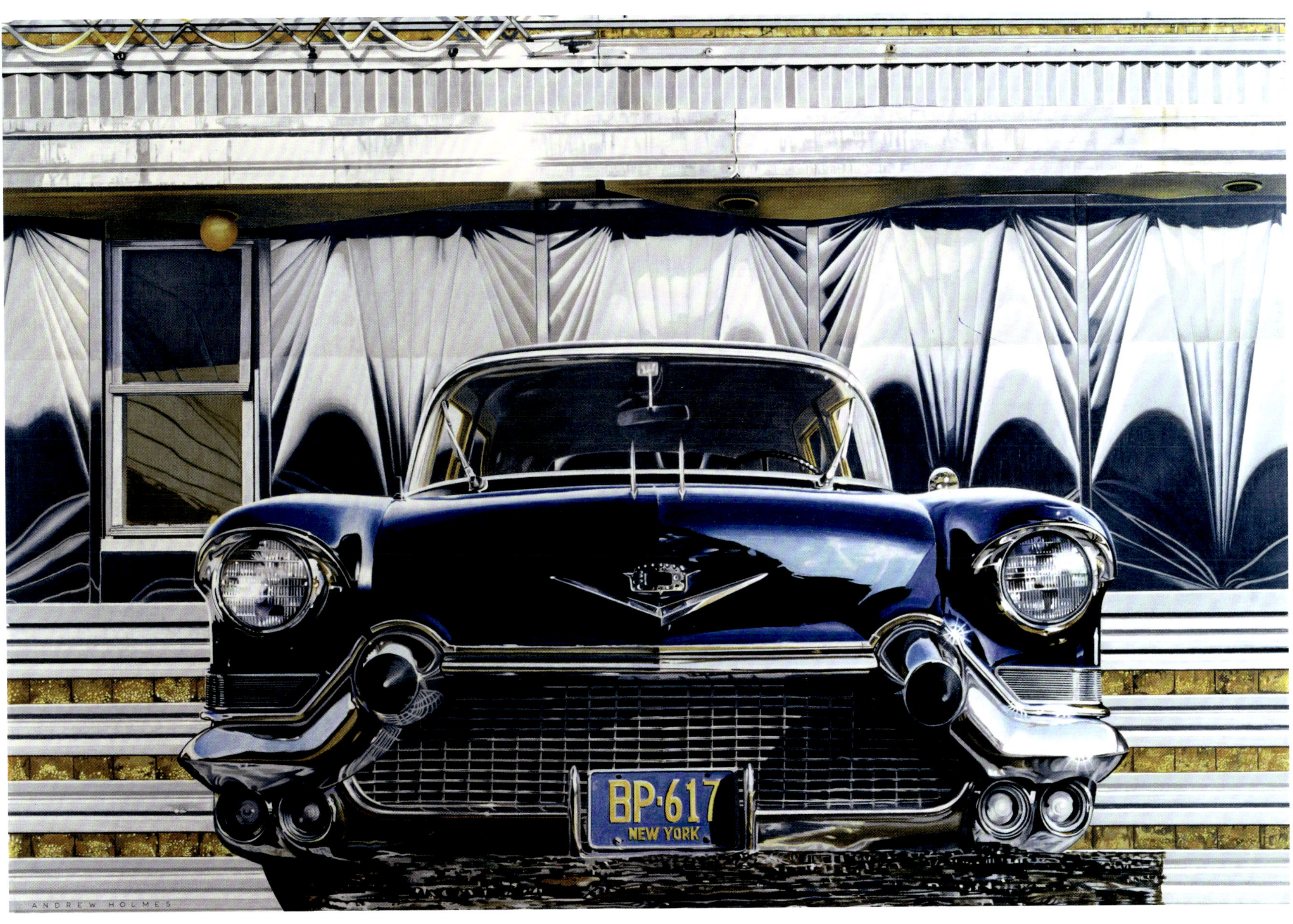

ANDREW HOLMES
BP·617
NEW YORK

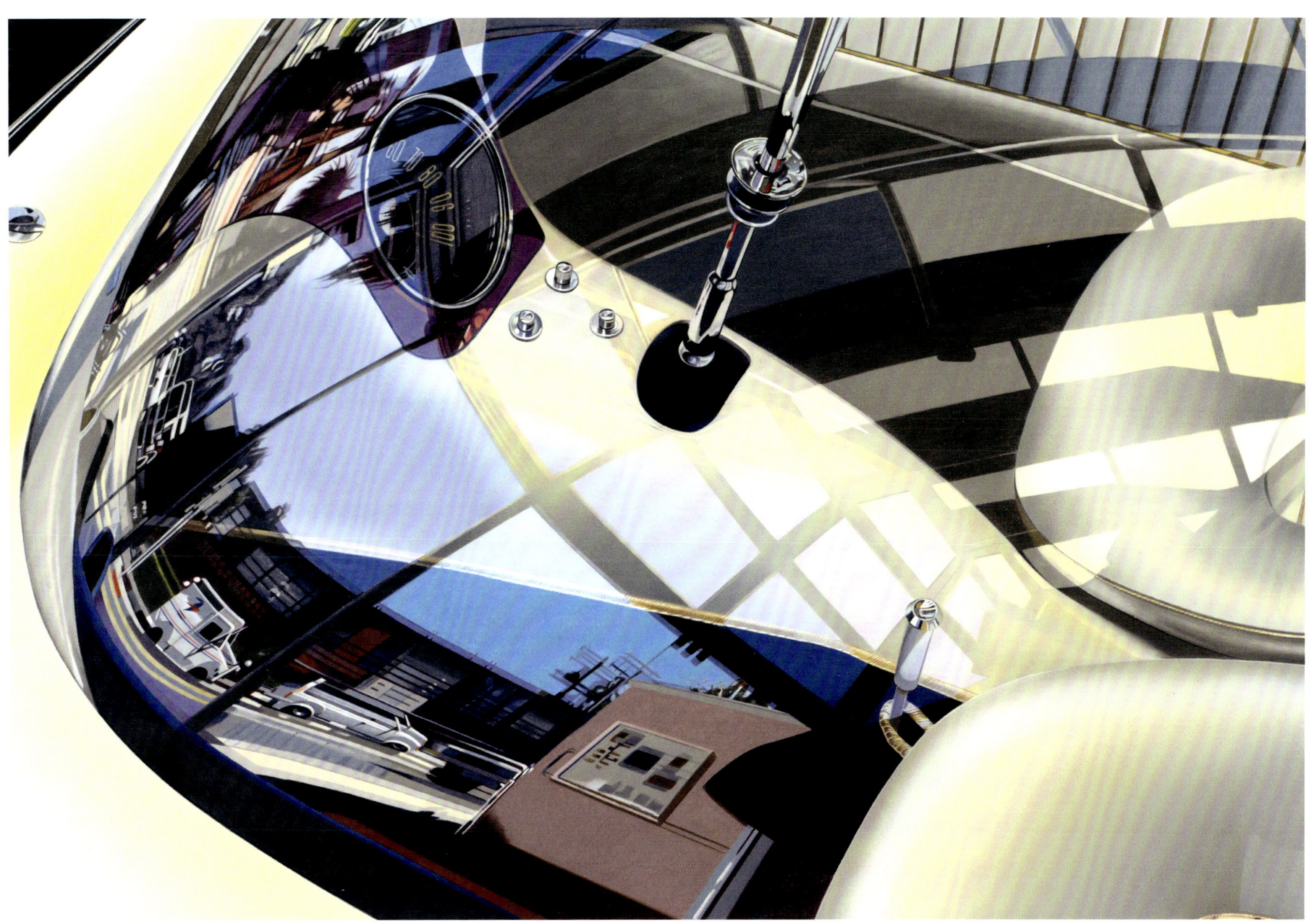

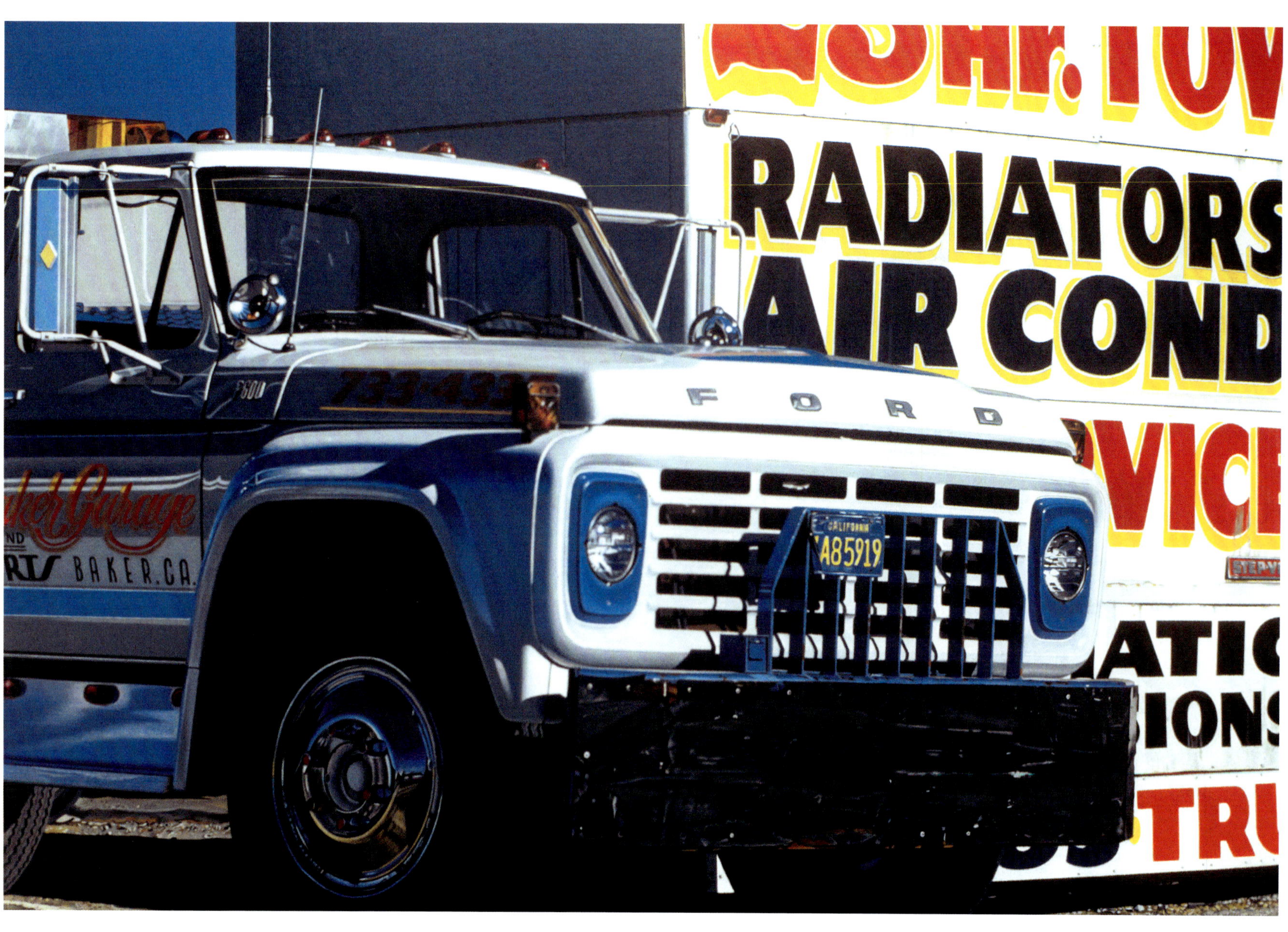
24 Hr. TOW
RADIATORS
AIR COND
VICE
ATIO
IONS
TRU
F600
733-493
FORD
aker Garage
RTS BAKER.CA.
CALIFORNIA
A85919

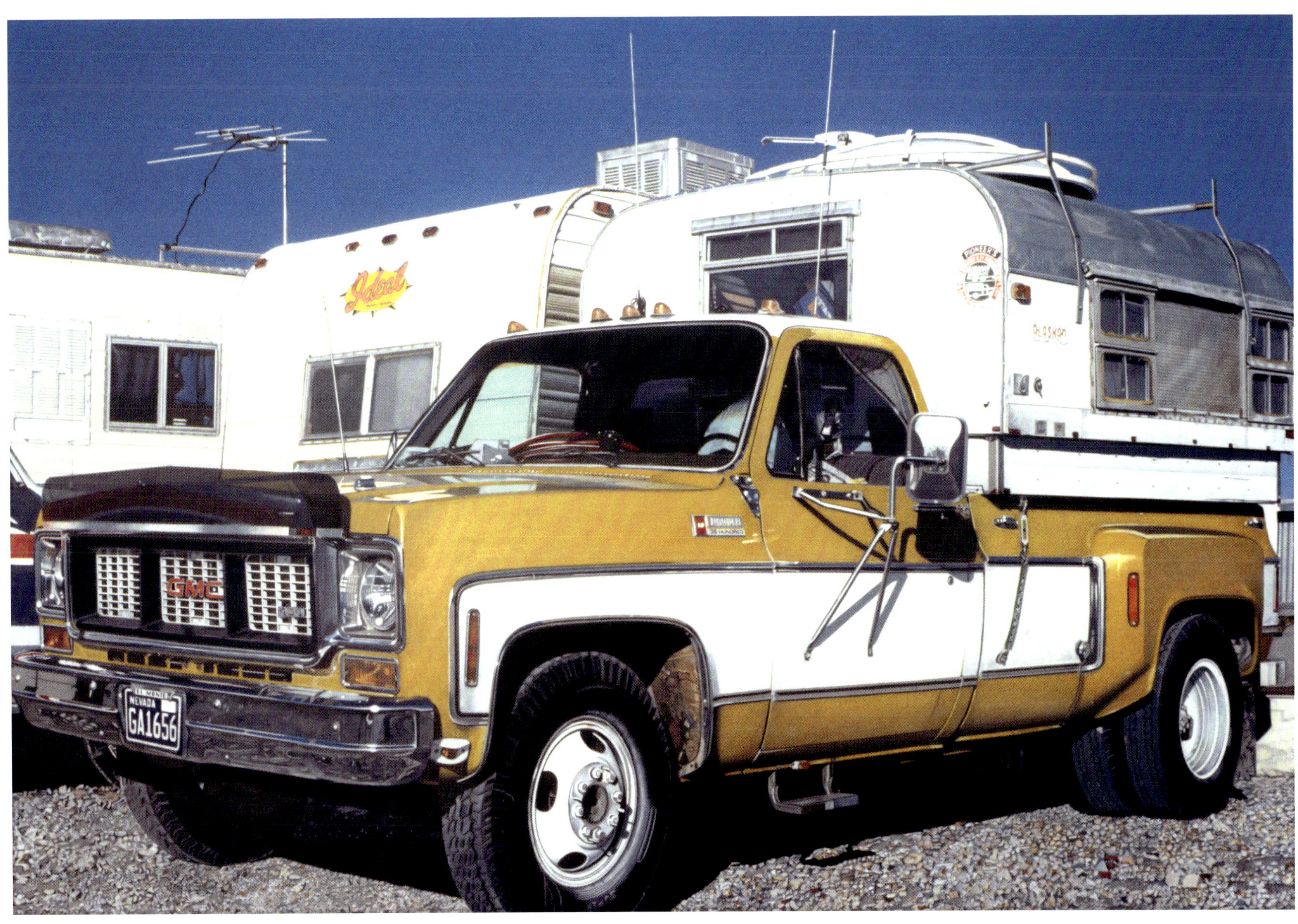

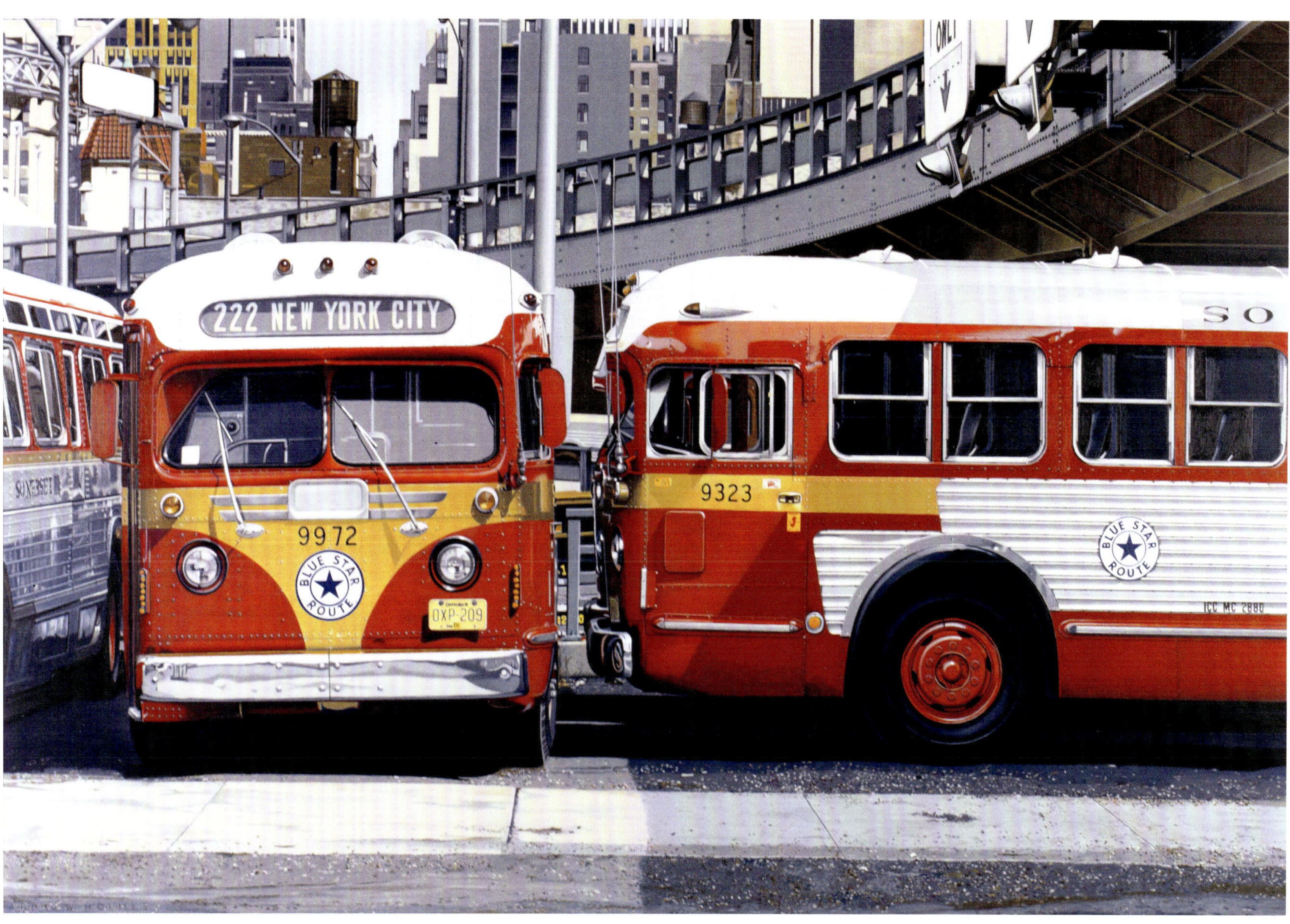

222 NEW YORK CITY
9972
BLUE STAR ROUTE
OXP 209
SO
9323
BLUE STAR ROUTE
ICC MC 2880
ONLY

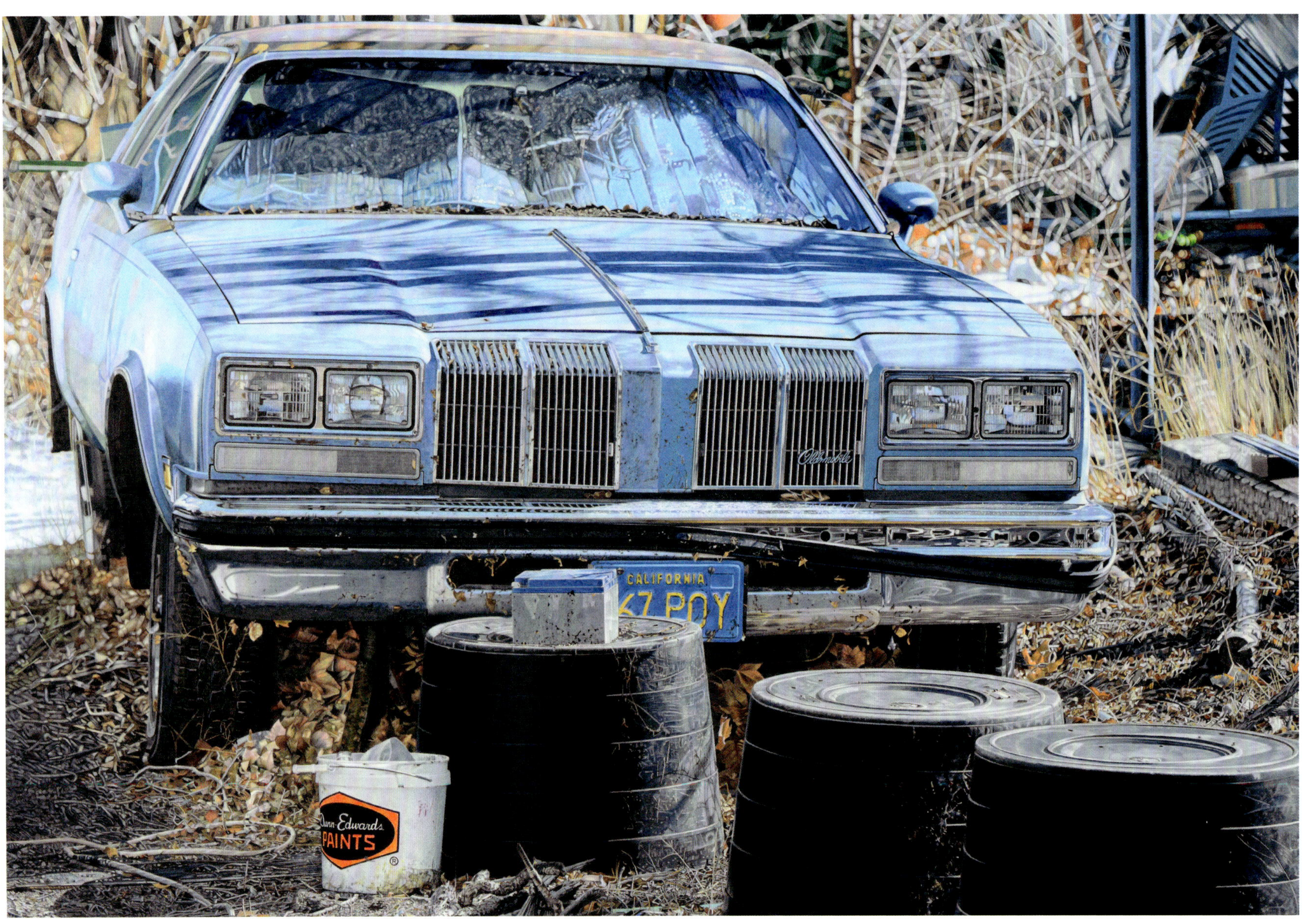
CALIFORNIA
47 PDY
Dunn Edwards
PAINTS ®
Oldsmobile

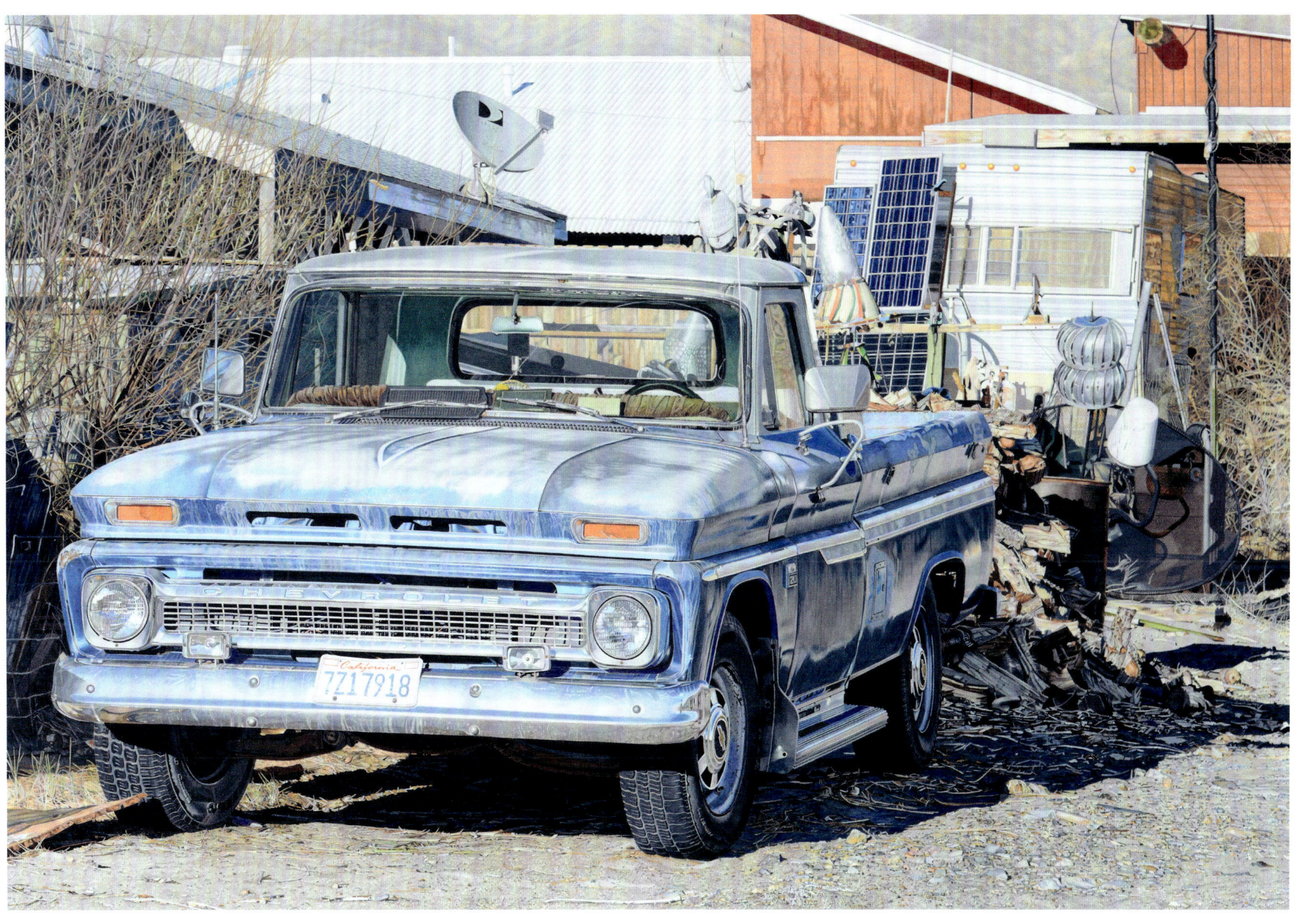

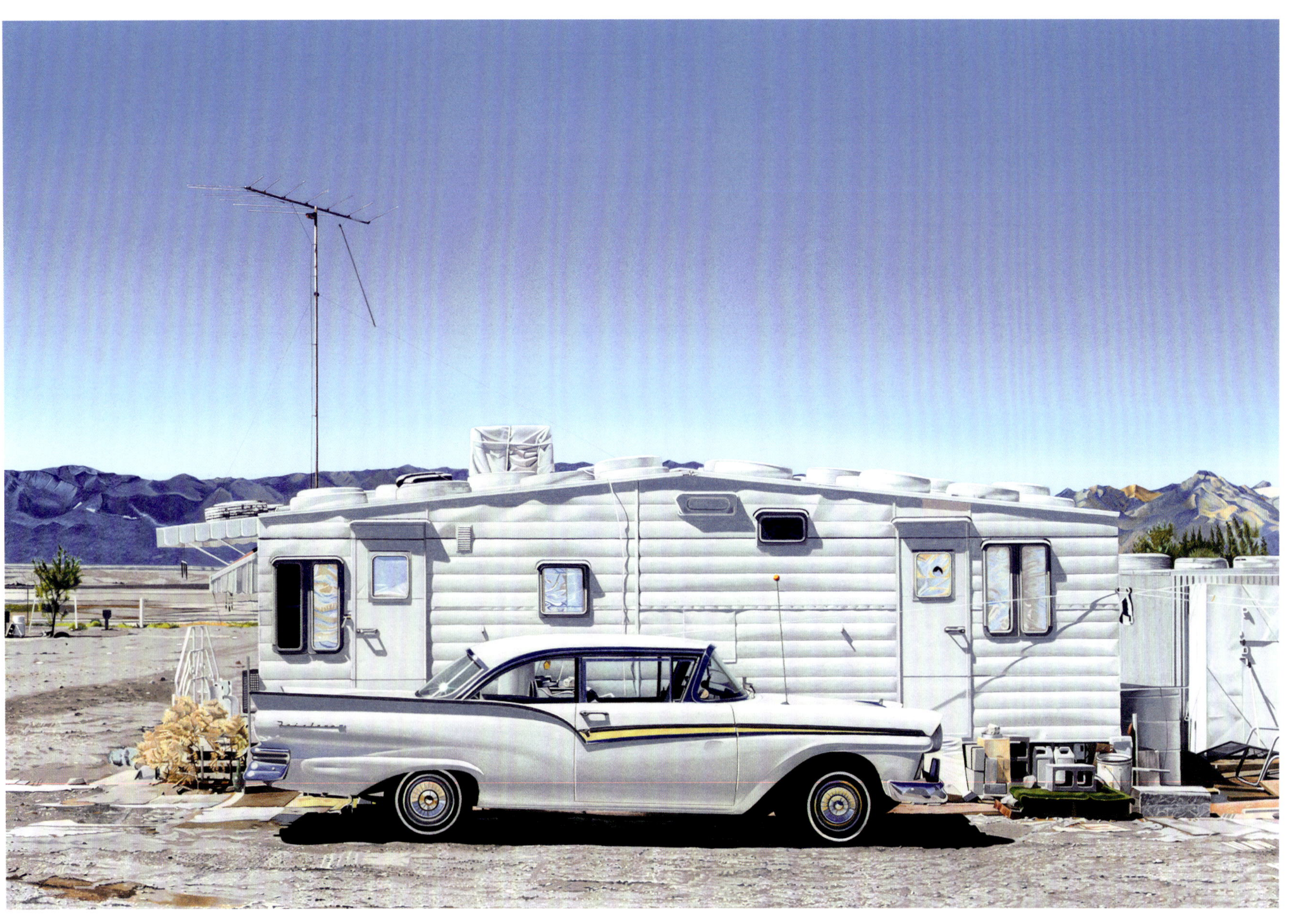

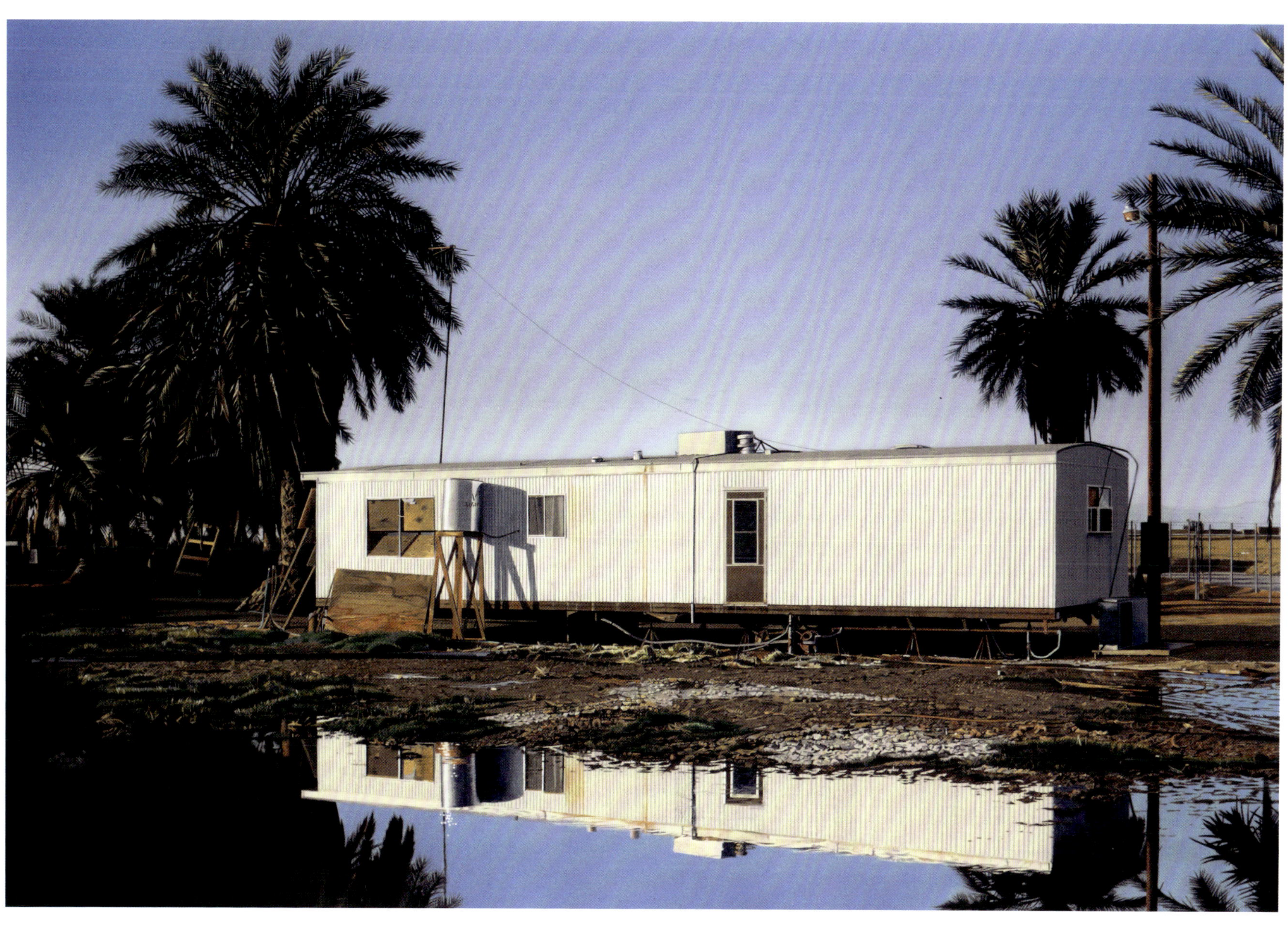

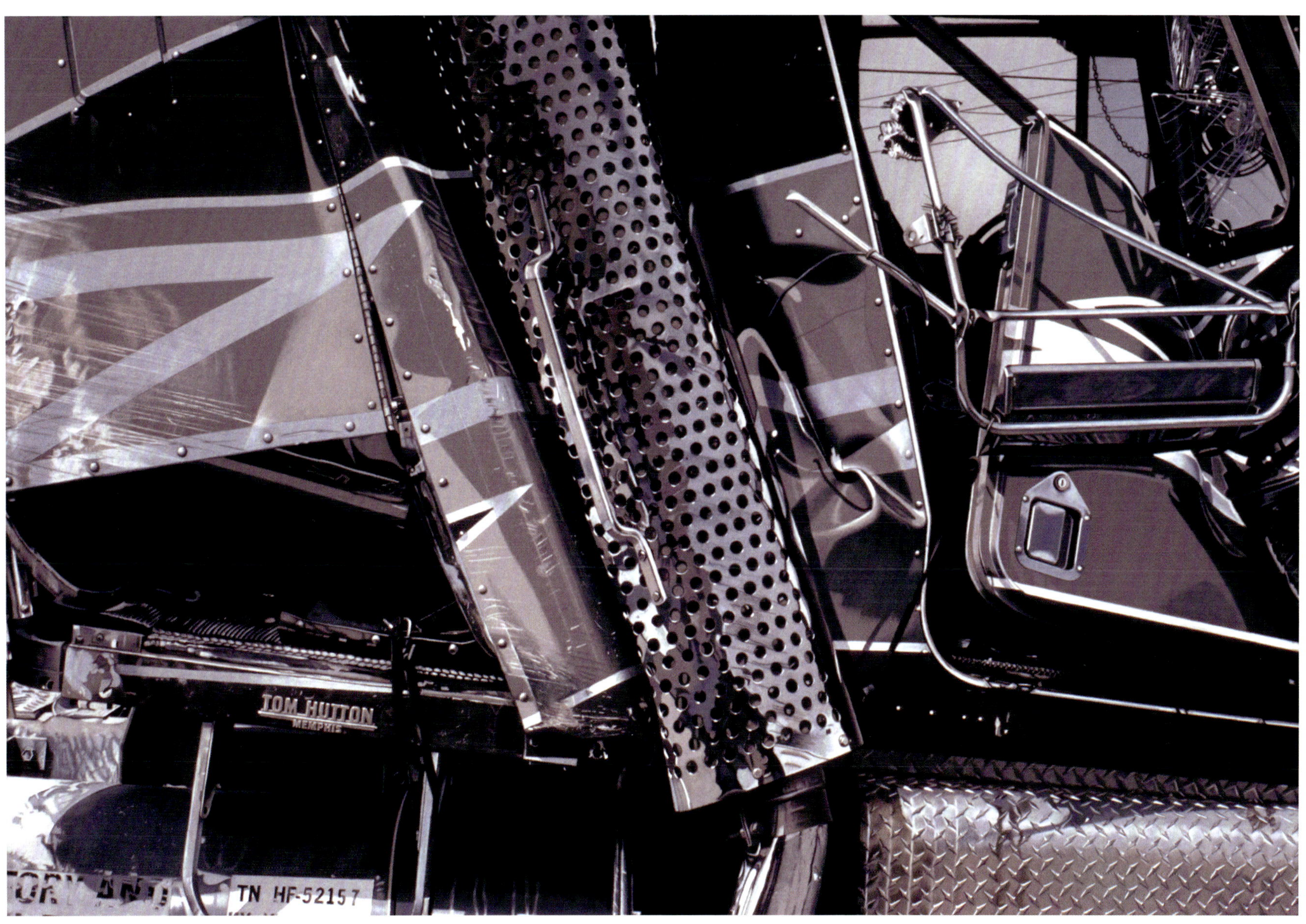

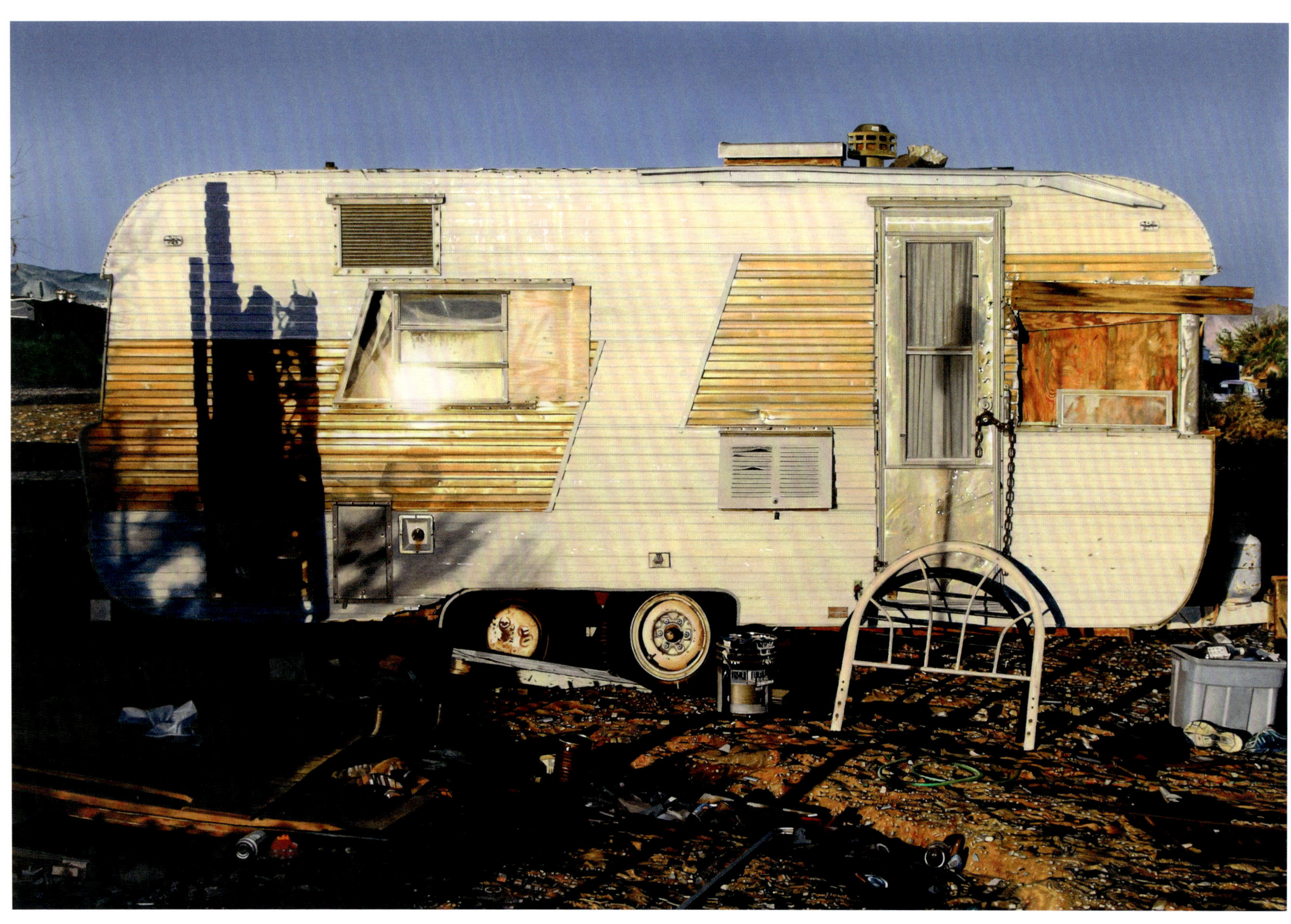

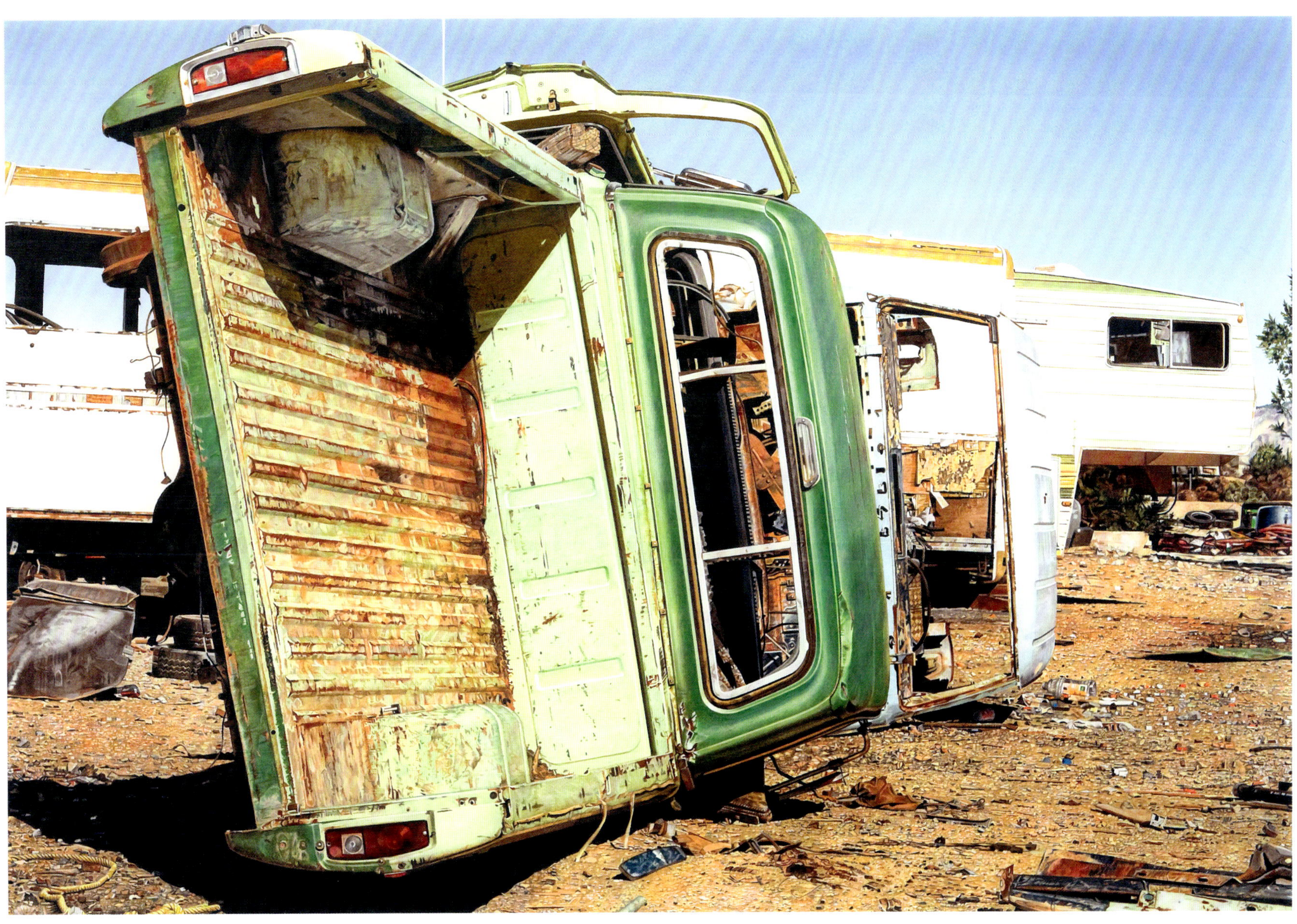

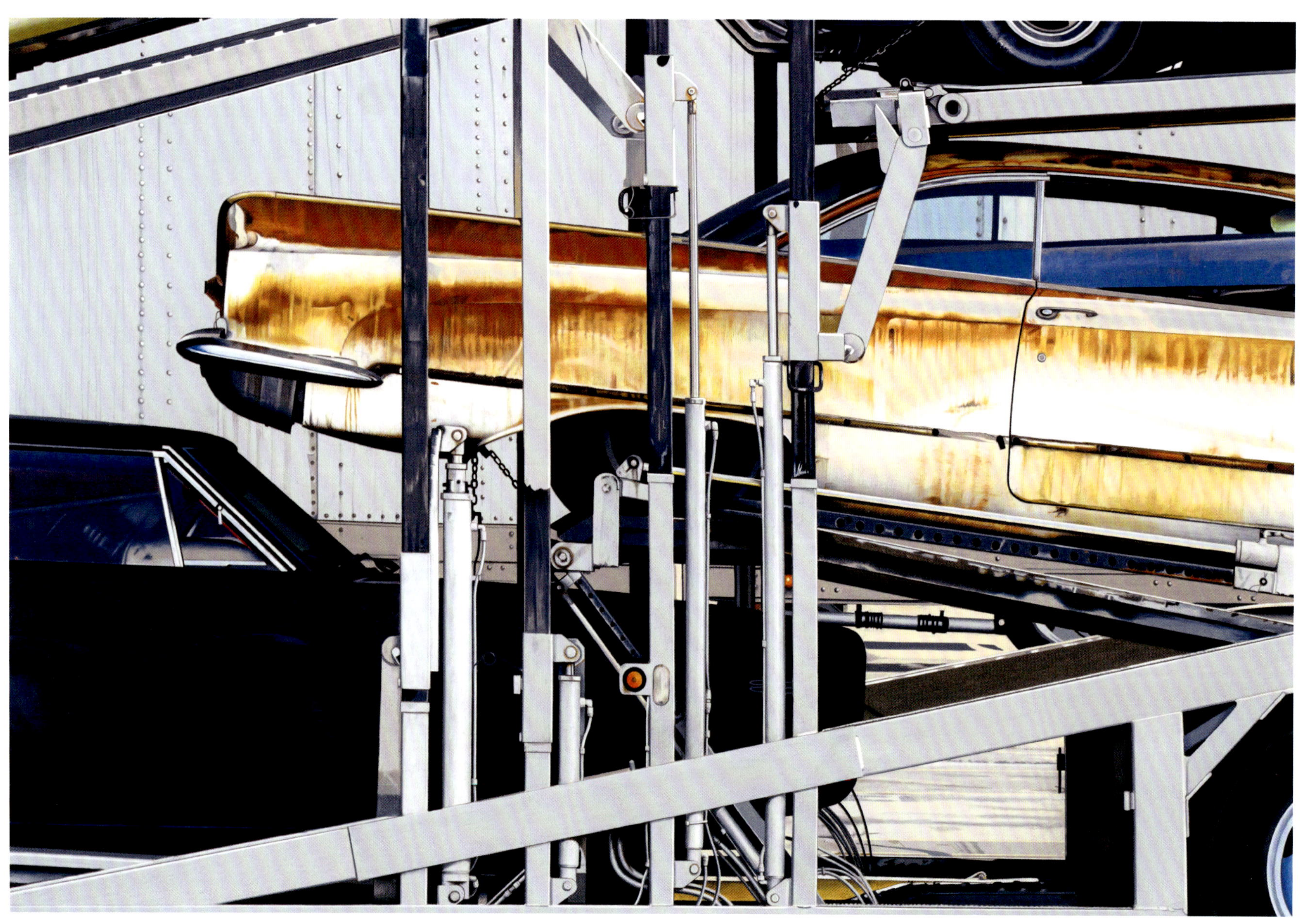

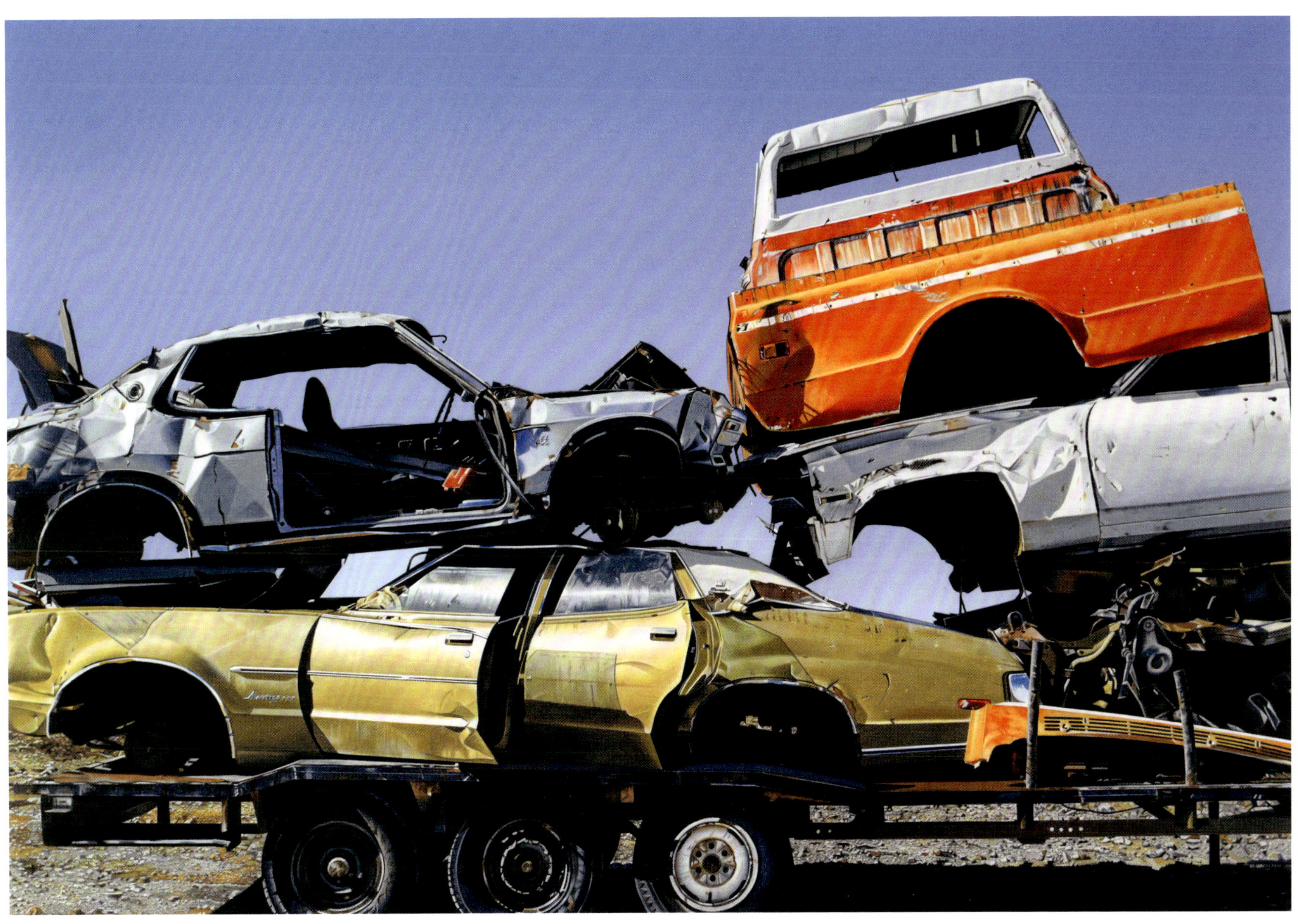

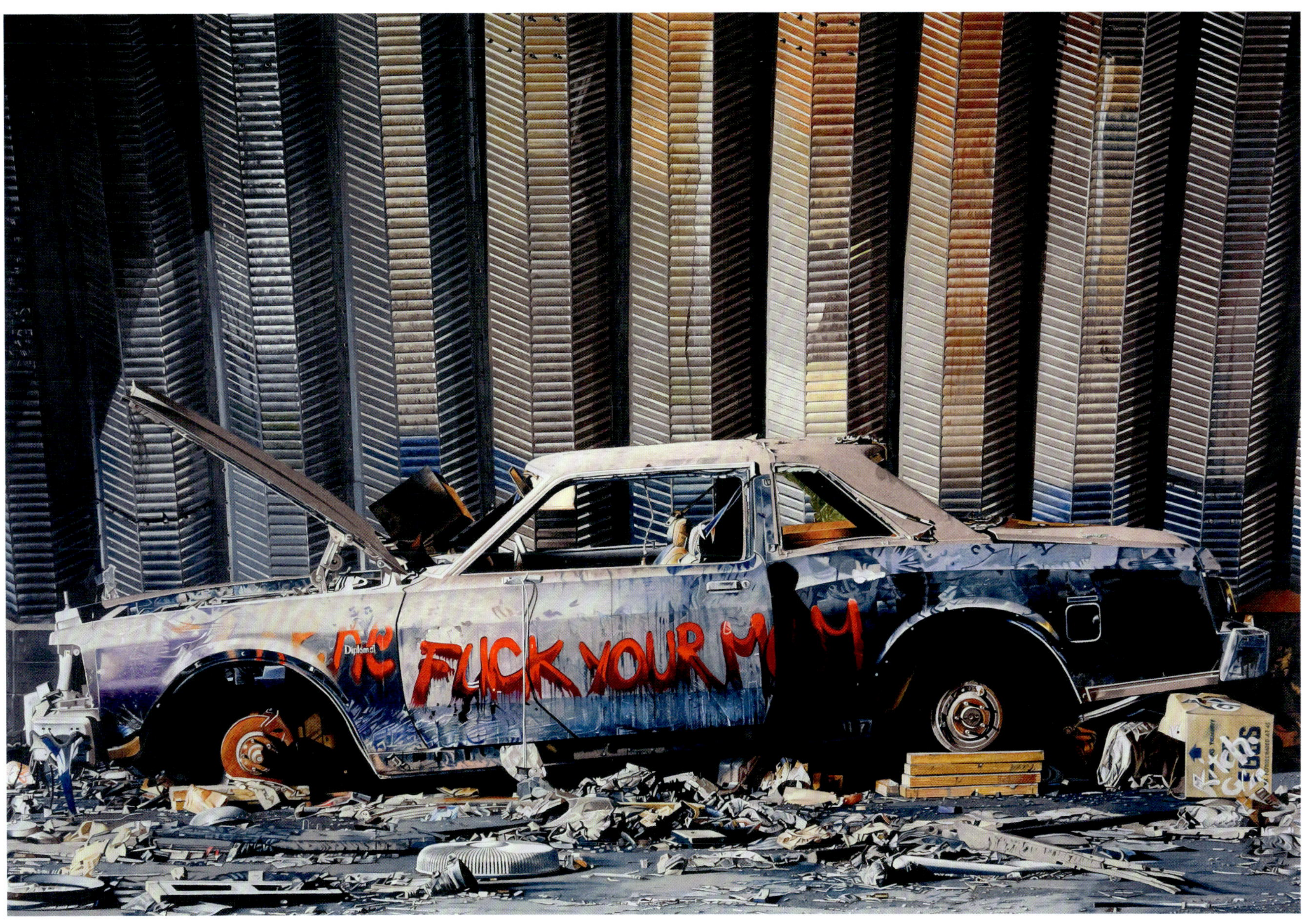

Diplomat
FUCK YOUR M M
EGGS

## The Romance of Anonymity Mark Fisher

Andrew Holmes belongs to a generation of British architects who discovered the USA in the late 1960s. This was a period that saw the climax of the American Dream, a seductive transatlantic force that had been filtering into Britain during the 1950s. To a British visitor, the USA seemed like another planet. It was 'God's Own Country', with more food, more industry, more roads and bigger cars than anywhere else in the world. On the East Coast, the great Saturn V launch platforms at Cape Kennedy were sending Americans to the Moon, while on the West Coast gasoline was so cheap that rental companies included it in the hire charge.

In the beginning, Holmes was attracted to the great urban centres. His first colour-pencil drawings of 1950s Cadillacs were made from photographs he took on visits to New York. It was mainly out of admiration that he chose to draw these extravagant rolling sculptures, but there was also his enthusiasm for pop music. The Cadillac was the car Chuck Berry sang about, and Elvis Presley gave to everyone he knew. Harley Earl's voluptuous styling represented both the embodiment of the American Dream and the antithesis of G-Plan furniture.

*Cadillac* (1974), Holmes's first drawing, reflects an appreciation of craftsmanship and a shameless love of the things he chooses to draw, which has continued in his subsequent work. In reaction to the raw newness of America, he selected low-key images that had been marked by time, and presented them in a relaxed, understated way, as if discovered by accident.

By 1977, Holmes had discovered Los Angeles, and he has returned many times since. The American Southwest is depicted as an ephemeral, sprawling world sustained by transport – an artificial oasis so convincing that the desert has become invisible to its inhabitants. Just as the consumer culture requires a constant supply of new products and new consumers, the colonisation of a landscape that is naturally hostile to human settlement requires constant reinforcement.

Holmes loves this transitory environment and claims that he feels more at home at the Milliken Avenue Truck Stop in Ontario, California, than anywhere else in the world. But no matter how much he enjoys it, as an artist his obsessions and skills are different from those of the people whose world he records. Though cut off from his native culture, he remains an alien in the culture that temporarily surrounds him; a condition that tends to exaggerate experience. The commonplace, which has become invisible to the natives, can seem remarkable to the visitor.

The subject of much of Holmes's work is blue-collar America – redneck culture, novelty, disposable goods, junk. Blue-collar Americans advertise their lives and their lifestyles through their possessions, and the objects themselves are repositories for fantasy. One of the great surprises in Holmes's work is the way it shows that, while the evaporation of the American Dream in the second half of the twentieth century has changed blue-collar lives, it has not affected their aspirations. In Holmes's first drawings, Cadillacs are the status symbols of the 1960s. In *Video Rewind* (1988-2018), two low-riders (middle-aged coupes revitalised by dropped suspension) are parked outside a Hispanic store, low-rent symbols of that same American Dream.

In his paintings and drawings, Holmes concentrates on the tactile qualities of his carefully chosen subjects. He explores light and colour, exaggerating and altering their values in an attempt to recapture the feelings he experienced as he photographed the object. The pictures seem very still. Sometimes this contradicts the dynamism one might expect of the arrangement; even a composition with a dramatic perspective chopped by the picture frame is rendered static by the foreshortening effect of a long-focus lens. Cars, trucks, buses and bikes are always stationary, and the people we might expect to find working with the vehicles are somewhere else, out of the picture. What we see is the everyday working world, but the people are invisible.

After Holmes has composed a drawing, he gives it an ambiguous title, finding his 'text' in the subject itself. In Holmes's search for resonant images of America, the sprawling topography of the conventional truck – one of the great achievements of redneck design – rates highly. The old-fashioned 'conventionals' (trucks with the engine mounted in front of the cab, under a long hood), which Holmes portrays, are preferred by owner-operators, the self-employed drivers who tow trailers on contract all over the continent. The Kenworth, with its classically styled vertical radiator and a great slab-sided cab, has more in common with a Beaux-Arts building than a modern vehicle. Almost every element, from fender to smokestack, is individually expressed as a turbulence-generating, chrome-and-lacquer-decorated, add-on accessory. To the men who own and drive these machines, such old-fashioned styling represents a muscular affirmation of their free-ranging lifestyle. Like twentieth-century cowboys, they ride the Interstates, sleeping in the caboose, dining in truck stops and socialising on CB radio.

Holmes conveys the love the owners feel for these machines in the reverence with which he draws them. In *Tested* (1989), a three-quarter view of a Peterbilt tractor hitched to a tank, the colours of tractor and trailer match, a warm burgundy complementing the golden reflections the sunset lays over the chrome. The composition compressed by the lens combines with deep shadows to play down the form of the truck and emphasise the graphic qualities of the image.

The touch of the pencil is soft and the highlights flare and blend with reflections to create a mystical mood. In *Lord* (1987), a side-elevation of a gold and white Kenworth with hood up and the logo 'Jesus Is Lord' painted on the side, the truck gleams against the sky with the slightly iridescent quality characteristic of holy pictures. In more recent drawings Holmes seems less concerned with detail. Behind the neutral facade of realism he concentrates more on the overall impression of the scene than on the fastidious representation of the inanimate objects it contains.

In his truck drawings, Holmes extracts a sensual appeal from redneck design, without touching on the downside of the American Dream. The contradictions, however, have become increasingly obvious. Just as *Video Rewind* (1989) confirms the importance of the high-powered automobile as a virility symbol among poor urban immigrants, so *Ideal* (1991) commemorates the myth of the frontier spirit among the suburban middle class. Two pick-ups fitted with truck-tops stand baking in the sun, the identity of the ideal outdoorsman confirmed by a six-pack and a gun-rack. In *Taco* (1990), the energy of an immigrant store is juxtaposed with parked-up Honda Gold Wings, the WASP retiree's recreational motorcycle of choice. Within his disingenuous postcard framing of the scene, Holmes summed up an inherent contradiction of the end-of-the-century USA economy: if the increasingly rich and ageing white population continues to buy its toys abroad, how will the new immigrants earn their way into the middle class?

Holmes switches easily between the mechanical crafts of video and photography, and the handicrafts of painting and drawing. It is easy to suppose that because the handcrafted works bear witness to a huge investment in time and technique, they are more significant. For Holmes the physical and social structures that shape the environment are as important as the material qualities of the objects together with the sensuous pleasures of form and colour on paper.

The drawings share Holmes's preoccupation with the invisible systems that sustain urban America. For a long time he seemed to be concerned with recording carefully chosen subjects that might be regarded as symbolic of larger issues. Almost all the images capture attempts by individuals to stamp their identity on the world, whether by shooting at a road sign, customising a truck, or building a villa so desirable that it has to be protected by armed guards. Each image is framed without irony, as a moment recorded with all the pride of ownership; yet taken together the drawings become machine-like, exhibiting the paradoxical loneliness of anonymity among the crowd.

This bleak view contradicts the superficial beauty of his drawings. It is as if Holmes is trying, like a Country and Western songwriter, to wrap dark messages in sunny melodies. His romantic images seem to endorse the redneck culture of the Southwest, yet his compositions emphasise its underlying anonymity.

His exhibitions with their cool reference to the infinite grid of the LA
basin reflect the Cartesian subdivision of the city. The borders of the
expansive frames of the drawings keep the images apart. Likewise,
the trucks, cars and buildings in the drawings are isolated by their
frames. It remains one of the few places where true loneliness can
be enjoyed.

# The Harvest of a Quiet Eye Cedric Price

To realise these pictures, they should be looked at in conditions that fully display not only their colour but also their materials. Their validity and particular quality are inherent in the process of such realisation.

Whereas many pictures lose little through reproduction and a distortion of their original size, the works of Andrew Holmes, because of their several visual convolutions – if not 'tricks' – deftly played in their production, are subject to further ramifications when they are photographed, reproduced by some other process, and indeed projected as transparencies. Recalling that the works are invariably based on photographs taken by the artist, the whole process of creating these images becomes an extremely intriguing intellectual conundrum for the viewer.

However, over and above all that, these works are a delight to look at since the subject matter is carefully allowed to be enriched and distorted in the two-dimensional display provided. We might think that we see such objects just as shown but, in the vagaries of the Los Angeles sun, we do not – we just delight in being reminded in permanent form of what we thought we saw. Look again at the collection of trucks, their radiators, tanks and exhausts exploding with chrome pyrotechnics. Can we look at the original for as long and perceive with such clarity of detail all its facets, folds and fractures? Holmes rejects the loss of identity caused through parallax, the field of human perception and perspective, and feeds a richer meal than the original. But the pretence must be maintained, and made acceptable for this visually luxurious treat to be enjoyed. The realism is what we want to see. The artist's eye is 'at it' as ever.

But what of the subject matter? Is it chosen for itself, its context or its suitability for Holmes's particular attention? The West Coast of the United States – or more accurately Los Angeles – is the quiet sunlit home of most of the subjects of the bulk of his work.

Here in LA, the trucks, buses, autos and occasional rail stock stand motionless under the even, ever brilliant sky. Mostly they shine and glisten, though frequently they show evidence of recent hard usage. Rust, dust and sweat are evident, but all is at rest; people very seldom intrude, and the chrome-encrusted diners and Spick-n-Span

stores and offices and gas stations give only an occasional glimpse or reflection of a human being or a fleeting vehicle. The bars are closed and the autos and trucks driverless. The sky is always cloudless and the sunlight even. This all-pervading repose is slightly sinister and expectant. The artist spreads his subjects wider than the canvas – blank walls and roofs run on, while furniture and trucks lose their legs and wheels. The sky is a merciless illuminator, enabling the polished surface to establish its shape through the distortion of its reflections.

It is interesting that backgrounds, when used, become little more than backdrops in most of the works, and that this intentional flatness does not jar at all. For in enjoying Holmes's work one is constantly summoned to recognise that in the world of colour the sensation takes place within oneself. One must not confuse stimulus with sensation, nor indeed mistake paint for colour.

Holmes enjoys playing tricks – with breathtaking deliberation and industry – not only on the viewers but himself. Although the use of up to thirty different crayons on a single drawing or eleven colours on a screen print is impressive in itself, it is in the choice of subjects and, in my opinion, the limiting of the image in content and extent that Holmes's particular artistry lies. Norman Rockwell, the modern realists, and the antique English miniaturists have all exercised a generous economy in the eventual product, while Holmes appears to add further self-imposed disciplines on the evolving range of his work.

For control is a particular attribute this artist displays consistently. In so doing he will carry the observer with him on this journey through the physical, psychophysical, psychological, and aesthetic nature of colour because of the delight he provides.

In conclusion, I may well have answered my own question: why are Holmes's works so static? I think the answer is that it is in the beauty and clarity of investigations that movement is found.

**Gas Tank City** Drawings 1974–2024

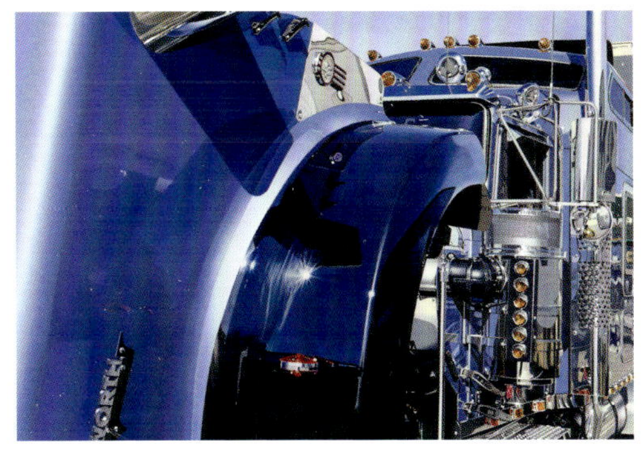

**13** *Worth*, 2000

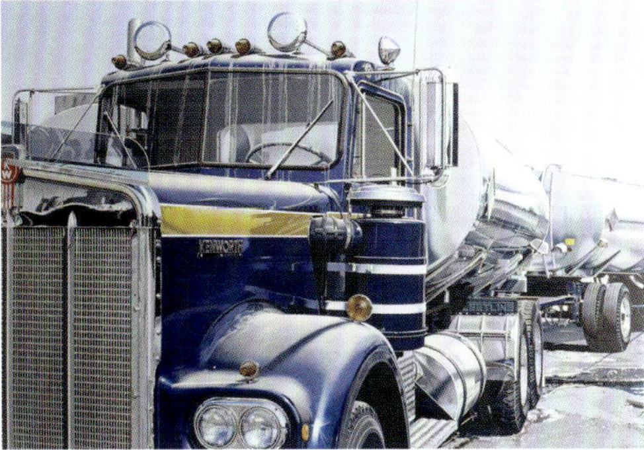

**14** *After The Rain*, 1976

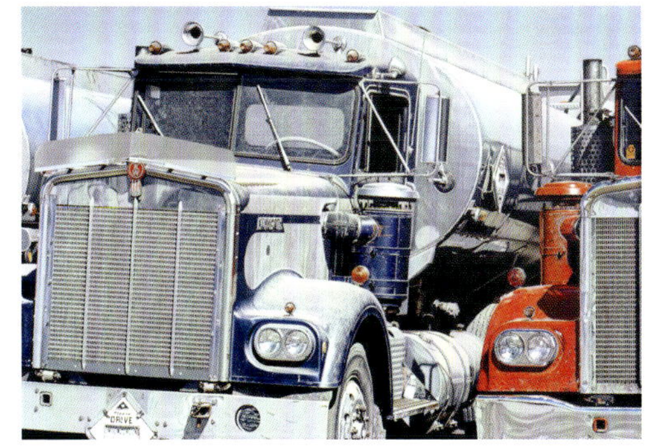

**15** *Drive*, 1989

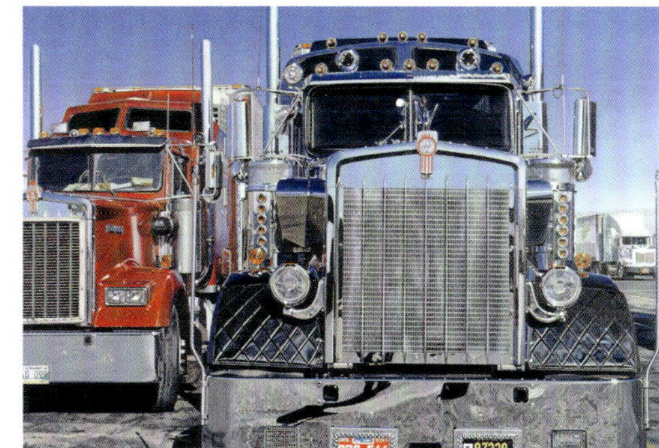

**17** *2KW+1*, 2001

**18** *One*, 2004

**19** *One Too*, 2006

**20** *Peterbilt*, 1976

**21** *Scarlet And Black*, 1977

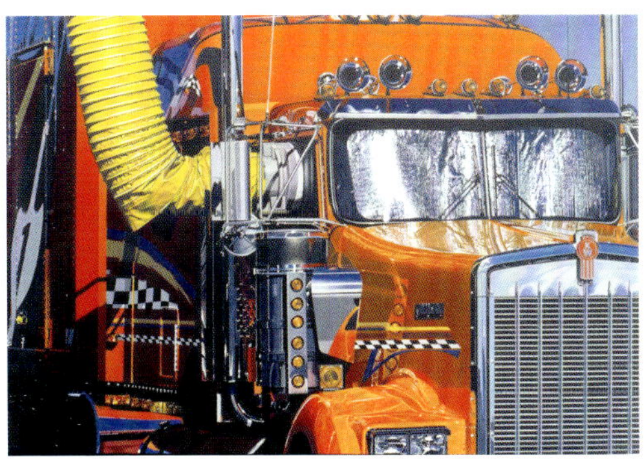

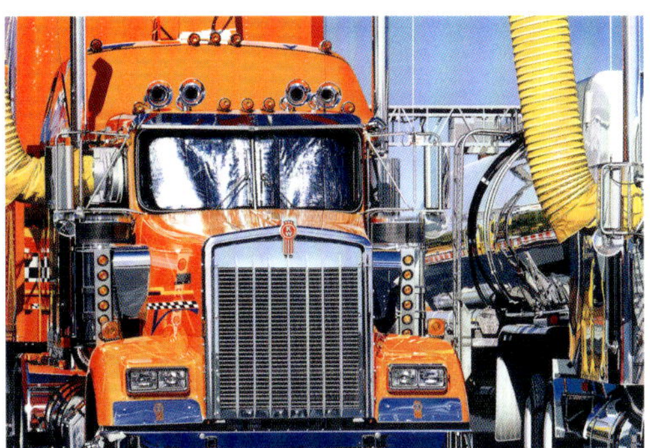

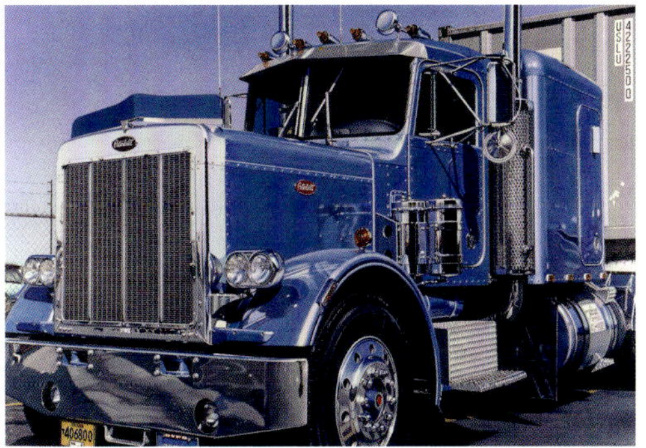

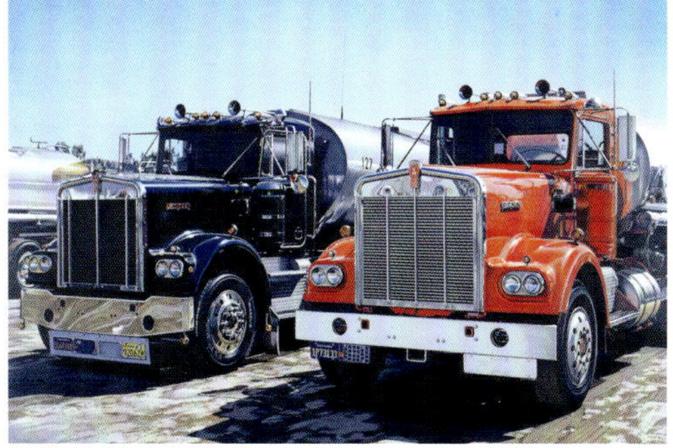

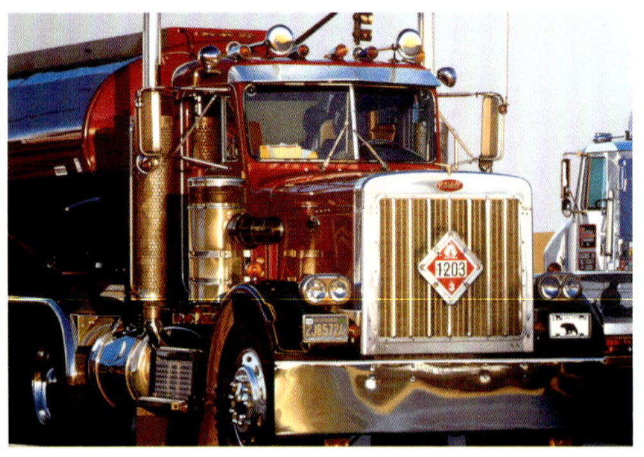

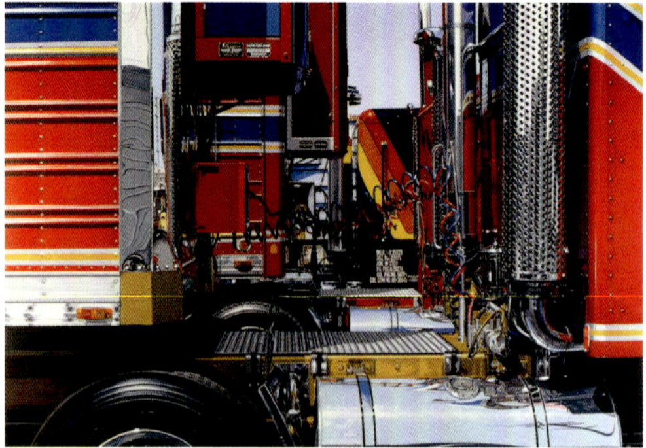

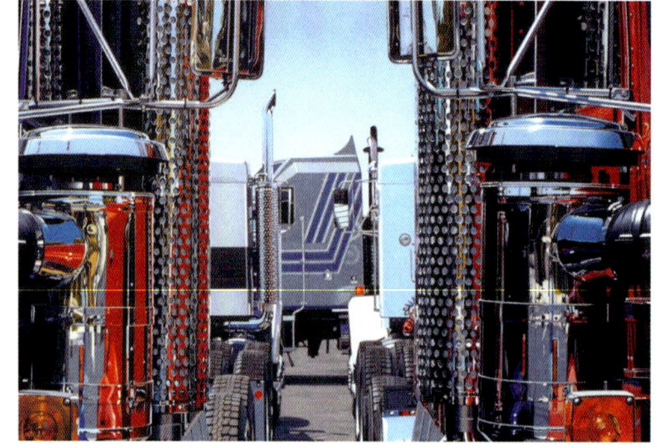

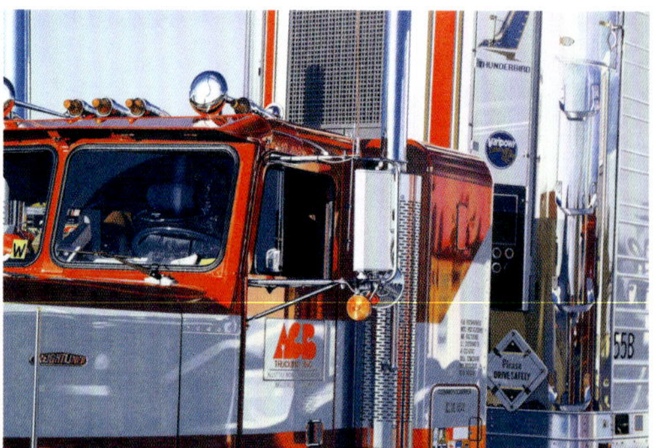

**23** *Tested*, 1988

**24** *Avenue*, 1980

**25** *Street*, 1986

**27** *Ace*, 1989

**28** *CT*, 2003

**29** *Joy*, 2024

**31** *Lord*, 1987

**32** *Apportioned*, 1993

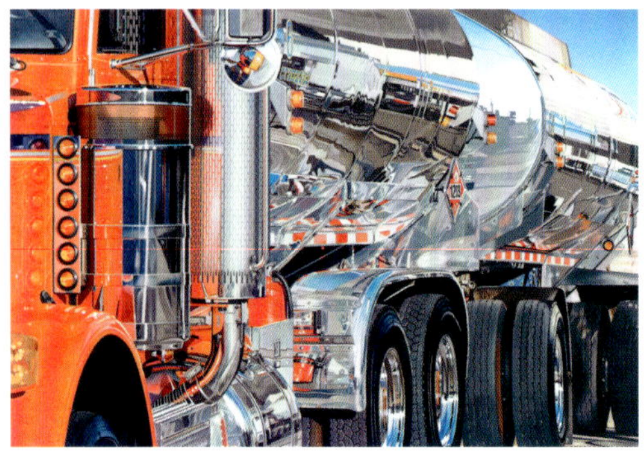

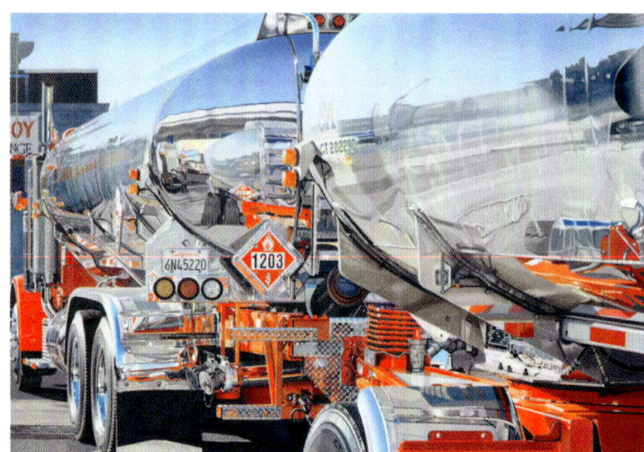

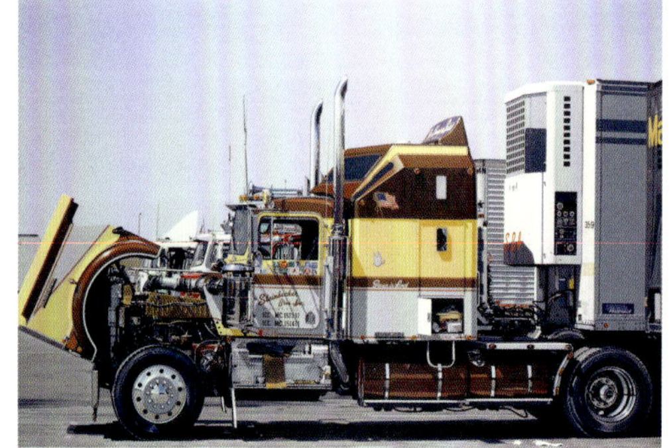

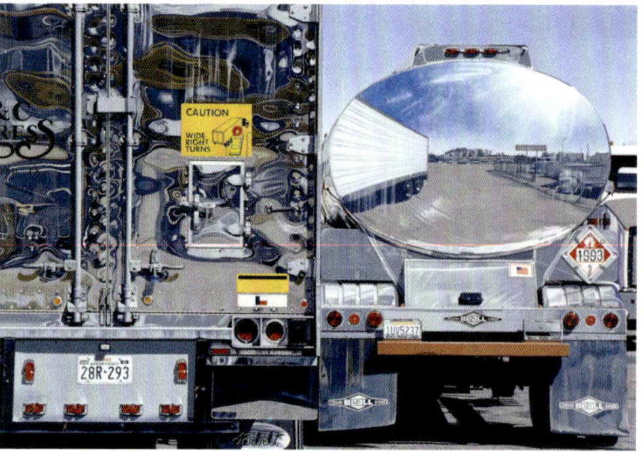

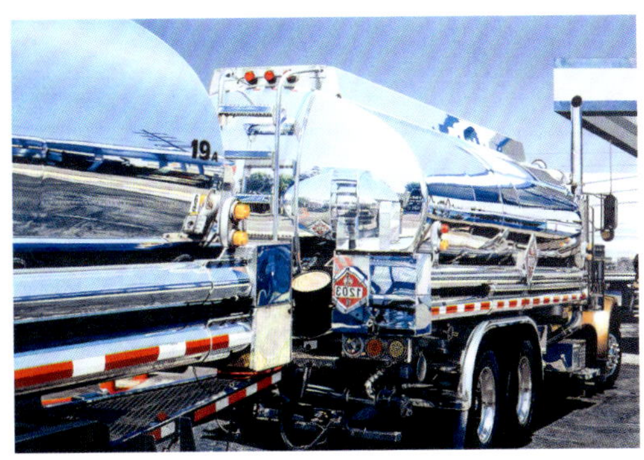 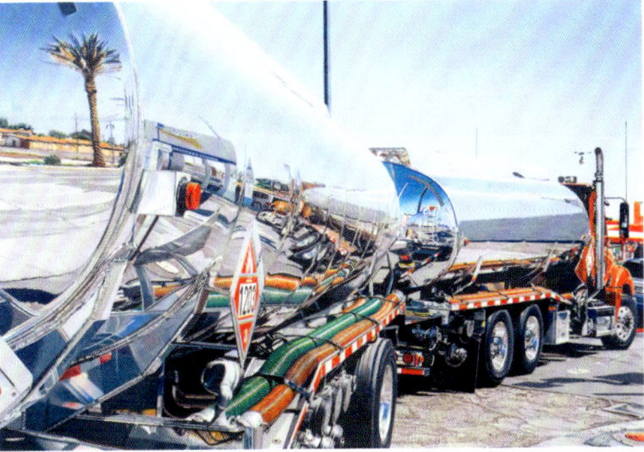 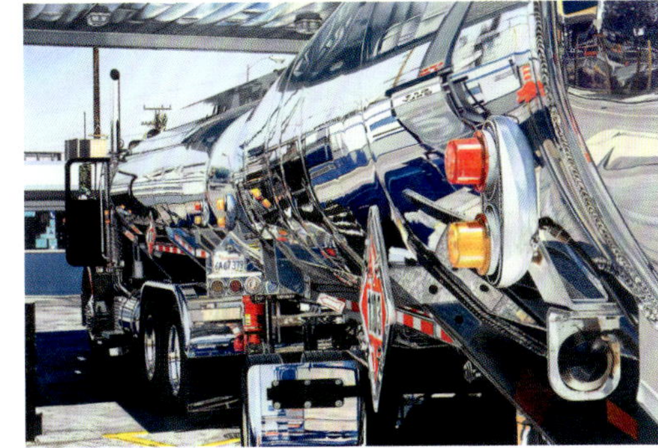 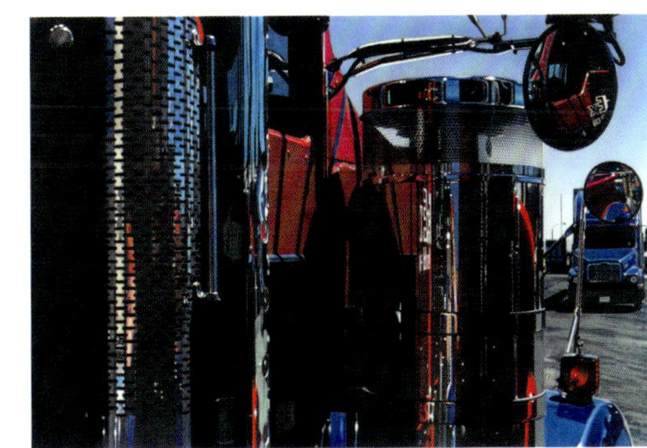

**33** *Mr Fine*, 2009  **34** *Niland*, 2010  **35** *Gas Only*, 2008  **37** *Ex*, 2003

**38** *Shutoff*, 2011  **39** *QC*, 2011  **40** *Sugartrux*, 2006  **41** *Vernon*, 2010

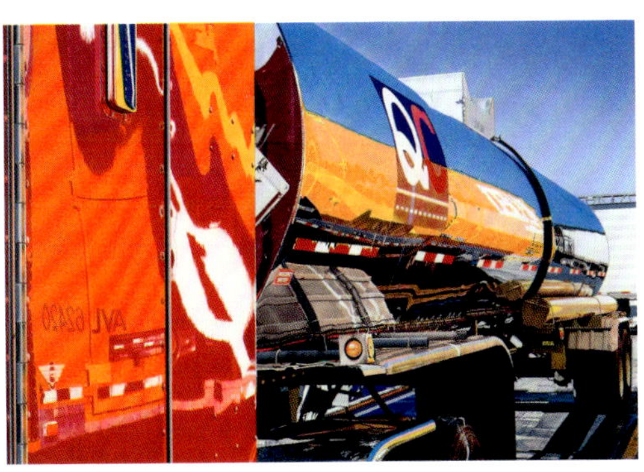 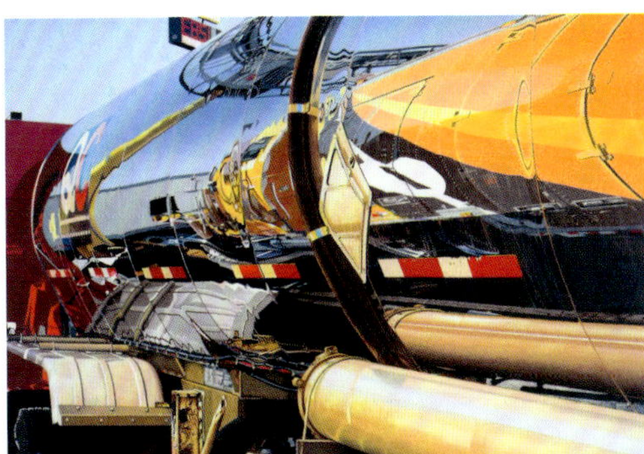 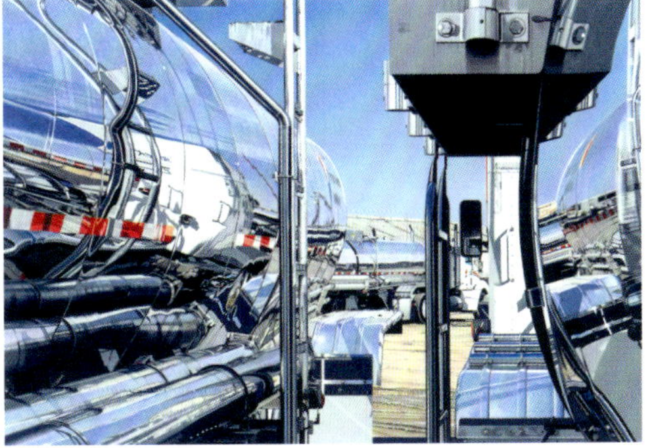 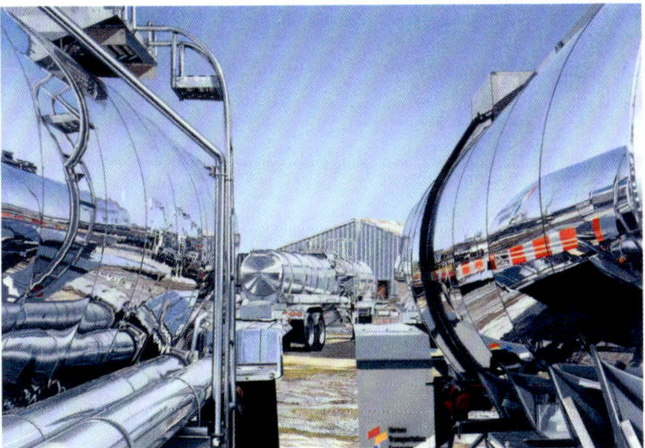

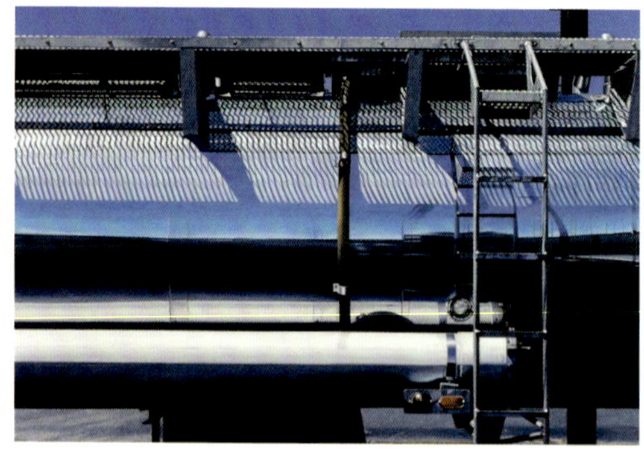

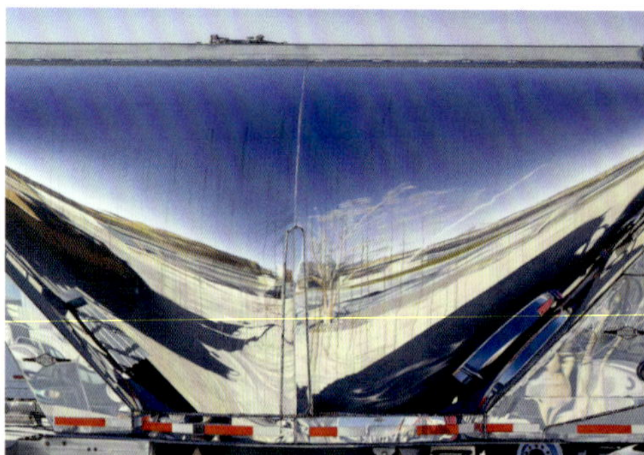

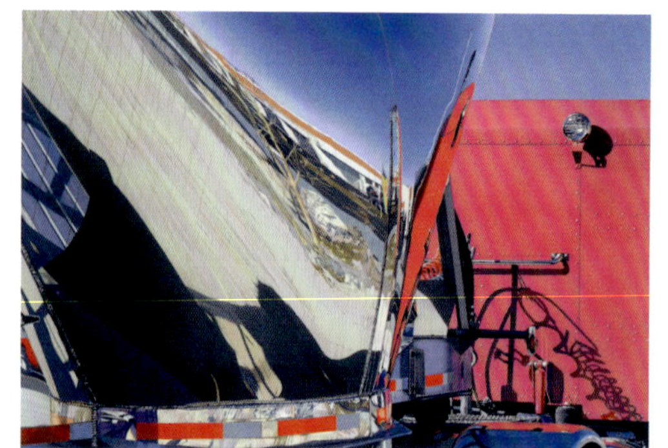

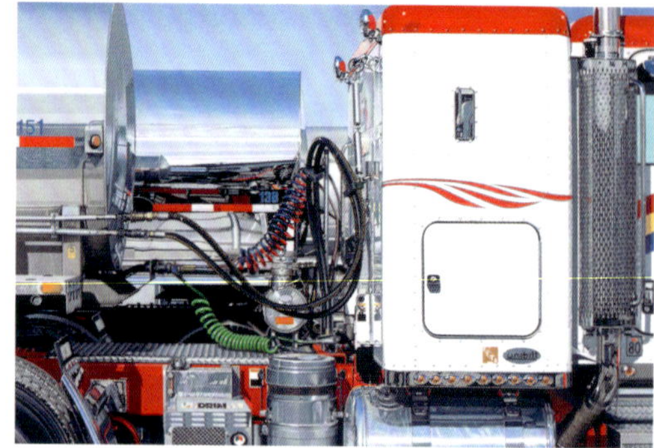

**43** *Long Range, 2000*

**44** *L, 1999*

**45** *B, 1999*

**47** *Unibilt, 2006*

**48** *No Smoking, 1996*

**49** *Now, 2006*

**51** *Paramount, 2008*

**52** *Van, 1995*

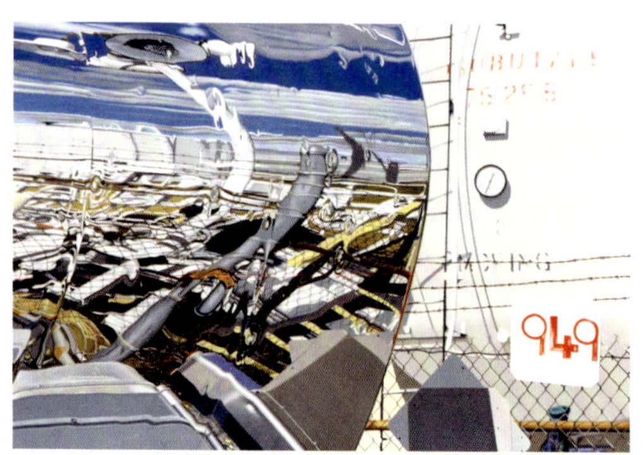

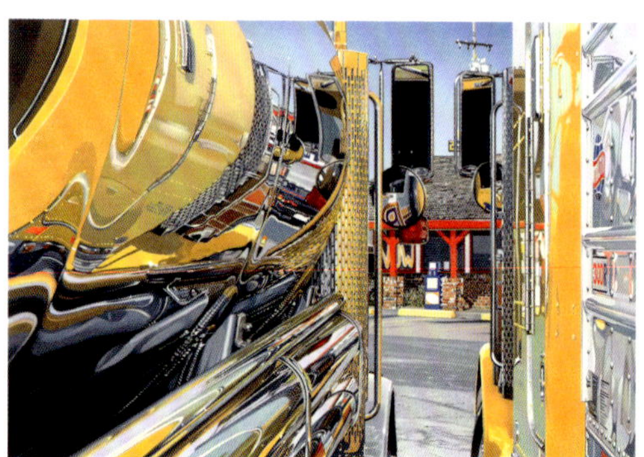

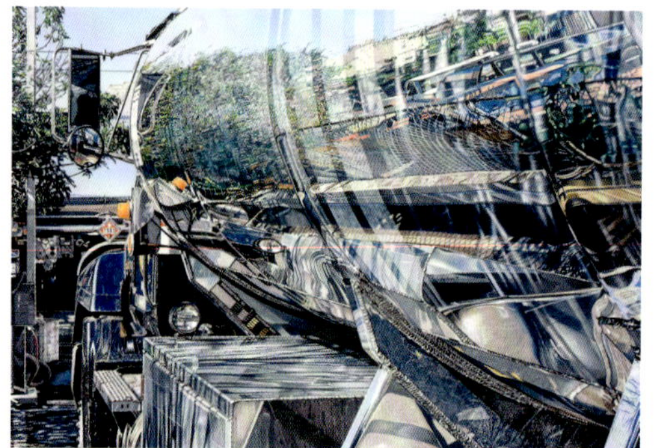

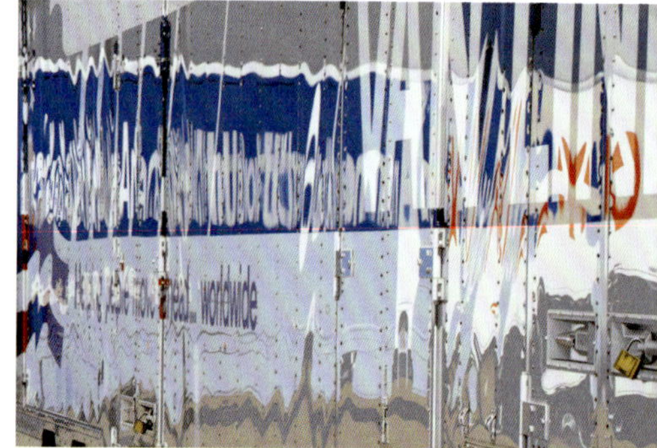

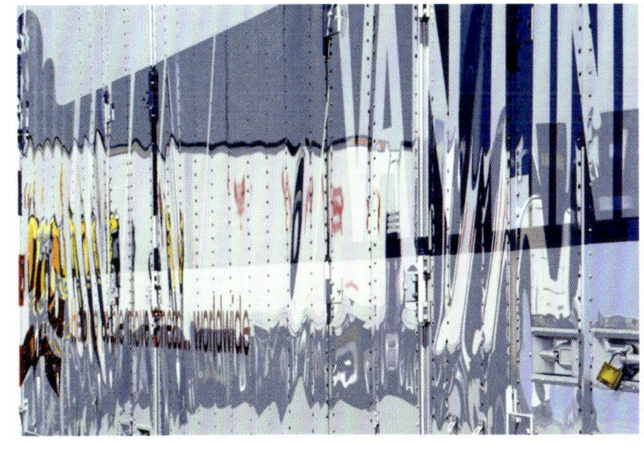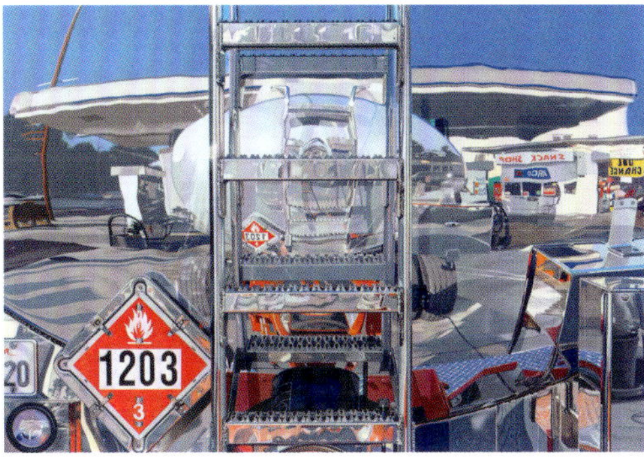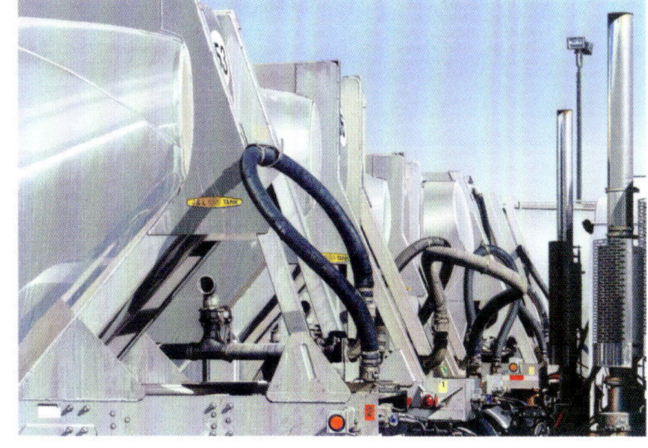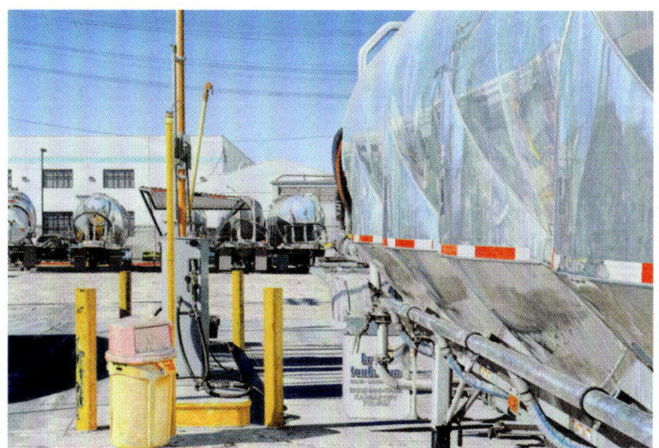

**53** *Lines*, 1997     **55** *Oil Change*, 2004     **56** *J&L Tank*, 2004     **57** *Tucson*, 2021

**59** *Profile*, 1999     **60** *Die Sel*, 2009     **61** *The Lot*, 2009     **63** *Reliance*, 1979

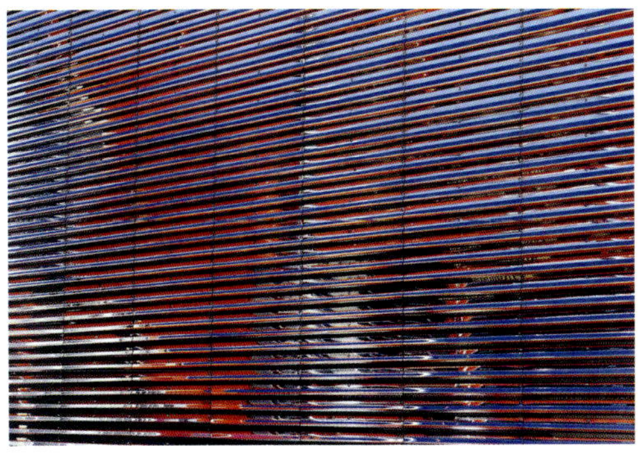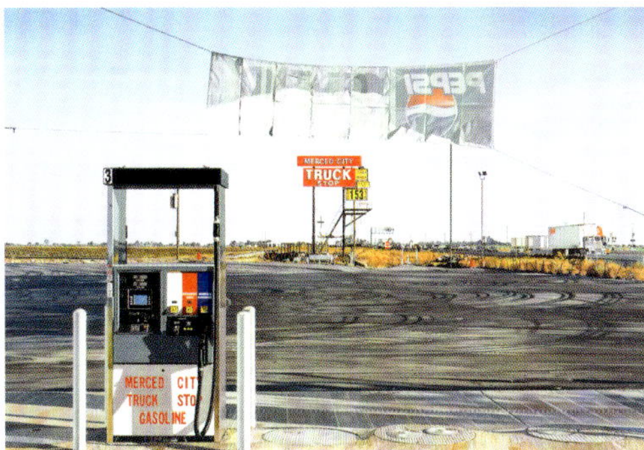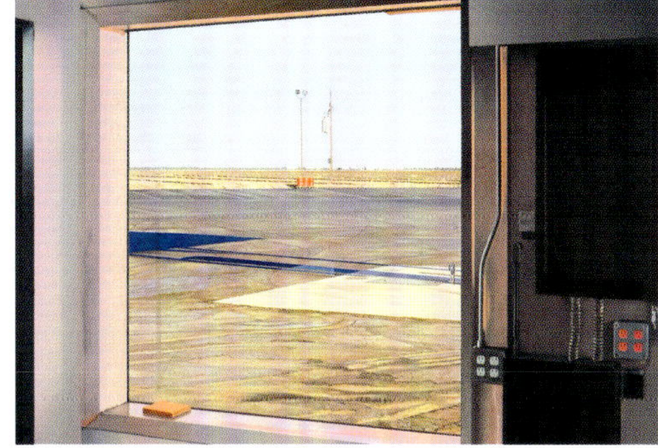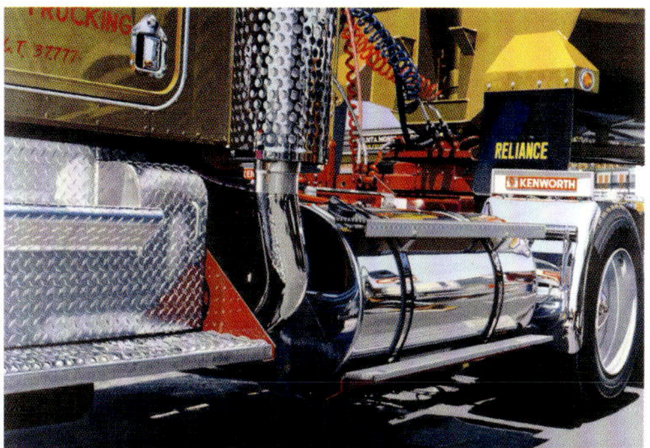

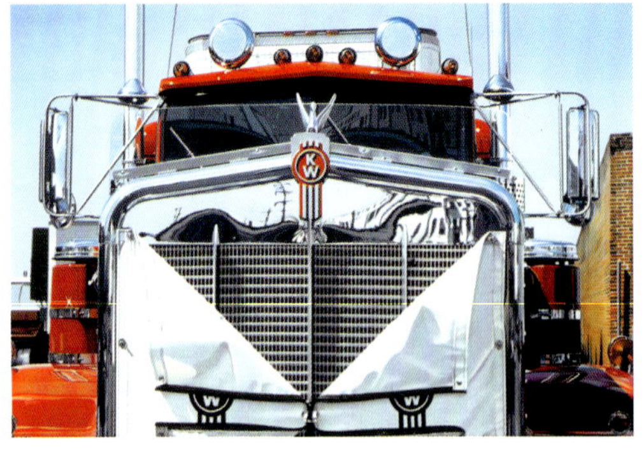 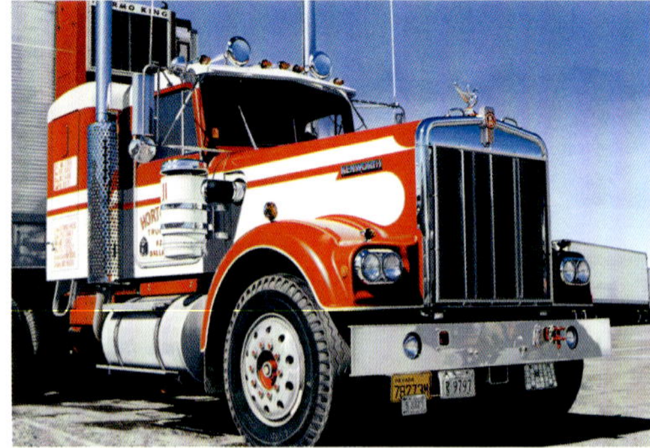 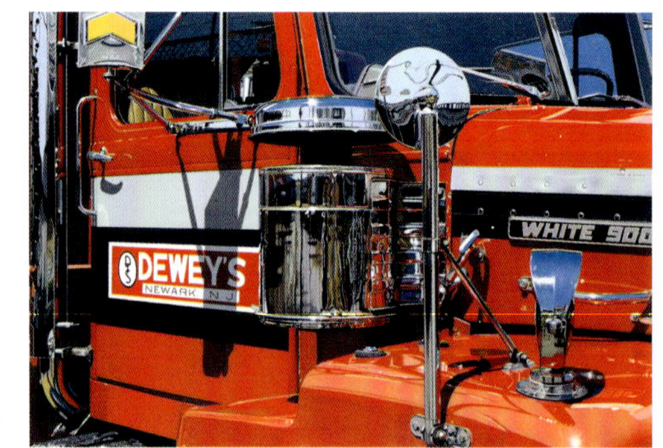 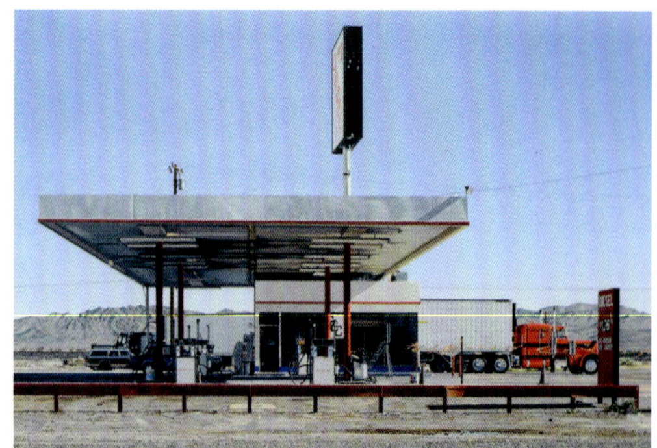

**64** *KW, 1976*

**65** *Thermo King, 1977*

**67** *White, 1986*

**68** *Diesel #2, 2020*

**69** *Propane, 2019*

**71** *Center, 1976*

**72** *Stainless, 1999*

**73** *Tanks, 1990*

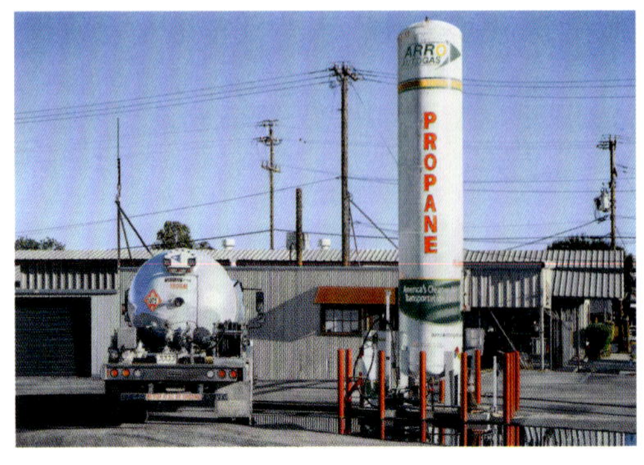 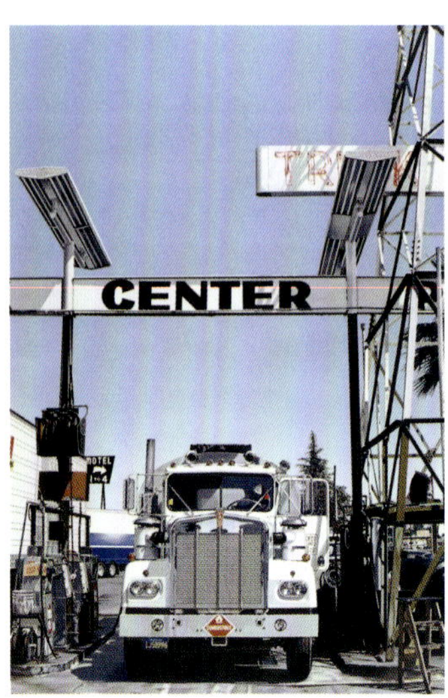 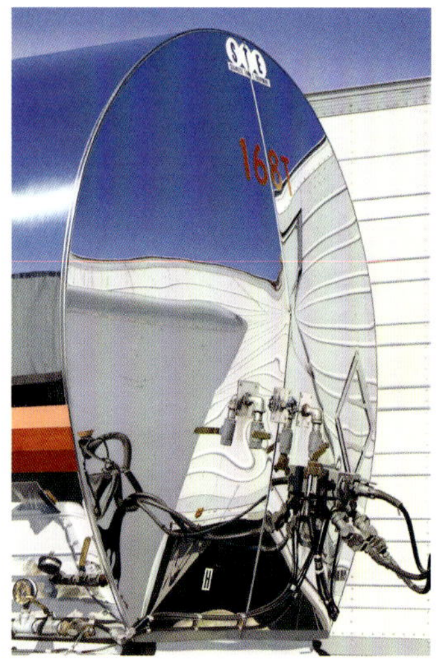 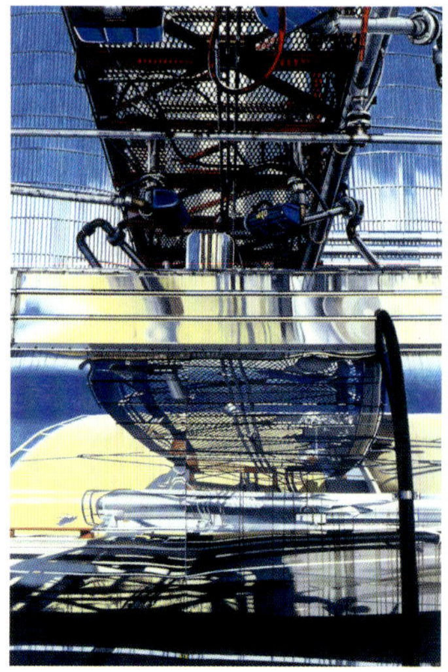

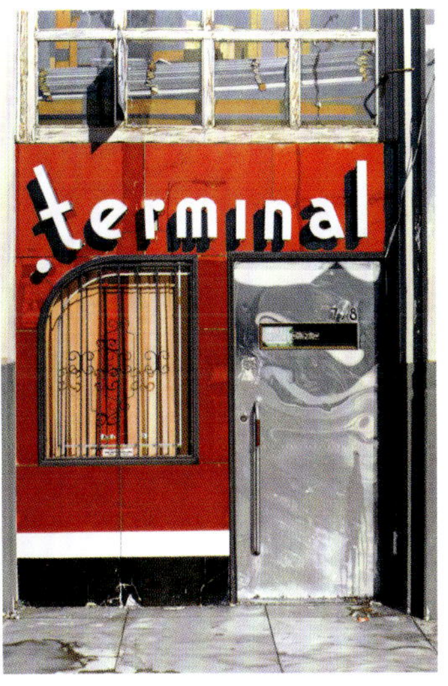 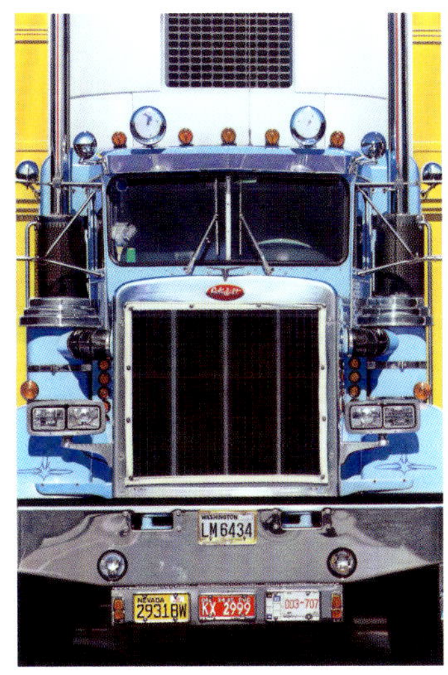 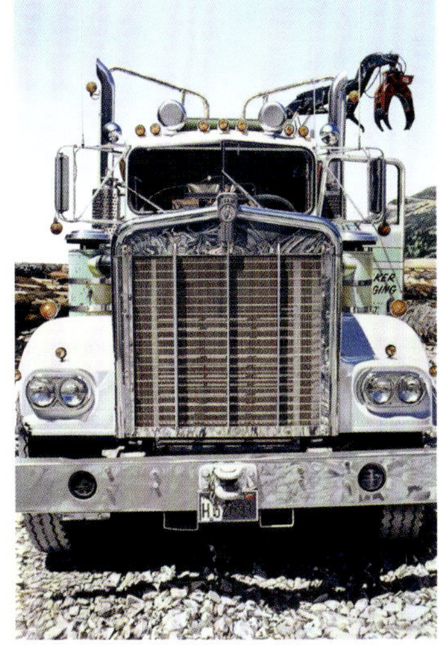 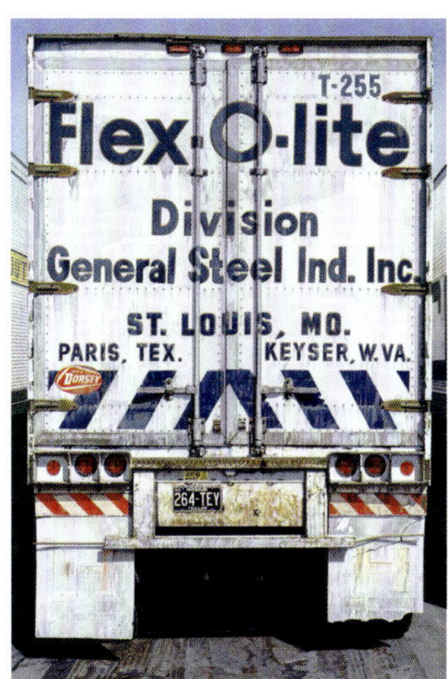

**75** *Terminal*, 1979

**76** *Nevada*, 2003

**77** *Log*, 1976

**78** *Steel*, 1992

**79** *Dane*, 1991

**81** *Blue LA Revision*, 1979–2018

**82** *Telephone*, 1974

**83** *Make Call*, 2020

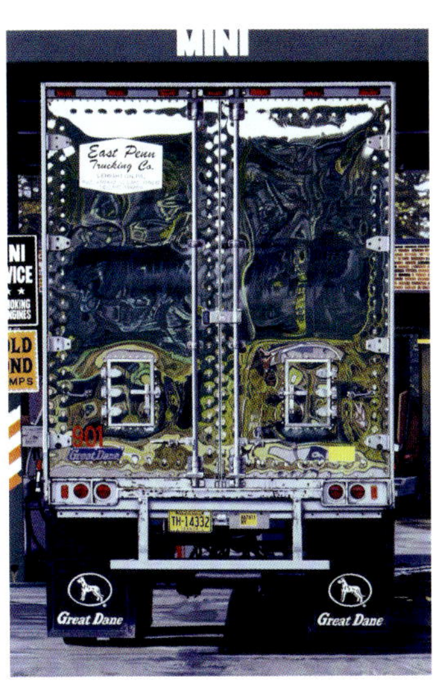 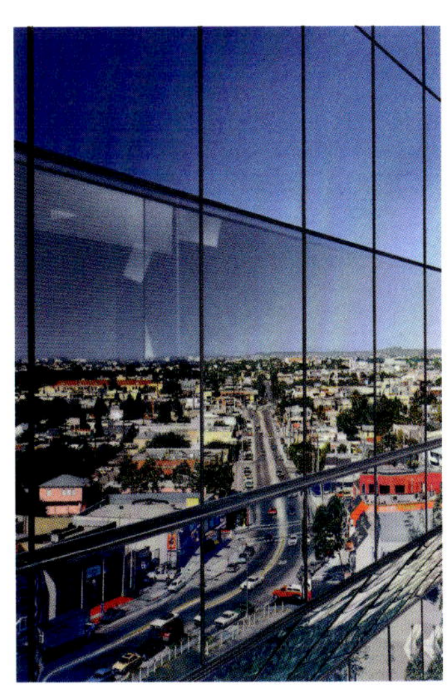 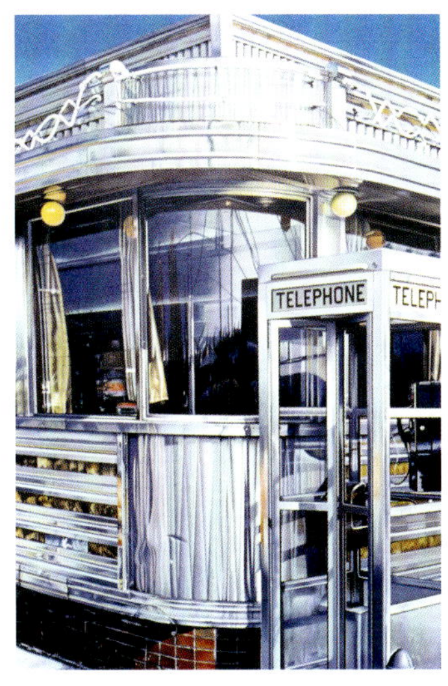 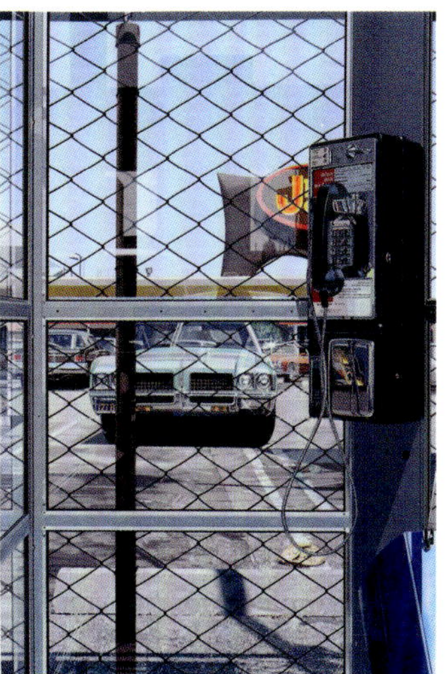

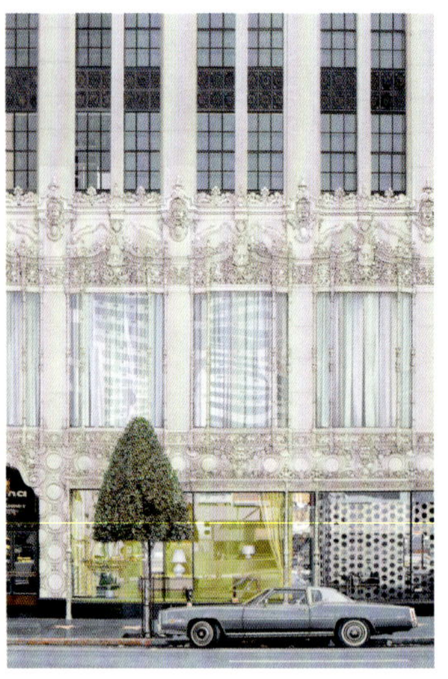 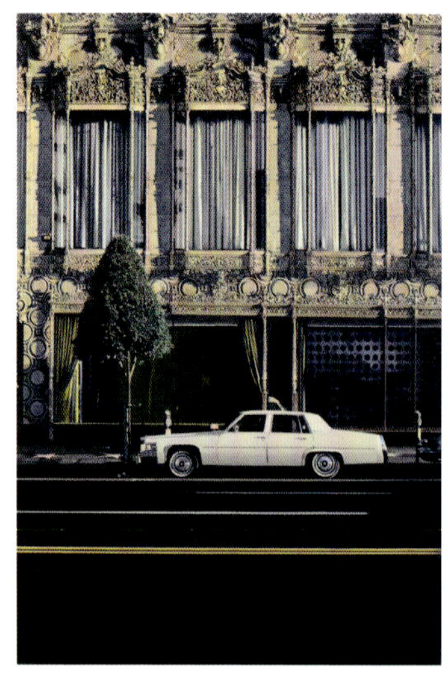 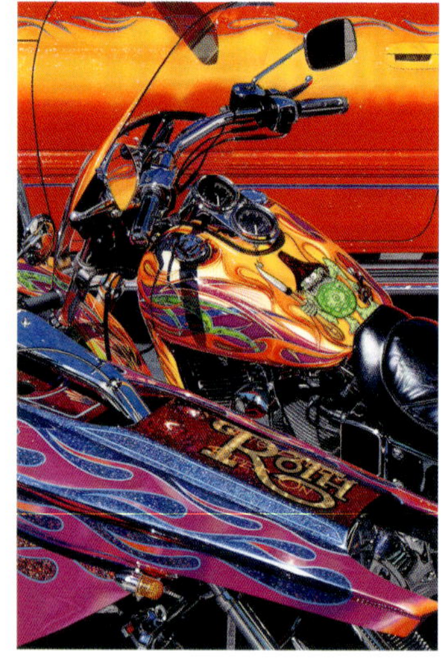 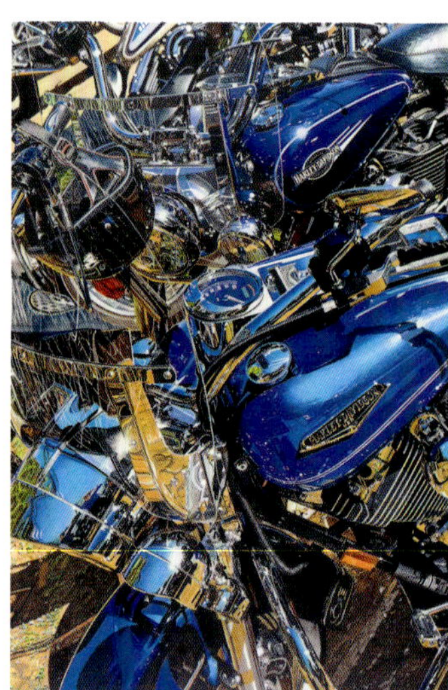

**84** *Hollywood Eldorado*, 2019

**85** *El Capitan*, 2019

**87** *Roth*, 2005

**88** *Kanan*, 2010

**89** *Rock Store*, 2007

**91** *Mulholland*, 2008

**92** *Road King*, 2009

**93** *Vegas*, 2005

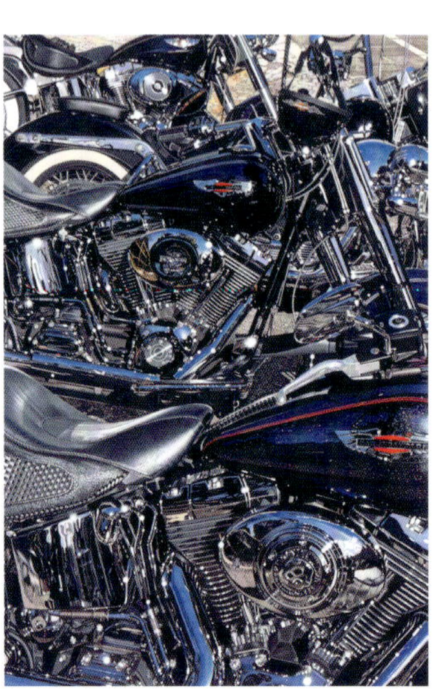 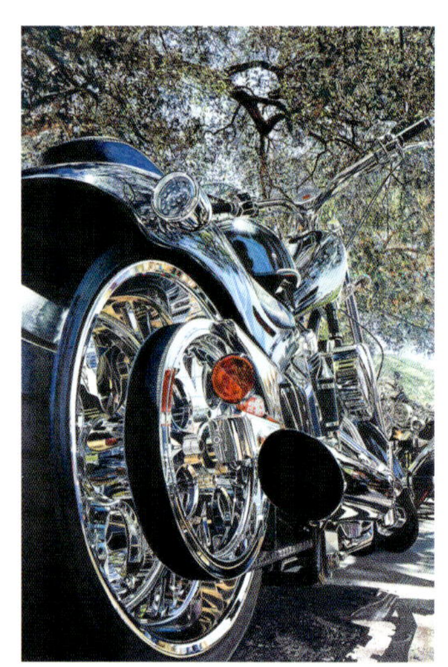 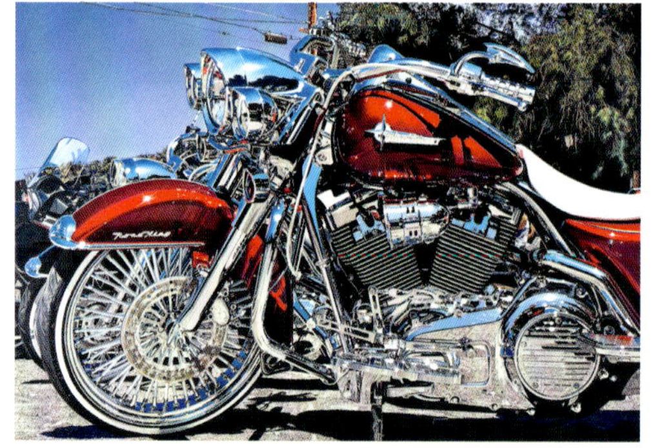 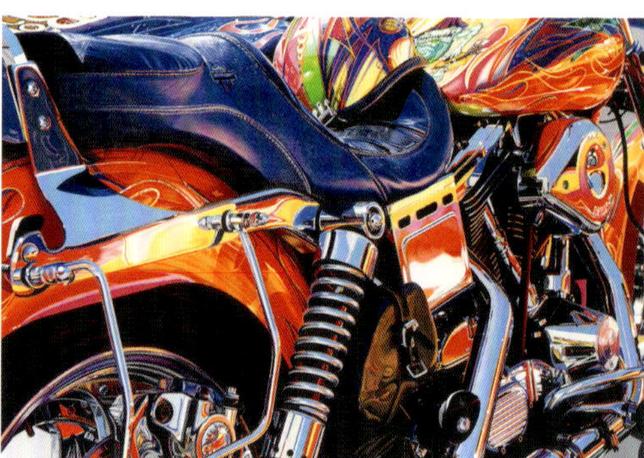

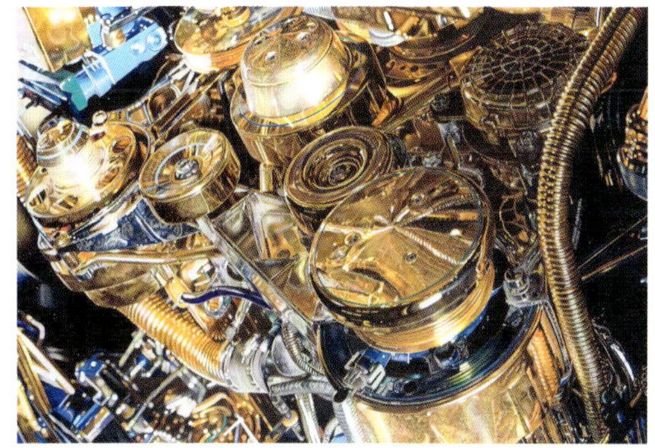

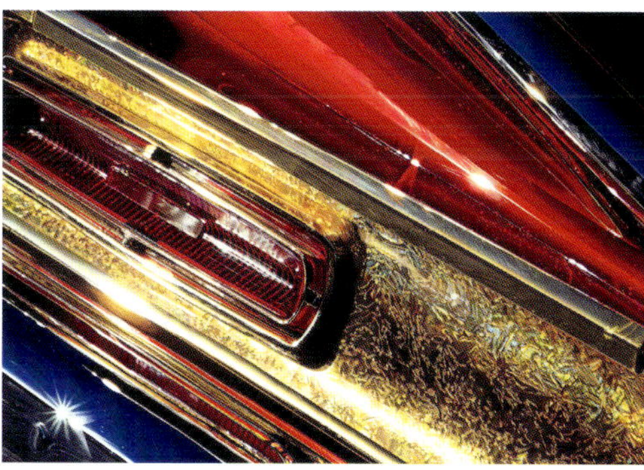

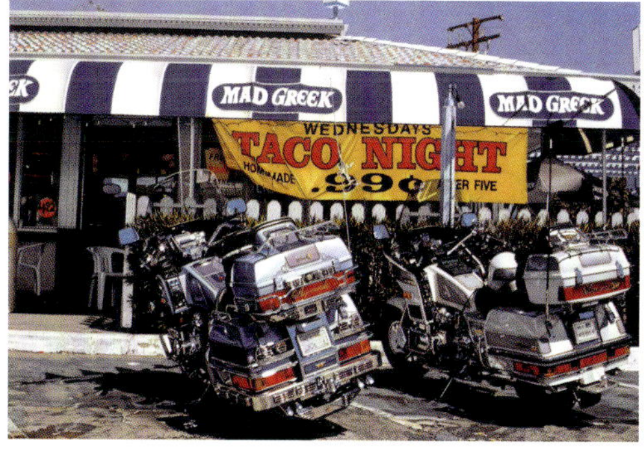

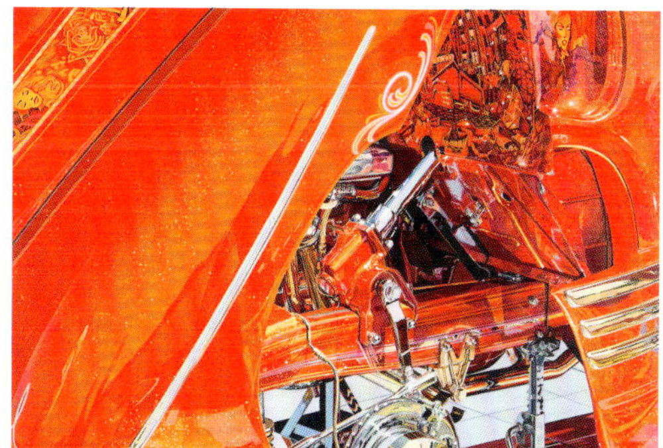

**94** *Elite, 2007*

**95** *Mario, 2006*

**97** *Taco, 1990*

**98** *Summer Blast, 2011*

**99** *Halloween, 1996*

**101** *Elk, 1998*

**102** *Discount, 1994*

**103** *Alamo, 1994*

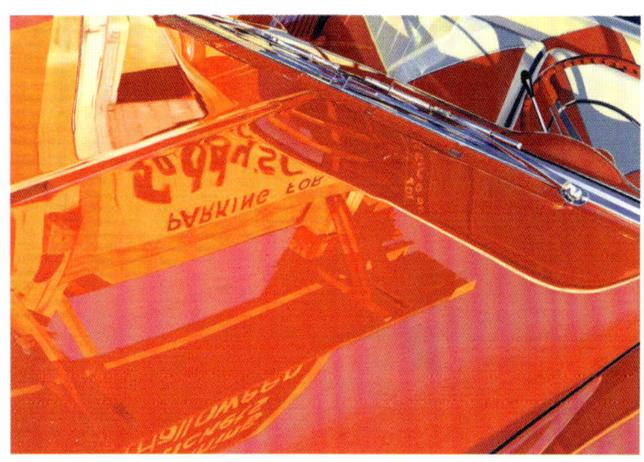

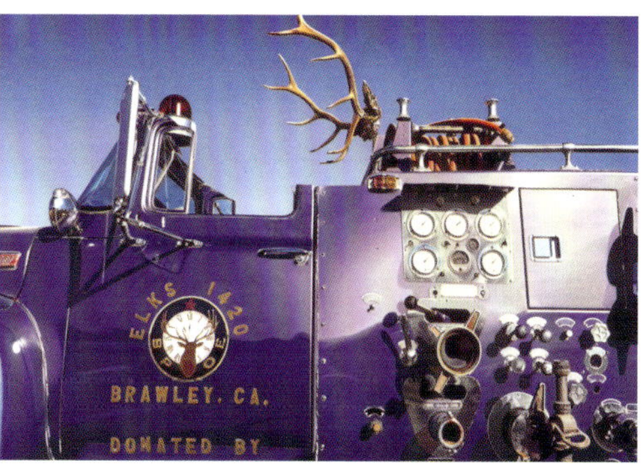


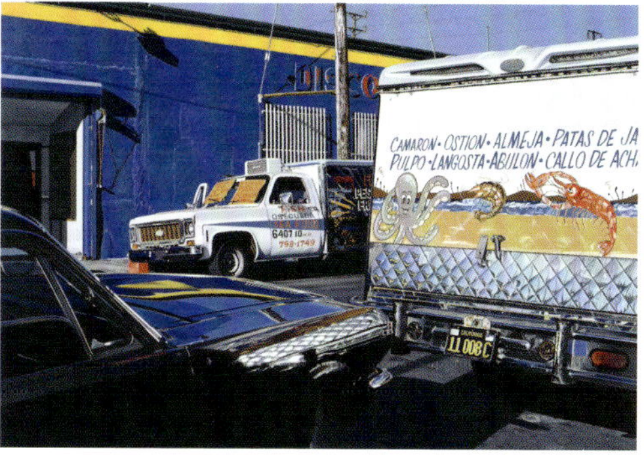

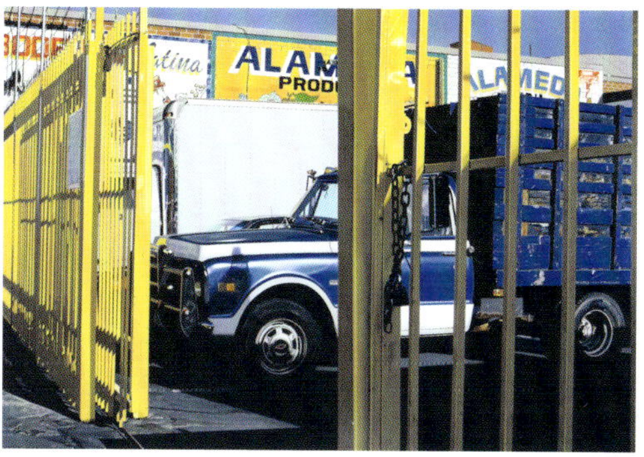

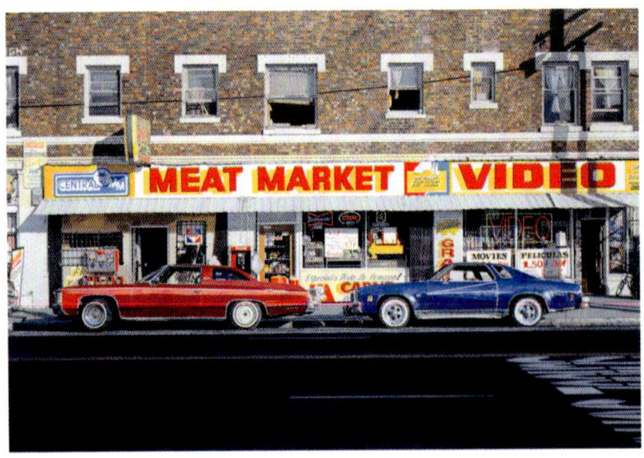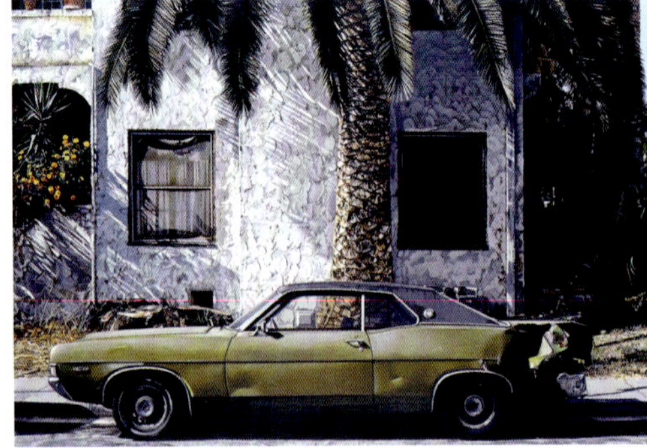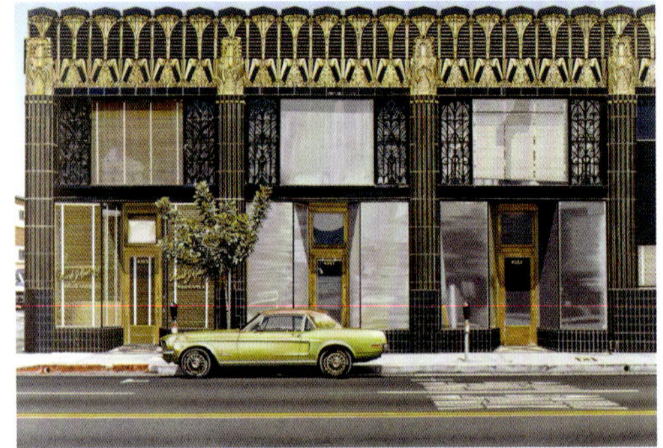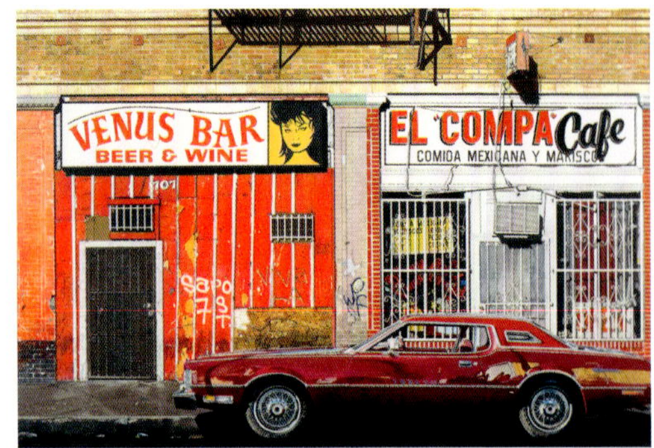

**105** *Video Rewind*, 1988–2018

**106** *Crash*, 1992

**107** *Insurance*, 1978

**109** *Venus Bar*, 2012

**110** *Oakland*, 1980

**111** *Queen's Boulevard*, 1978

**112** *Office Building*, 1980

**113** *Box Office*, 1980

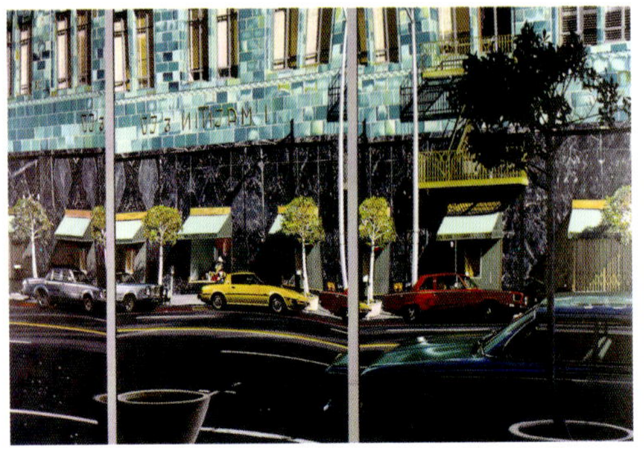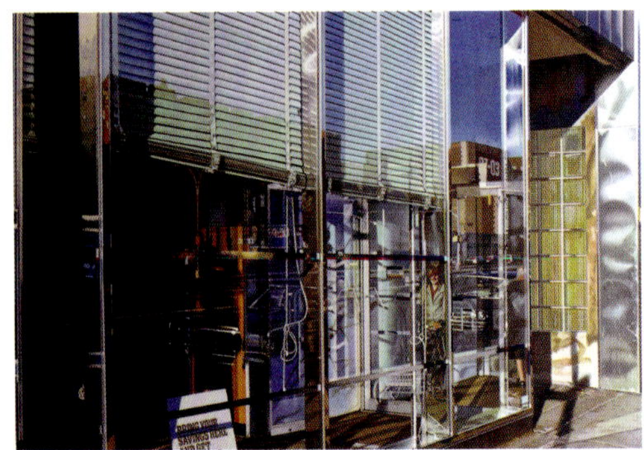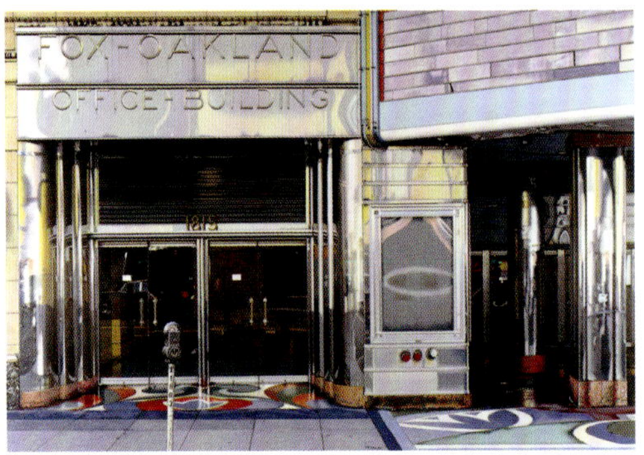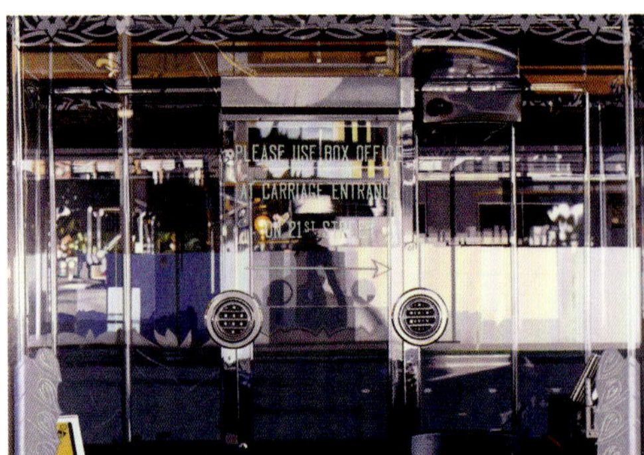

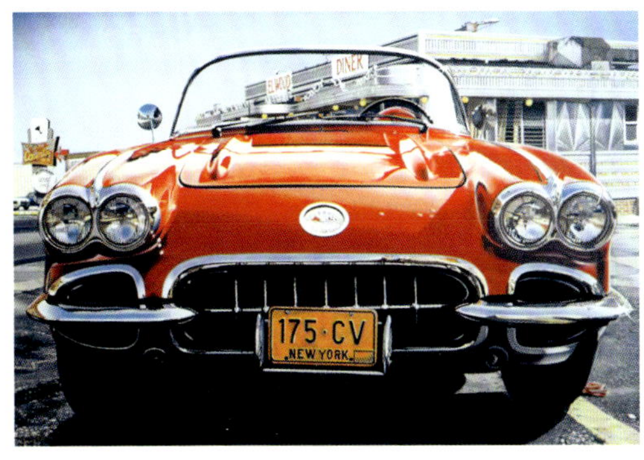

**115** *Corvette, 1974*

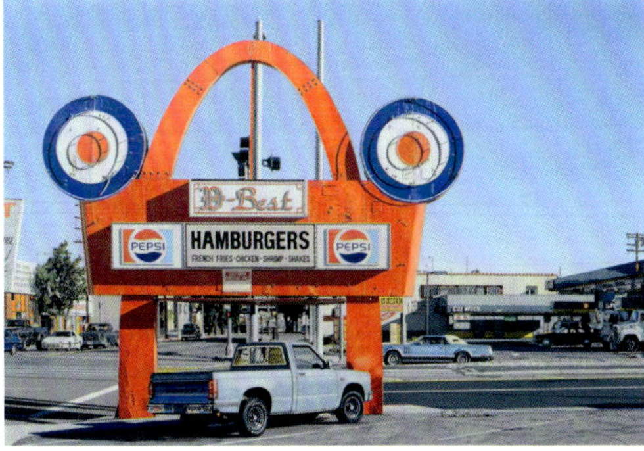

**116** *D-Best, 2020*

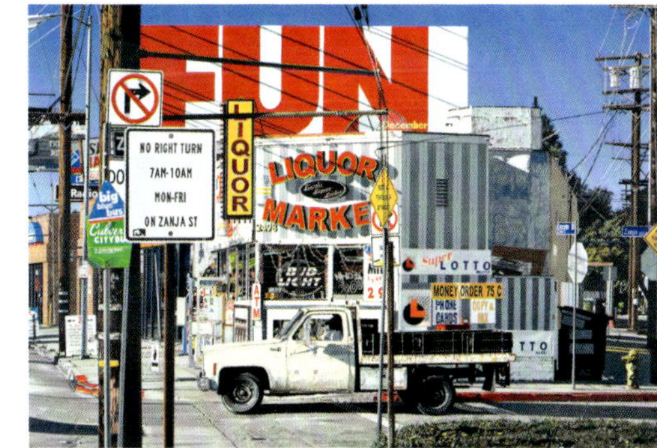

**117** *FUN, 2009*

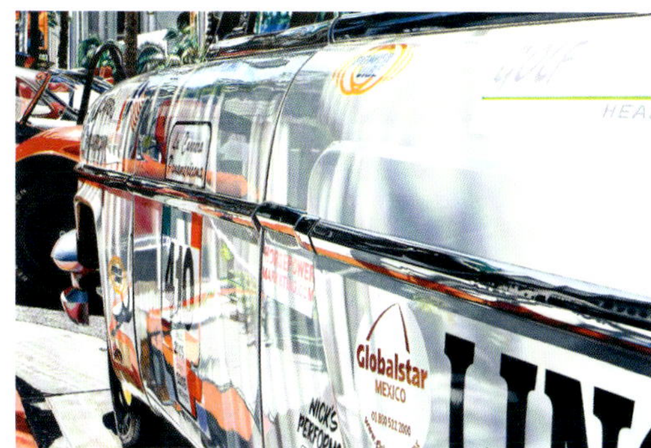

**119** *Power Vibe, 2007*

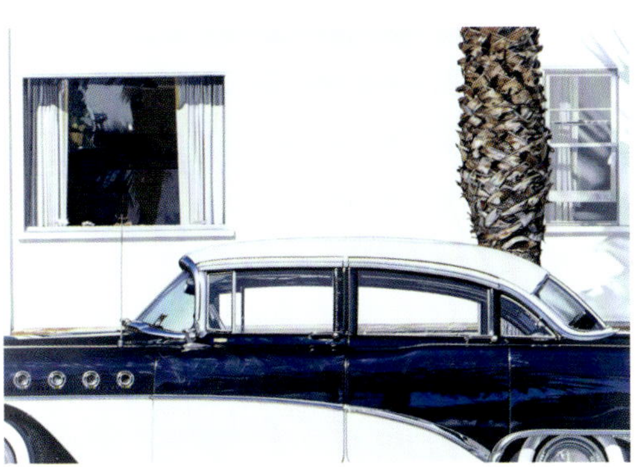

**120** *Roadmaster, 1977*

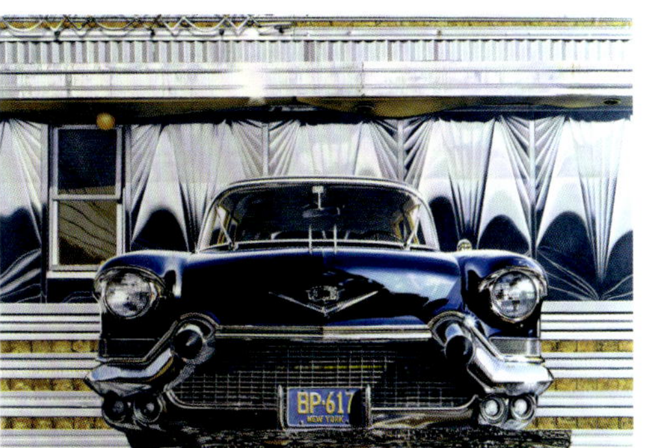

**121** *Cadillac, 1973*

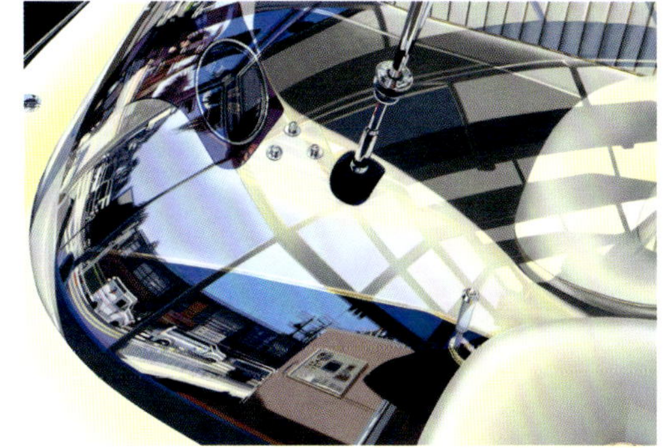

**123** *US Mail, 1996*

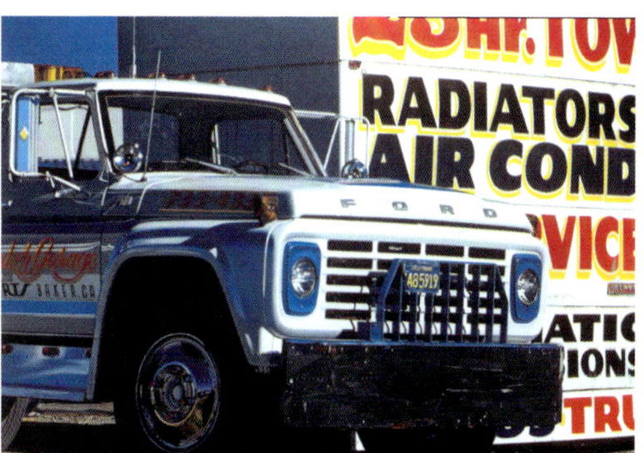

**124** *Vice, 1991*

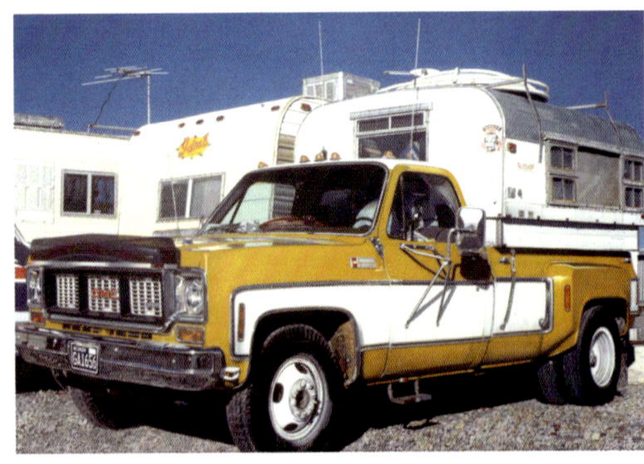

**125** *Ideal*, 1991

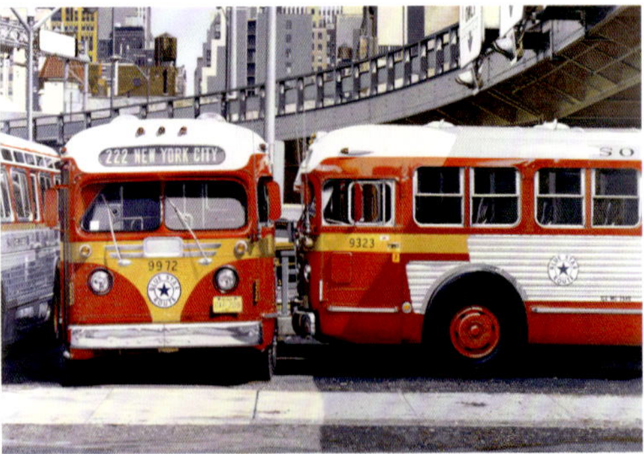

**127** *Blue Star Route*, 1978

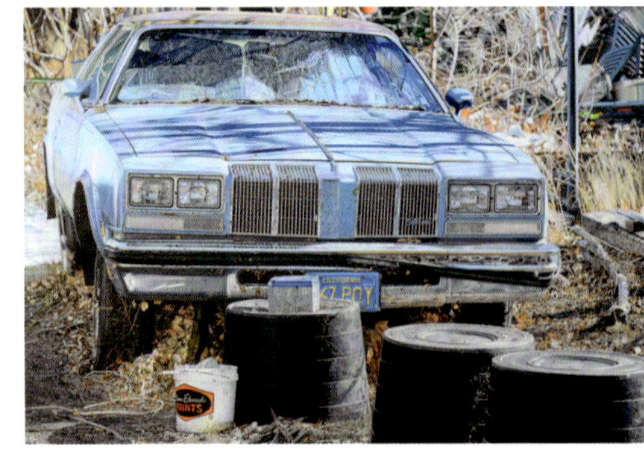

**128** *Independence*, 2020

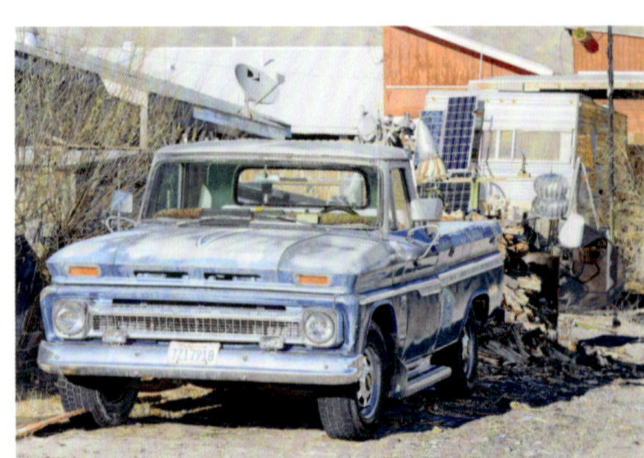

**129** *Keeler*, 2023

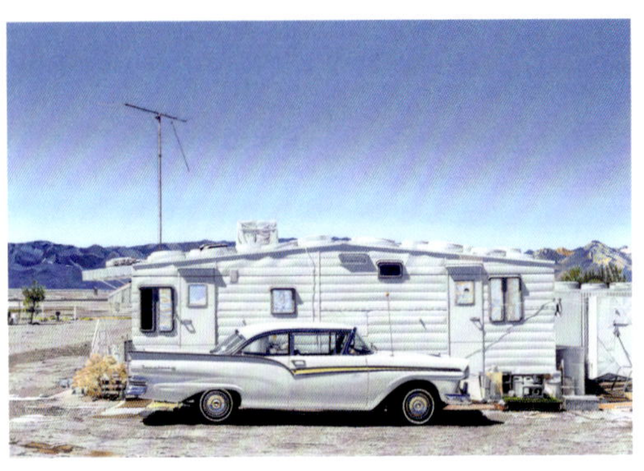

**130** *Fairlane*, 2005

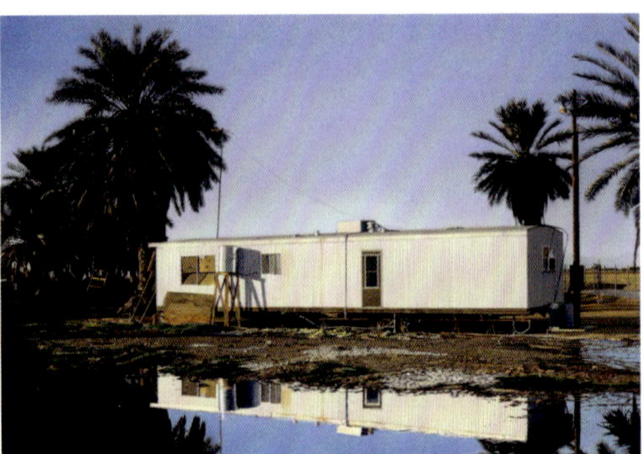

**131** *Salton City*, 2004

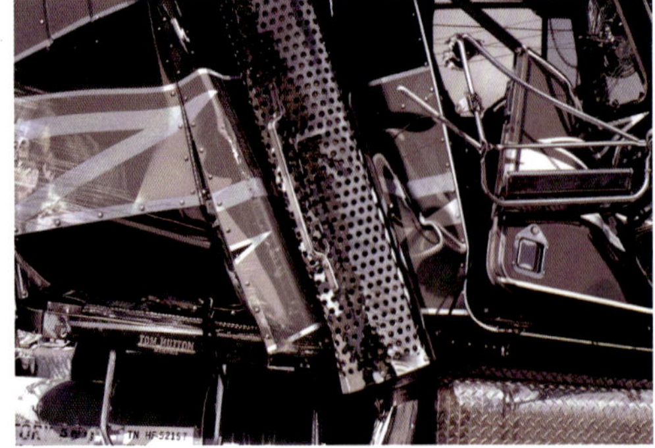

**133** *Memphis*, 1994

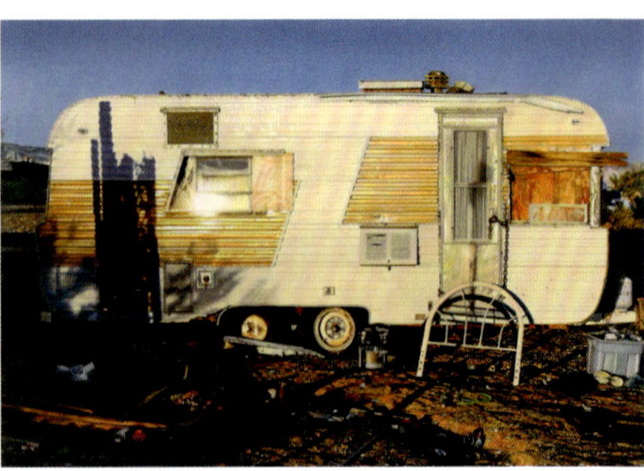

**134** *Slab City: Victory*, 2012

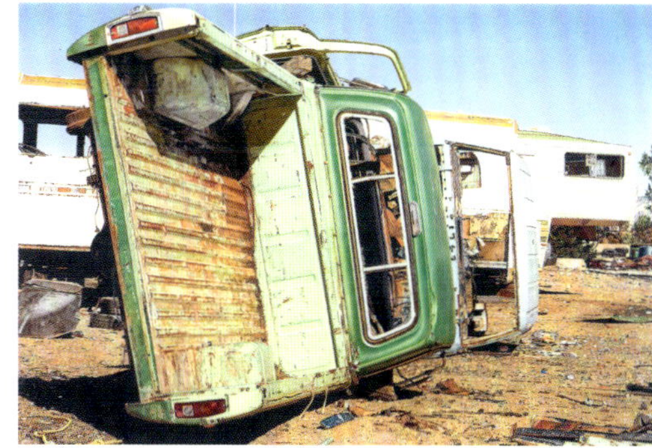 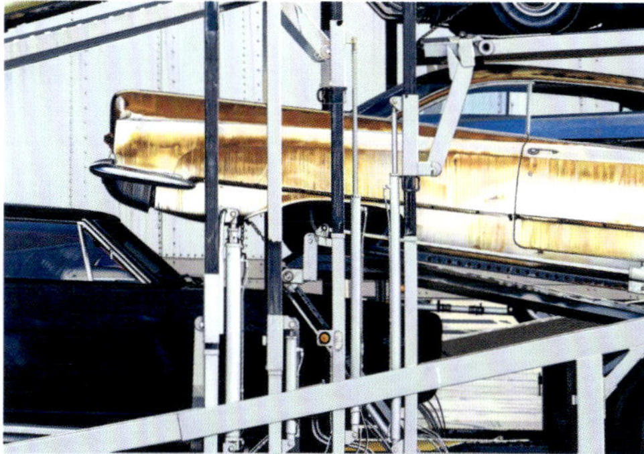 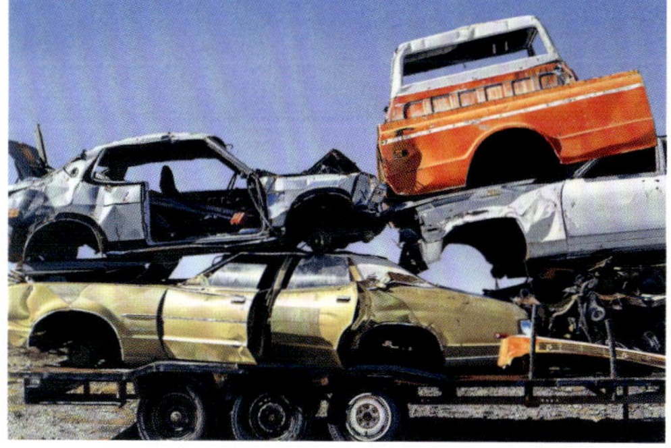 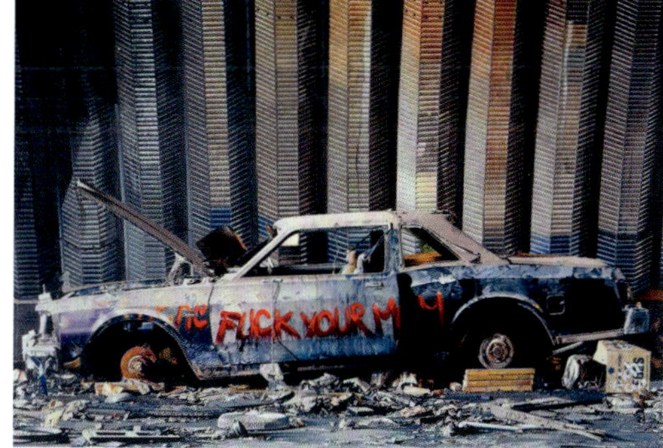

**135** *Imperial Valley: Death, 2012*

**136** *Accidents, 1998*

**137** *Wrecks, 1995*

**139** *Fuck Your Mum, 2012*

# Acknowledgements

It is now over fifty-five years since the work represented in this book was started. It was planned from the beginning as a series of one hundred drawings, all the same size. I realised even then how long it would take, and that I would need in the most part to travel alone. In the intervening years this Quixotic sally has had its Sancho Panzas, its Rocinantes and its Inns.

Initially, the method was to travel by Greyhound bus, but that gave no opportunity to stop. That limitation meant hiring a car. The original photography was done travelling by day and staying in motels by night. The cars evolved from mini to economy to compact. Over time, seedy motels became motel chains, then Airbnb. A manual Nikon 35mm camera, with a separate Weston V Master Light Meter with an Invercone, has transformed into a digital Nikon D800E. Kodachrome changed to Ektachrome VS, which in turn became Photoshop. Meanwhile, 20/20 vision deteriorated to be assisted by a pair of glasses when using the camera and two pairs of glasses when drawing.

Intermissions from this routine were provided by a number of staunch and tolerant friends in New York and Los Angeles: Kathy Garner, Jennifer Janis, Eileen Lipp, Robin Parkinson, Peter Szego, Kathryn Wiedener, Janet Ziff, Stuart Ziff, and early on by their parents. In the course of the project, mattresses on the floor became mattresses on beds.

Quixote was guided by visions, but the driver preferred *The Thomas Guide Los Angeles Updated Zip Code Edition*, and the perfect pocket-sized *A Guide to Architecture in Los Angeles and Southern California* by David Gebhard and Robert Winter.

Reconnoitres were undertaken in company and on these expeditions Mike and Elizabeth Davies, Celia Davies, Sarah Granville, Anna Hart, Maureen Hedges, and Bernice Holmes offered patience, tolerance and a break from the intensity of concentration. At night, in Independence, Ursula Esser drove her old trusted faded green jeep Nellie, and together with Maureen braved the possibility of snakes, the interference of a giant owl, and held the lights, while the artist photographed a grove of silver trees in the otherwise empty desert landscape.

Being a Visiting Scholar at the Getty Research Institute (GRI) at the Getty Center, Los Angeles, was life changing and a privilege. Angie Donougher eased the way. Sabine Schlosser quietly made an installation of images and music happen, and explained the protocol of talking face to face rather than emailing. Using this protocol I discovered John Kiffe in the basement of the GRI. There in the dark he is the master of the digital file and the inkjet print, a great spender of time on the detail and finesse necessary in his craft, welcoming to someone happy to learn.

I had time there to visit old friends. A multitude of thanks are due to George Barris, customiser, the De Alba Family, Mario, Adrian and Mario Junior, extraordinary builders of lowriders, to George Herms, Leonard Knight, 'Lil Daddy' Dennis Roth, and Bob Spina. They all accepted a tall Englishman, made him feel at home, showed and shared their phenomenal work.

I'll be forever indebted to Mississippi Fred McDowell for his inspiration. That's the way it's supposed to be. Jimmie Dale Gilmour and Butch Hancock got it. They immediately understood the project and participated. Motown commissioned work, and The Four Tops put it on the sleeve of *Reach Out I'll Be There*. Along the way Quixote thought he heard celestial music but in reality The Buckaroos, The Chambers Brothers, Junior Brown, Clifton Chenier, The Clark Sisters, Freddy Fender, Clarence Fountain and The Blind Boys of Alabama, D L Menard, Augie Meyers, and Irma Thomas all played live and in person for the traveller. He visited Inns, but The Rock Store, Bob's Big Boy at Toluca Lake, The TravelCenter on Milliken Avenue, Ontario, on Route 10, Love's Travel Stop at Ripon, on Route 99, stood in. The conversations with nameless drivers over the lunch counters provided the stories I still tell today.

Starting at the Architectural Association, Alvin Boyarsky, genius and chairman, understood a difficult character, and offered exhibitions often at very short notice. David Greene loved the work, and sharpened the mind, as he has that of many students and colleagues. Paul Oliver, without whom I would have left the AA halfway through my first year, brought musicians to talk to us: John Cage, Morton Feldman, and Xenakis. He showed that my enthusiasms were not misplaced. Because of this connection, David Pelham, art director of Penguin Books, thought I would be just the person to design the cover of *The Story of the Blues*.

The lessons learned in doing covers and artwork in the analogue way made it easier, I hope, for others to cope with the particularities acquired in making books.

The editorial clarity and patience of David Jenkins and the digital precision and flexibility of design ideas of Joana Niemeyer have eased the way to the book you see here. It is the result of the careful photography of the drawings, in most cases their digital scanning, and the advice and the exacting precision of the Photoshop work by my son, Jackson Holmes, over many years.

At various times critics have written in incisive, profound, and honest ways, often revealing something I had not realised myself about the work.

Thomas E Crow was Tom Crow when I first met him, forty-five years ago, before the Internet made it a must to distinguish himself from others with the same name. He understood from the very beginning the connection between the drawings I made, the things I saw, and the music I listened to. In our conversations over many years he has encouraged a sometime wavering confidence in observations and enthusiasms that no one else seemed to share. His recognition of this when he wrote 'Andrew Holmes is the master over all that is deep, distinguished, and soulful in the popular cultures of both the US and UK' is treasured. With his wife Catherine Phillips they have been generous, gentle and kind anchors always.

Mark Fisher, despite being the hardest working man in show business, apart from James Brown, found time to see and think about a variety of work, making allusions and drawing conclusions simply by observing what was there. His critical thinking was always tough and to the point. There was no escape from his sharp eye and brain. It always revealed a human understanding of what motivates an artist of whatever sort, visual or musical.

Cedric Price, a man full of surprises and delight, drew an astonishing parallel with William Wordsworth in the title of his essay. *A Poet's Epitaph* is not an obvious link to make, but forty years later I find it comforting that all the work may not have been in vain.

In common things that round us lie
Some random truths he can impart,
The harvest of a quiet eye
That broods and sleeps on his own heart.

Andrew Holmes
March 2024